The Great Awakening at Yale College

The American History Research Series

William R. Taylor
State University of New York at Stony Brook

Arthur Zilversmit
Lake Forest College

General Editors

**Salem-Village Witchcraft: A Documentary Record
of Local Conflict in Colonial New England**
Paul Boyer and Stephen Nissenbaum,
University of Massachusetts, Amherst

The Great Awakening at Yale College
Stephen Nissenbaum, University of Massachusetts,
Amherst

The Response to John Brown
Richard Scheidenhelm

Lincoln on Black and White: A Documentary History
Arthur Zilversmit, Lake Forest College

Forthcoming

**How Revolutionary Was the American Revolution?
New York as a Case Study**
Larry R. Gerlach, University of Utah

Thomas Mott Osborne and Prison Reform
Jack M. Holl, Williams College

The Passaic Textile Strike
Paul L. Murphy, University of Minnesota

The Negro in the New Deal
Paul B. Worthman, Wellesley College, and
Linda Gratz Worthman

The Great Awakening at Yale College

Stephen Nissenbaum
University of Massachusetts

Editor

Wadsworth Publishing Company, Inc., Belmont, California

"There is a great aptness in persons to doubt of things that are strange; especially elderly persons, to think that to be right which they have never been used to in their day, and have not heard of in the days of their fathers."

—Jonathan Edwards,
speaking at the 1741 Yale commencement

ISBN–0–534–00101–7
L. C. Cat. Card No: 74–167899

Printed in the United States of America

1 2 3 4 5 6 7 8 9 10—75 74 73 72

Series Introduction

This volume forms part of a new series of source readers designed to acquaint students with one of the major tasks of historical study. The series is directed to the problem of how a society makes up its mind, how individuals and groups within such a society take stock of what is happening to them, of what they are becoming.

Ordinarily, history courses are concerned with one phase of this problem. They take account of the many different kinds of decisions members of a society are forced to make, and they take some account of the process through which these decisions are made: the election of candidates to office, the framing of new legislation, the arbitrating of conflicts between groups, the revision of existing institutions, and the creation of new institutions. In such courses the student is fed assessments of the mood of the country and the attitudes held by particular groups. He reads about periods in which problems seemed staggering and prospects for survival dim. He also reads of periods of enormous optimism when no problems seemed beyond solution and when visions of the future took on a utopian glow. He studies accounts of wars fought and the aims that were employed to justify them. In general, however, the decisions studied and the assessments made are on a massive, usually national, scale: they are the decisions of governments or comparatively impersonal representatives of governments or the corporate decisions of masses of men who determine, for example, to move westward, who make their way to new American cities, or who seem to demand a vast bloodletting to regain their national honor. What the student misses is the pulsebeat of historical experience, the chance to tap the thought processes of men in the course of their deliberations and on a scale that makes close observation and analysis possible. Ordinarily, the student is asked to take the self-appraisals Americans have made at various times in their history on faith, on the say-so of the historian himself or of the authorities that he selects to speak for him. The object of this series is to place the student where he himself may feel the pulse and try to determine the nature and quality of the changes contemporaries see taking place. The object, in short, is to place the student in a situation where, on a limited and manageable scale, he must *act* the historian.

The books of readings have therefore been designed to provide the *initial* step in the investigation of a problem of intellectual or social history. They are intended to be provocative rather than comprehensive, and they are not designed to be, like most source readings, free-standing units of study. Rather, they are to provide the student with incentives to enter the library and investigate further. In this sense, they are designed to be a historical bridge rather than an island. At every point our emphasis has been that of freeing and activating the student's initiative rather than confining and guiding it along predetermined lines. It is for this reason that the editorial apparatus has been minimized in all volumes. In our own earlier use of some of these materials, in fact, we had provided no editorial apparatus whatsoever—not a word. Among the more modest objectives of this kind of teaching is the desire on our part to get students back into libraries and especially into reference collections. Most headnotes either prejudge the significance of the reading, summarize it, or contain biographical information about the author that is easily obtainable elsewhere. We suggest a few books by way of bibliography, and again, our assumption is that an introductory student of history ought to be encouraged to use a card catalogue and standard reference aids such as the *Harvard Guide to American History* and the *Dictionary of American Biography*.

We want students to initiate their understanding of the period by puzzling over a body of closely related sources. It has been our experience that students, after some initial confusion, become intensely interested in probing the pulse of a particular historical setting without someone standing over them and telling them what they should be concluding. It is wrong to assume that only upperclassmen and sophisticated students are capable of this kind of undertaking. Freshmen often produce work that would do honor to our graduate students. They become critical, skeptical readers of standard secondary works.

Our larger objective, of course, is to counteract the deadening effect of most historical study from which a student emerges with a kind of mini-version of scholarly truth—only to shed it within the next 90 days.

In selecting topics and readings for this purpose, three criteria—focus, scale, relatedness—have proved most important. In seeking to meet these criteria, moreover, other criteria normally employed in selecting source readings have had to be abandoned, comprehensiveness most of all. Where the tactics and the process of thought are to be examined, it has seemed advisable to prefer the battle, so to speak, to the war. Since our object is to excite students to question historical evidence, it has seemed important to find bodies of documents that are closely interrelated, suggestive, and resonant of meaning. It has thus seemed preferable, for example, rather than presenting students with a scattering of documents which illustrate the sources of social conflict in colonial America, to focus narrowly upon the experience of the few hundred inhabitants of Salem Village at the time of the witchcraft trials. Instead of attempting to canvass the conflicting, often contradictory attitudes of Southerners and Northerners on the eve of the Civil War, we have chosen instead to examine the attitudes that developed in response to John Brown's raid on Harper's Ferry. Instead of trying to display the significance of the Great Awakening as it swept through the colonies after 1740, we have decided to examine its effect on those in and around the hotseat of Yale College. In short, we have chosen to work microcosmically, to understand the whole of a development by close examination of a part. We have also sought out moments of crisis, conflict, and drama in which the student can observe contending ideas at play. It seemed better, for example, to study American religious thought in the early nineteenth century by focusing on the upheaval of the revivals rather than by examining the comparatively unchanging nature of theology and church institutional life. We have attempted to confront our students with American Protestantism in a fever fit where the contradictions both of revivalists and those who opposed them are highlighted.

The general editors of the series agreed upon several criteria to govern their editing of the volumes. We made no effort to include the "classical" statements of particular ideas—Winthrop on the social covenant or Emerson on nature. In part, we eschewed this kind of inclusiveness because most other readers possess it. Our most important objective, however, was to achieve an interrelatedness of documentation. We have striven for texts that express the thinking of particular groups or communities. Wherever possible we looked for documents that form part of an actual controversy or running debate even when the participants were little known or obscure men. For this reason, we have tried to offer whole, unabridged texts as often as we could with a minimum of editing in order to present the student with a scholar's text in which the original design and flavor have not been destroyed or deleted.

We tried to design these readers so they can be used in several ways: to supplement more general readings in an introductory survey course or in addition to more theoretical readings in a course in intellectual or social history. One or two of them can even be useful in some courses in American literature. Whatever the kind of course in which they are used—and some new courses, we believe, will be built around them—they are designed to give students a more active role in their courses by providing them with some experience in inquiry learning, in learning by discovery, as they would in a good scientific laboratory experiment. This presumably means that these readings might be used as the basis for problem exercises of the kind suggested in the study guides at the close of each volume. They could also, of course, be assigned as independent reading for the preparation of more extensive term papers. For that reason, each volume contains a list of related further readings. Doubtless, imaginative teachers will discuss other ways to present students with these new kinds of source readers. It has been our experience that students seize upon sources of this concrete, specific kind where historical problems are of a manageable scope and where it is possible to exercise their historical judgment with greater precision and to acquire some of the skills that will equip them to do more advanced and more far-ranging analysis.

William R. Taylor
Arthur Zilversmit

Contents

Introduction   *1*

One   Awakening the Campus, October 1740–July 1741   *11*

1.   Samuel Hopkins: Memoirs, 1721–1741   *13*

2.   George Whitefield Comes to New Haven, October 1740   *21*

3.   George Whitefield Writes to the Students at Harvard and Yale, July 1741   *24*

4.   Gilbert Tennent to George Whitefield, New York, April 25, 1741   *26*

5.   Ebenezer Pemberton: "The Knowledge of Christ Recommended," April 19, 1741   *28*

6.   David Brainerd: Memoirs, 1732–1741   *37*

Two   A Divisive Commencement, September 1741   *53*

7.   Daniel Wadsworth: Diary, September 1741   *55*

8.   Samuel Johnson to George Berkeley, October 3, 1741   *57*

9.   Proceedings of the Yale Trustees, September 9, 1741   *58*

10.   Jonathan Edwards: *Distinguishing Marks of a Work of the Spirit of God*, September 10, 1741   *61*

Three   Schism in the Church, September 1741–May 1742   *109*

11.   Governor Talcott to Colonel Lynde, Hartford, September 4, 1741   *111*

12.   Thomas Clap to the Boston *Post-Boy*, New-Haven, September 21, 1741   *113*

13.   New Haven Church Members: Memorial to the Congregation, December 28, 1741   *116*

14.   Thomas Clap to Jonathan Dickinson, New Haven, May 3, 1742 *117*

15.   Covenant of the New Haven Separate Church, May 7, 1742 *119*

Four   Official Countermeasures, October 1741–May 1742   *123*

16.   The New Haven Ministerial Association Petitions the General Assembly, October 8, 1741   *125*

17.   The General Assembly of Connecticut Responds to the Petition, October 1741   *126*

18.   Resolution of the New Haven Association, November 1741   *127*

19.   The Guilford Resolves, November 24, 1741   *128*

20.   Governor Law's Address to the General Assembly, May 1742 *132*

21.   Committee of the General Consociation: Presentation, May 1742 *135*

22.   General Assembly: The Anti-Itineracy Act, May 1742   *136*

Five   Controlling the Campus, November 1741–November 1742 *141*

23.   Jonathan Edwards: Account of David Brainerd's Expulsion, November 1741   *143*

24.   Boston *Evening Post*: Account of the Troubles at Yale, April 26, 1742   *145*

25.   John Cleaveland: Diary of a Yale Freshman, 1742   *146*

26.   The General Assembly: Report on Yale, May 1742   *164*

27.   Benjamin Colman to George Whitefield, Boston, June 3, 1742 *167*

28.   Thomas Clap to Solomon Williams, New Haven, June 8, 1742 *169*

29.   Eleazar Wheelock: Diary, June 1742   *171*

30.   Eleazar Wheelock to His Wife, New Haven, June 28, 1742   *172*

31.   Thomas Clap to Solomon Williams, New Haven, July 16, 1742 *174*

32. John Maltby to Eleazar and Mrs. Wheelock, New Haven, November 18, 1742 *176*

Six Controlling the Colony, June 1742–June 1744 *179*

33. Resolutions of the General Association on the Revival, June 15, 1742 *181*

34. The General Assembly Condemns the Shepard's Tent, October 1742 *183*

35. Timothy Allen to Eleazar Wheelock, New London, February 27, 1743 *185*

36. John Davenport's Recantation, July 18, 1744 *188*

37. The General Assembly Repeals the Toleration Act, May 1743 *191*

38. The General Assembly Strengthens the Anti-Itineracy Act, October 1743 *192*

39. Benjamin Colman to Governor Law, Boston, January 21, 1745 *194*

Seven Two Commencements, September 1743–September 1744 *197*

40. David Brainerd Visits New Haven, September 1743 *198*

41. Eleazar Wheelock to Thomas Clap, September 1743 *202*

42. Thomas Clap to Eleazar Wheelock, New Haven, November 17, 1743 *204*

43. Chauncy Whittelsey: *A Faithful Improvement of our Talents,* September 9, 1744 *206*

44. Proceedings of the Yale Trustees, September 12, 1744 *217*

Eight The Cleaveland Expulsions, November 1744–April 1745 *219*

45. A Letter to the New York *Post-Boy,* March 17, 1745 *221*

46. Thomas Clap to the New York *Post-Boy,* New Haven, April 18, 1745 *223*

47. Thomas Clap et al.: *Judgment of the Rector and Tutors,* 1745 *224*

48. John Cleaveland: "A Just Narrative of the Proceedings," 1745
232

49. Eleazar Wheelock to John Cleaveland, Lebanon, March 9, 1745
245

50. John and Ebenezer Cleaveland: Memorial to the General Assembly, April 1745   *246*

Appendix A: The Yale Community   *253*

Appendix B: New Light Ministers in Connecticut   *259*

For Further Investigation   *261*

Introduction

George Whitefield arrived in New England in September 1740 and sailed for England in January 1741. In four months he traveled 800 miles from Massachusetts to Virginia and preached 130 sermons; by the time he left the New World, the years of religious revival known as the "Great Awakening" had begun. Benjamin Franklin, a rather detached observer of the phenomenon, later described its effects on life in Philadelphia in this way:

> It was wonderful to see the changes soon made in the manners of our inhabitants; from being thoughtless or indifferent about religion, it seemed as if all the world were growing religious; so that one could not walk through the town in the evening without hearing psalms sung in different families in every street.

Such a development, you might expect, would win the whole-hearted approval of America's religious establishment. As it happened, Whitefield's activities quickly produced as much ministerial hostility as support. In many places, Whitefield was simply not invited to preach. But even this step only increased the size of his audience, as Franklin makes clear:

> He was at first permitted to preach in some of our churches; but the clergy, taking a dislike to him, soon refused him their pulpits and he

was obliged to preach in the fields. The multitudes of all sects and denominations that attended his sermons were enormous.

Before very long, the Great Awakening had divided the ministry, and the rest of the public, into opposing camps—"Old Lights," those who opposed the revivals, and "New Lights," who supported the movement. Between 1741 and 1745 the American people debated the issue —in churches, town meetings, and published tracts—as they had not debated any issue in their century-old history. When Whitefield (the name is pronounced *Whit-field*) returned to America for another evangelical tour early in 1745, both sides were prepared: the New Lights welcomed him with invitations; the Old Lights—including the entire Yale faculty—cordially and publicly demanded that he stay away from their territory. The Great Awakening was not only the first large-scale American religious revival; it also marked the first time that American opinion had been polarized throughout the British colonies. Not until the Revolutionary War a generation later would a single issue inflame the whole society. At once disruptive and unifying (like the Revolution), the Great Awakening was our first national experience.

    In our own time, when revivalism seems old-fashioned and unavoidably associated with religious and social conservatism, it is hard to get a real sense of the Great Awakening in its mid-eighteenth century setting. It was an unprecedented, disruptive, even radical event— an episode that split apart established institutions—families, churches, communities—and put them back together again in new and unfamiliar ways. Just as it is already difficult from a 1970 perspective to see the early 1960s as a "new frontier," so it is almost impossible on the face of it to see hellfire preachers like George Whitefield and his fellow revivalists as the purveyors of a "new light." On the surface they appear quite the opposite: in trying to purvey old-time religion in the Age of Reason, weren't they the real conservatives? And weren't the "Old Lights," Whitefield's opponents, really the far-sighted liberals who realized that Calvinism was finished and that the time for a more "reasonable" religion was at hand?

    The answers to these questions depend, at least in part, on the places you chose to look. In Massachusetts, to which the history books generally direct our attention, the debate can be construed (if you're not listening carefully, at least) in just these terms—reactionary revivalists versus liberals. This interpretation is possible because the Bay

Colony had one highly articulate and prolific spokesman for each position: the great Jonathan Edwards of Northampton speaking in favor of the revival in a series of published sermons and books, and Rev. Charles Chauncy of Boston's First Church replying in kind to each of Edwards' efforts. The debate also has the appearance of a classic confrontation between conservative and liberal: Edwards pleading for a resurgence of Puritan piety in an increasingly secular world, Chauncy attacking revivalistic excess and proposing a cool, almost rationalistic brand of religion. It is all too easy to conclude from this debate that the issues were exclusively theological, and, even in this context, that Edwards and the New Lights were reaching back to the seventeenth century while Chauncy and the Old Lights were pointing the way to the nineteenth.

But when the scene shifts to Connecticut, this scenario disappears. Here there were no first-class pamphleteers to seduce our attention, no pens—no minds, even—who successfully raised the debate to a level of theological abstraction. Here the struggle did not take the form of a "pamphlet war"; even on the surface, it was a more earthly struggle in which the theological issues were inextricably linked to social control in individual towns and churches.

And in Connecticut the theological issues themselves blatantly violated the "liberal-conservative" model that seems to emerge elsewhere. The Connecticut "Old Light" leadership, for example, far from being progressive crypto-Unitarians like Charles Chauncy, were hardline Calvinists whose orthodox credentials were at least as secure as those of Jonathan Edwards himself.

Thomas Clap, the Rector (President) of Yale-College during the Great Awakening, was also one of the important Old Light leaders in Connecticut. Born in 1703, he graduated from Harvard and, in his twenties, became minister to the Congregational church in Windham, Connecticut. In the mid-1730s, Clap allied himself with Jonathan Edwards in an effort to prevent the ordination of one Robert Breck, a Massachusetts minister with suspected liberal (non-Calvinist) leanings. Clap's role in the "Breck affair" established his reputation as a staunch defender of theological orthodoxy—and prepared the way for his appointment to the Yale rectorship late in 1739. Yet when the revival first swept the colony and the College late the next year, Clap turned on it and its votaries with the same blunt force he had exerted on the liberal Robert Breck just a few years earlier. Ironically, by 1744 he was engaged in a nasty pamphlet war with his erstwhile ally, Jonathan Edwards.

Clap's double role as Yale president and Old Light spokesman is one reason that the present collection of documents is focused on the institution he directed. But an even more important reason is that Yale College itself was a center of New Light revivalism. Virtually all the touring revivalists—*itinerants,* they were called—stopped for a time in New Haven, and for good reason, as the Yale students (and many townspeople, as well) were among their most responsive audiences. Because the head of the College and his entire staff opposed the revival, the Yale campus inevitably seethed with political as well as religious tension in the five years between 1740 and 1745. For this reason, it is an almost ideal "laboratory" for examining the troubles that wracked much of American society during these years. And because this book will generally be read on college campuses, the choice of Yale as its setting may evoke for some readers a special resonance. Similarities between the battles at Yale during the 1740's and the troubles on many college campuses in the 1960's are sufficiently obvious that they need not be described here.

In other respects, though, eighteenth century colleges were far different from their modern university counterparts. First, there weren't very many of them. In the 1740's, Yale was one of only two colleges in New England, and one of only three in the whole of British America. It was, furthermore, under strict ecclesiastical as well as civil control. Founded in 1701 to present an orthodox Calvinist counterpoise to 65-year-old Harvard (which had just betrayed *its* Calvinist heritage by appointing a theologically "liberal" president), for years it remained a small institution: graduating classes between 1701 and 1745 averaged only 11 students. Along with the undergraduates, the campus contained a handful of graduate students working for their M.A.'s, and the faculty consisted of two or three young tutors (themselves recent graduates) and the rector himself. There was no resident administrative apparatus; the faculty handled routine administrative matters. Each faculty member was responsible for the education of an entire entering class; members of the class of 1745, for example, spent their entire four years at Yale studying under Rector Clap alone. There were no specialized professorships as we know them today. Students generally lived in a single dormitory on campus, although boarding with a New Haven family was not uncommon.

The early history of Yale had not been exactly placid, although the problems that the College faced in the years before 1740 had resulted not from student discontent but from inadequate support from Connecticut's colonial legislature (known as the General Assembly).

For years Yale lacked a permanent home. Hartford and New Haven fought bitterly to acquire the new College; at one point, in 1719, the situation was so chaotic that most of the faculty and student body simply moved without authorization to the town of Wethersfield and carried on "Yale-College" in that place.

In other ways, too, the college and its tiny faculty were weak. The Trustees—a self-perpetuating group of 12 Connecticut ministers —held most real power over the institution. They, not the rector or his assistants, made all important administrative decisions: for example, they determined the nature of the curriculum and decided the appointment of tutors and the admission of students. (Even today, the Trustees or Regents of many universities technically retain these functions—for instance, the awarding of degrees—but, in fact, the actual power over such matters is generally in the hands of the resident faculty and administration). The rector himself was little more than the head teacher. In addition he led prayers twice a day, lectured to the entire Yale community on the Sabbath, and held disciplinary powers over the students. He did not, however, have a vote on the Board of Trustees (though he did sit in on their meetings), and he held his office at the Board's pleasure. He was, in other words, more the hireling of the Trustees than the leader of the College.

From the moment Thomas Clap took over the rectorship early in 1740, he worked single-mindedly to increase the power and prestige of the office and to consolidate the position of the College itself. To accomplish both these ends, for the first five years of his long tenure (he kept the office until 1766) he lobbied with important political figures to obtain a new College charter from the General Assembly. This effort coincided, of course, with the Great Awakening, and it is not surprising to find that Clap was quick to use the student unrest pervading Yale in these years as an argument to convince the legislature of the need for an independent college with a strong resident administrator. Early in 1745 the General Assembly granted the new charter; it satisfied Clap's expectations in every respect. He was given the title of "President" along with extensive legal and discretionary power. Exercising his new authority, Clap issued a new, elaborate, and harsh set of "College Laws," with regulations and penalties covering every conceivable aspect of student life—from the library to the dining commons. (One provision permitted faculty members to "break open any college door to suppress any disorder.")

The 1745 Charter and "College Laws" make for interesting reading, but they are not included here, for a simple reason: this is not a collection of documents about "college life" in the eighteenth century (valuable as such a collection might be), any more than it is a set of readings about all aspects of the Great Awakening. It is an attempt to capture both the College and the revival at their points of intersection, in those moments and from those angles at which the *institution* and the *event* begin to shade into one another. Whatever may be lost in breadth of coverage by this editorial decision is hopefully gained back in depth. Within the limitations of available space, it has become possible to include, uncut, virtually every relevant document.

The Great Awakening at Yale College covers the effect of a single event on a single institution over a period of barely four years. But the documents printed here include the widest possible range of human discourse, from the most private (diaries, personal letters) to the most public (published tracts, legislative enactments). Some of them are as brief as a few sentences; others are too long to read at a single sitting. Some are filled with intrinsic drama and life; others are listless and boring. Some are composed in the most impeccable eighteenth-century style; others probably seemed as illiterate when they were written as they seem "quaint" today. The printed page is a cheat: it takes the most varied forms of human expression—diary entries penned in the light of still-fresh experience, autobiographical memories coolly compiled years after the events they describe, letters designed to convey information (but not too much!) to a barely-trusted colleague, letters designed to win favors, sermons delivered with a public voice to audiences of students or legislators, passionate petitions, impersonal laws, prayers—and reduces them all to an identical, opaque format. It takes constant work to realize, while one is reading them, that the documents printed here were not written for the *purpose* of being printed here. Only history textbooks are written to be read by history students.

A Chronology
of The Great Awakening in New England

1740

September–October. George Whitefield's tour of New England. Revivals in many churches.

December–March [1741]. Gilbert Tennent's tour of New England.

1741

July. Jonathan Edwards, "Sinners in the Hands of an Angry God" (revival sermon).

July–September. James Davenport's tour of Connecticut.

1742

Frequent itinerant tours of the area by young ministers (including some recent college graduates without regular pastorates).

The beginning of church "separations."

May. Isaac Stiles, "A Prospect of the City of Jerusalem" (anti-revival Connecticut election sermon).

May. Anti-itineracy Act passed by the Connecticut legislature.

May–June. Davenport's second visit to New England (ending in his expulsion).

June–August. Davenport's third visit (jailed in August, expelled in October).

July. Charles Chauncy, "Enthusiasm Described and Cautioned Against" (anti-revival sermon).

1743

Appearance of "lay exhorters" (laymen functioning as preachers).

Increase in church "separations."

March. Davenport's fourth visit. The New London "book-burning."

March. Edwards, *Some Thoughts concerning the Recent Revival of Religion.*

May. Toleration Act repealed by the Connecticut legislature (to prevent the "separates" from taking advantage of it).

May. Convention of anti-revival ministers in Boston.

July. Convention of New Light (pro-revival) ministers in Boston.

September. Chauncy, *Seasonable Thoughts on the State of Religion in New England* (long attack on the Great Awakening).

October. Second anti-itineracy act passed by the Connecticut legislature.

1744

Summer. Davenport's recantation.

November–February [1745]. Whitefield's second visit to New England.

1746

Edwards, *A Treatise concerning the Religious Affections.*

A Chronology
of The Great Awakening at Yale College

1701

Yale College founded as a bastion of religious orthodoxy in response to the "liberalization" of Harvard.

1708

The Saybrook Platform in Connecticut provided centralized ministerial control of the colony's churches by means of country-wide "consociations." (The Saybrook Platform replaced the Cambridge Platform of 1648, which had insured a large measure of autonomy to the individual congregation.)

The Toleration Act passed by the Connecticut General Assembly (the colonial legislature) permitted freedom of worship to most non-Congregationalists and absolved them from paying taxes to support the established churches.

1734–1736

The Little Awakening, a religious revival more localized than the Great Awakening of the 1740s, which spread through the Connecticut River Valley from northern Massachusetts through southern Connecticut.

1740

April. Thomas Clap installed as Rector (President) of Yale.
October. George Whitefield in New Haven.

1741

March. Gilbert Tennent in New Haven (preaches 17 sermons).

April. Ebenezer Pemberton in New Haven, "The Knowledge of Christ Recommended."

August–September. James Davenport in New Haven. His confrontation with Joseph Noyes.

September. Commencement. Jonathan Edwards in New Haven, "Distinguishing Marks of a Work of the Spirit of God." Yale Trustees warn unruly student dissenters of expulsion.

November. Expulsion of David Brainerd, a Yale senior.

December. Secession from the New Haven Church.

1742

Winter. "New Light" ministers preach to the seceders from the Church. Some Yale students attend their preaching.

April. The Yale campus is closed on account of dissension. Students return home.

May. Formation of the New Haven sepaeate Church (New Light). Committee of the Connecticut legislature recommends firm action against student dissenters.

Summer. Formation of the "Shepard's Tent" at New London.

September. Yale reopens.

1743

May. The Connecticut legislature repeals the Toleration Act.

September. David Brainerd's unsuccessful attempt to receive his degree.

1744

September. Chauncy Whittelsey's commencement sermon, "A Faithful Improvement of Our Talents." Yale Trustees pass the "21-year-old" restriction on future admissions.

December. Expulsion of the Cleaveland brothers.

1745

Winter. Yale students reprint Locke's *Essay on Toleration*.

February. George Whitefield in New Haven.

May. Yale receives a new charter from the legislature. The College is reorganized.

1757

President Clap organizes a Church for Yale College.

ONE

Awakening the Campus, October 1740–July 1741

When George Whitefield arrived in New Haven in October 1740, nineteen-year-old Samuel Hopkins (1721–1803) was just beginning his senior year at Yale. Some fifty years later, toward the end of a long and distinguished career, Hopkins recalled in his autobiography the way he and other students on the Yale campus had responded to Whitefield's visit [#1]. By the time he set down his recollections, Hopkins was recognized as one of the most significant theologians of his time—the heir of his teacher Jonathan Edwards and the most systematic exponent of the "New Divinity," as the ideas that were forged in the revivals came to be called.

As Whitefield traveled through England and America soliciting donations for his Georgia orphanage, he kept a journal of his experiences, designed like his earlier journals for almost immediate publication. Whitefield's account of his trip down the Connecticut River valley from Northampton, Massachusetts, to New Haven [#2] was published in England late in the spring of 1741. It was not long before copies crossed the Atlantic, and the journal was read by many of the same New Englanders who had been discussed in its pages— discussed in a manner they must occasionally have found embarrassing. Whitefield, back in England since early in the year, composed a letter in July to the students at Yale and Harvard [#3] that was at least partially intended to mitigate the effect of his earlier comments about New Haven and Cambridge.

But by the time Whitefield wrote this letter, it was apparent that life in the two towns had changed. His own technique of evangelical itineracy, or traveling from one pulpit to another in an attempt to arouse the kind of spiritual concern that the local minister had failed to evoke, was in 1740 strange and disconcerting to New Englanders —people assumed that a pastor's role was fulfilled when he ministered to his own congregation and were surprised by the possibility that he might visit a colleague's parish without prior invitation. Whitefield's effect on the audiences to which he preached, however, was often electrifying, and his example was quickly imitated by sympathetic ministers with whom he had come into contact.

The first of these domestic itinerants to reach New Haven was Whitefield's friend Gilbert Tennent (1703–1764), a Presbyterian clergyman from New Jersey who had warned as early as 1739 about "The Danger of an Unconverted Ministry," in a sermon that urged people to attend churches other than their own if the local pastor preached without sufficient conviction. Tennent opened his tour of New England in December 1740, after he had spent several days traveling with Whitefield in New Jersey. He remained some two months in Boston—the major town in the area—and then began to travel down the New England coast through Rhode Island and Connecticut. Tennent reached New Haven late in March. While no account has been preserved of the seventeen sermons he preached there (at least three of them in the college hall), at the end of his trip Tennent did write Whitefield a letter in which he reported on his New Haven experiences [#4].

The one sermon delivered at Yale by an itinerant minister that was later published, "The Knowledge of Christ Recommended" [#5], was preached in April 1741, by Ebenezer Pemberton (1704–1777), a Harvard graduate who was pastor of the Presbyterian Church in New York. Two years before, Pemberton had led a revival in his church, and he was the only minister in New York City who had invited Whitefield to his pulpit in 1740.

The last document in this section, like the first, is excerpted from an autobiographical memoir [#6]. David Brainerd (1718–1749), a Yale sophomore during the 1740–41 academic year, wrote this account late in his brief career to serve as an introduction to the journal he began to keep about the time of Whitefield's visit. While Brainerd describes his pre-student years at some length and ends his account as early as January 1741—he deliberately destroyed his journal for the following crucial year of his life [#24]—his memoir is placed at the end of this section because it provides a most intensive and sophisticated record of the inner struggles which many young people in New Haven and elsewhere were undergoing in this period. Brainerd's description stands—as it was certainly intended to stand—as a "model" of religious conversion at the time of the Great Awakening.

1

Samuel Hopkins: Memoirs

1721–1741

I was born at Waterbury in Connecticut, on the Lord's day, September 17, 1721. My parents were professors of religion; and I descended from christian ancestors, both by my father and my mother, as far back as I have been able to trace my descent. I conclude I and my ancestors descended from those called *Puritans* in the days of queen Elizabeth, above two hundred years ago, and have continued to bear that denomination, since, and were the first settlers of New-England. This I have considered to be the most honourable and happy descent, to spring from ancestors, who have been professors of religion, without interruption during the course of two hundred years, and more: and many of them, if not all *real christians*. And I have considered it as a favour that I was born on the sabbath, and was perhaps publicly dedicated to Christ by baptism on the day in which I was born; and if not, certainly soon after.

As soon as I was capable of understanding, and attending to it, I was told that my father, when he was informed that he had a son born to him, said, if the child should live, he would give him a public education, that he might be a minister or a sabbath-day-man, alluding to my being born on the sabbath.

I was the first child of my parents that lived. They had one before, which was not alive when born, or died as soon as born. My

Samuel Hopkins, *Sketches of the Life of the Late, Rev. Samuel Hopkins, D.D., . . . Written by Himself* (Hartford, 1805), pp. 23–38.

mother was twenty years old when I was born, and my father thirty.

I have considered it as a great favour of God, that I was born and educated in a religious family, and among a people, in a country town, where a regard to religion and morality was common and prevalent; and the education of children and youth was generally practised in such a degree that young people were generally orderly in their behaviour, and abstained from those open vices, which were then too common in seaport and populous places. I do not recollect that I ever heard a profane word from the children and youth, with whom I was conversant, while I lived with my parents, which was till I was in my fifteenth year.

I from my youth was not volatile and wild, but rather of a sober and steady make, and was not guilty of external irregularities, such as disobedience to parents, profanation of the sabbath, lying, foolish, jesting, quarrelling, passion and anger, or rash and profane words; and was disposed to be diligent and faithful in whatever business I was employed; so that as I advanced in age, I gained the notice, esteem and respect of the neighbourhood. I was, in general, greatly careless about all invisible things; but was often plotting for something, which then appeared to me good and great in this life; and often indulged and pleased myself with vain and foolish imaginations of what I should be and do in this world. And sometimes, though rarely, had some serious thoughts of God, and about my soul and a future world of happiness and misery. And I once had a dream of the future judgment, in some measure agreeable to the representation made of it by Christ himself in the xxvth chapter of Matthew. I dreamed that I and a brother of mine, who was about two years younger than me, were sentenced to everlasting misery, and driven down to hell, with the rest of the wicked. This greatly impressed my mind, for a long time after. And the impression then made has not wholly worn off to this day.

As my father was a farmer, I was employed in labouring on the farm, with which business I was pleased, and made proficiency in it. I was frequently told, and often thought of the declaration of my father on the day on which I was born, *that he would bring me up to college,* as the phrase then was for a public education. But I felt no particular inclination to this; but was rather inclined to labour on a farm: But what always turned my mind against going to college, was the years of absence from my parents and their family, which were involved in it. Such absence was intolerable to my childish mind, and was sufficient to suppress the thought of going to learning.

But in the winter after I was fourteen years old, I retired much to a chamber in my father's house, and spent considerable time in reading, especially reading the bible; and began to feel more inclination to learning, and less to working on a farm; as our farming business did not go on so well as it had done, by reason of some particular circumstances which had taken place. When my father perceived this, he told me, if I was inclined to go to learning, he would put me to a place where I might be fitted for the college. To which I readily consented. Accordingly, I was put under the care and tuition of the Rev. John Graham of Woodbury, which joined West or Waterbury, his meeting-house being about ten miles from my father's house. Here I fitted for college, with a number of others; and was examined and admitted a member of college in September 1737, being sixteen years old on the seventeenth day of that month.

While a member of the college, I believe, I had the character of a sober, studious youth, and of a better scholar than the bigger half of the members of that society; and had the approbation of the governours of the college. I avoided the intimacy and the company of the openly vicious; and indeed kept but little company, being attentive to my studies. In the eighteenth or nineteenth year of my age, I cannot now certainly determine which, I made a profession of religion, and joined the church to which my parents belonged in Waterbury. I was serious, and was thought to be a pious youth, and I had this thought and hope of myself. I was constant in reading the bible, and in attending on public and secret religion. And sometimes at night, in my retirement and devotion, when I thought of confessing the sins I had been guilty of that day, and asking pardon, I could not recollect that I had committed one sin that day. Thus ignorant was I of my own heart, and of the spirituality, strictness and extent of the divine law!! In this time I was at home, in a vacancy at college; and several men, who were gross Arminians, entered into a dispute with me about doctrines and religion. I was in theory a Calvinist, and attempted to defend that scheme of doctrines, in opposition to them. In these we could not agree: But when we came to talk of practical religion, and of conversion, I agreed with them, allowing it to consist chiefly in externals, overlooking the real and total depravity of the heart, and the renovation and great change which must take place in that, in order to true conversion and the exercise of real religion, having never experienced any thing of this kind. My mother heard the conversation; and after the company was gone, she told me, she was surprized to hear me agree with them in their notion of conversion;

and that I should think real conversion was no more than that which I and they had described. This put me upon thinking, and raised a suspicion in my own mind that I was a stranger to real conversion. But it wore off, without any abiding conviction of my deficiency.

From this experience of mine, I have been led to fear, and, in many instances, to conclude persons to be strangers to true conversion, who appear to have the same or no better notion of it, than I then had, and talk much as I did on that head, while they profess to believe Calvinistic doctrines, though they choose to be considered as *moderate Calvinists*. There are many of this sort of professing christians, with whom I have been acquainted. When persons build upon such a false foundation, and set out in religion, and think themselves christians, without being *born of God,* and continue strangers to a true and sound conversion; they will be inclined to oppose or slight the most important and excellent exercises of experimental religion, and will be dry and fruitless christians, and ignorant of true religious affections and enjoyments. And it will be no wonder if they loose all their zeal for the peculiar doctrines of the gospel, and grow indifferent about them; if they do not gradually give them up, and renounce them.

While I was in this state and situation of mind, Mr. Whitefield came into New-England; and after he had preached in Boston, and other places, came to New-Haven, in his way to New-York. The attention of people in general was greatly awakened upon hearing the fame of him, that there was a remarkable preacher from England travelling through the country. The people flocked to hear him, when he came to New-Haven. Some travelled twenty miles out of the country to hear him. The assemblies were crowded and remarkably attentive; and people appeared generally to approve, and their conversation turned chiefly about him and his preaching. Some disapproved of several things which he advanced, which occasioned considerable dispute. I heard him when he preached in public, and when he expounded in private in the evening; and highly approved of him; and was somewhat impressed by what he said in public and in private; but did not in the least call in question my own good estate, that I remember. He preached against mixed dancing and frolicing of males and females together: which practice was then very common in New-England. This offended some, especially young people. But I remember I justified him in this in my own mind, and in conversation with those who were disposed to condemn him. This was in October 1740, when I had entered on my last year in college.

During that fall and the succeeding winter, there appeared to be much more attention to religion, than before, among people in general: And a number of ministers in New-England were aroused, and preached oftener than they had done, and appeared much more engaged and zealous, than before; and several came to New-Haven and preached in a manner so different from what had been usual, that people in general appeared to be in some measure awakened, and more thoughtful on religious subjects, than they had been before.

Early in the next spring, in March, Mr. Gilbert Tennent, who had been itinerating in New-England, in Boston and other places in the winter, came to New-Haven from Boston, in his way to the southward. He was a remarkably plain and rousing preacher, and a remarkable awakening had been produced by his preaching, and many hopeful conversions had taken place under his preaching, where he had itinerated. On his coming to New-Haven, the people appeared to be almost universally aroused, and flocked to hear him. He stayed about a week in New-Haven, and preached seventeen sermons, most of them in the meeting-house; two or three in the college hall. His preaching appeared to be attended with a remarkable and mighty power. Thousands, I believe, were awakened; and many cried out with distress and horror of mind, under a conviction of God's anger, and their constant exposedness to fall into endless destruction. Many professors of religion received conviction that they were not real christians, and never were born again; which numbers publicly confessed, and put up notes, without mentioning their names, but their number; desiring prayers for them as unconverted, and under this conviction. The members of college appeared to be universally awakened. A small number thought themselves christians before they came to college, and I believe were so. Several of these appeared with an extraordinary zeal, and concern for the members of college; and without paying regard to the distinctions of higher and lower classes, they visited every room in college, and discoursed freely and with the greatest plainness with each one; especially such whom they considered to be in an unconverted state, and who acknowledged themselves to be so, setting before them their danger, and exhorting them to repent, &c. The consciences of all seemed to be so far awakened as to lead them to hang their heads, and to pay at least a silent regard to their reprovers. And every person in the college appeared to be under a degree of awakening and conviction. The persons above mentioned, who thus distinguished themselves in zeal were two of them my class-mates, Buell and Youngs. The other was David Brainard. I attended to the whole, and approved of all they said and did. But retained my hope that I was a christian, and had little or no conversation with these zealous men. At length Brainard came into my room, I being there alone. I was not at a loss with respect to his design in making me a visit then; determining that he came to satisfy himself whether I were a christian, or not. And I resolved to keep him in the dark, and if possible prevent his getting any knowledge of my state or religion. I was therefore wholly on the reserve, being conscious that I had no religious experiences, or religious affections to tell of. In his conversation with me, he observed that he believed it impossible for a person to be converted and to be a real christian without feeling his heart, at sometimes at least, sensibly and greatly affected with the character of Christ, and strongly going out after him; or to that purpose.—This observation struck conviction into my mind. I verily believed it to be true, and at the same time, was conscious that I had never experienced any thing of this kind; and that I was a stranger to the exercise of real christianity. I then determined that no one should know from me, or any other way, if I could prevent it, that I was not a christian, until I should be converted: For it was mortifying to my pride to be thought to be no christian, having made a christian profession, and having had the character of a christian for some time; though I now knew myself not to be one. Brainard took his leave of me without bringing me to put off my reserve; and what he then thought of me, I know not; but believe he strongly suspected, if he did not without hesitation conclude, that I was not a christian.

My conviction fixed upon me. I saw I was indeed no christian. The evil of my heart, the hardness and unbelief of it came more and more into view; and the evil case in which I was, appeared more and more dreadful. I felt myself a guilty, justly condemned creature, and my hope of relief by obtaining conversion failed more and more, and my condition appeared darker from day to day, and all help failed, and I felt myself to be nothing but ignorance, guilt and stupidity. I now lost all desire to conceal my case from those whom I considered to be christians, and freely opened it to some of them. They appeared particularly to interest themselves in my condition, and often conversed with me, and asked me if I had any new views, &c. I constantly told them I was still the same, in an unconverted state, &c. Thus I continued for some weeks, generally retired, unless when I attended private meetings of young people, for prayer, &c. which were frequent then in college, and in the town.

At length as I was in my closet one evening, while I was meditating, and in my devotions, a new and wonderful scene opened to my view. I had a sense of the being and presence of God, as I never had before; it being more of a reality, and more affecting and glorious, than I had ever before perceived. And the character of Jesus Christ the mediator came into view, and appeared such a reality, and so glorious; and the way of salvation by him so wise, important and desirable, that I was astonished at myself that I had never seen these things before, which were so plain, pleasing and wonderful. I longed to have all see and know these things as they now appeared to me. I was greatly affected, in the view of my own depravity, the sinfulness, guilt, and odiousness of my character; and tears flowed in great plenty. After some time I left my closet, and went into the adjoining room, no other person being then there. I walked the room, all intent on these subjects, and took up Watts's version of the psalms, and opened it at the fifty-first psalm, and read the first, second and third parts in long metre with strong affections, and made it all my own language, and thought it was the language of my heart to God; I dwelled upon it with pleasure, and wept much. And when I had laid the book aside, my mind continued fixed on the subject, and in the exercise of devotion, confession, adoration, petition, &c. in which I seemed to pour out my heart to God with great freedom. I continued all attention to the things of religion, in which most appeared more or less engaged. There were many instances, as was then supposed, of conversion. I felt a peculiar, pleasing affection to those, who were supposed to be christians.

But two things appear, now, to me remarkable, with respect to my views and exercise which I have just now mentioned. *First,* I had not then the least thought or suspicion that what I had experienced was conversion, or any thing like it, nor did such a thought enter my mind, so far as I can recollect, till near a year after this, or if any such thought was suggested at any time, it was immediately rejected. I had formed an idea in my mind of conversion, what persons who were converted must be, and how they must feel, which was so entirely different from that which I had seen and felt, that I was so far from a thought that I was converted, that I thought I *knew* I was not, and made no scruple to tell my friends so, from time to time. *Secondly,* I do not recollect that I said a word to any person living of these exercises, or gave the least hint of them to any one for almost a year after they took place. I did not think they were worth speaking of, being nothing like conversion. And by degrees I ceased to recollect any thing of them, still hoping and looking for something greater and better, and of quite a different kind.

When I heard Mr. Tennent, as mentioned above, I thought he was the greatest and best man, and the best preacher that I had ever seen or heard. His words were to me, "like apples of gold in pictures of silver." And I then thought that when I should leave the college, as I was then in my last year, I would go and live with him, wherever I should find him. But just before the commencement in September, when I was to take my degree, on the seventeenth day of which month I was twenty years old, Mr. Edwards of Northampton came to New-Haven, and preached. He then preached the sermon on the *trial of the spirits,* which was afterwards printed. I had before read his sermons on justification, &c. and his narrative of the remarkable conversions at Northampton, which took place about seven years before this. Though I then did not obtain any personal acquaintances with him, any farther than by hearing him preach; yet I conceived such an esteem of him, and was so pleased with his preaching, that I altered my former determination with respect to Mr. Tennent, and concluded to go and live with Mr. Edwards, as soon as I should have opportunity, though he lived about eighty miles from my father's house.

After I had taken my first degree, which was in September 1741, I retired to my father's in Waterbury. And being dejected and very gloomy in my mind, I lived a recluse life for some months. Considering myself as a sinful lost creature, I spent most of my time in reading, meditation and prayer; and spent many whole days in fasting and prayer. My attention turned chiefly to my own sinfulness, and as being wholly lost in myself, of which I had an increasing conviction. But I also attended to the state of religion in the vicinity. There was a general and uncommon attention to religion, and much preaching by ministers who went from town to town, but opposition was made to the revival of religion, which now began to increase among ministers and people. Some considered it as an evil work, in the whole of it. Others allowed there was some good attending it: but objected greatly to many things which took place and were practised by the friends and subjects of the work, as imprudent and wrong. I was a strong advocate for the doctrines preached by the ministers who were instruments of promoting the revival, and for the practices of those who were the subjects of it, and were supposed to be converted. It is true, there were some things said and practised, which I did not understand, and fully see through. But as I considered them as christians, and myself as not one, and consequently ignorant and incapable of judging, I concluded they must be right. I spent days in fasting and prayer, seeking the promotion of that which to me appeared to be true religion, and the suppression of all opposition to it. I endeavoured to promote religion among the young people in the town: and encouraged them who were attentive and concerned to meet together for prayer, and to spend days of fasting and prayer together; especially those who were thought to be converted. When I saw persons, whom I considered to be unconverted, I felt disposed to pray for them that they might be converted and saved; and felt great concern for some individuals of this character.

2

George Whitefield Comes to New Haven

October 1740

Middletown and Wallingsford

Tuesday, October 23. Was much pleased with the Simplicity of our Host, and the Order wherein his Children attended on their Family Devotions. Preached to about 4000 People (great Numbers of which were considerably affected) about 11 o'Clock. Preached again

George Whitefield, *A Continuation of the Reverend Mr. Whitefield's Journal from a Few Days after His Return to Georgia to His Arrival at Falmouth on the 11th of March, 1741* [The *Seventh Journal*] (London, 1741), pp. 50–52.

in the Afternoon at *Wallingsford,* fourteen Miles from Middletown; and then rod to New-Haven, fourteen Miles further, where I was most affectionately received by Mr. Pierpoint, Brother to Mr. Edwards of Northampton. As I came along, I found wonderful Freedom in my Soul for declining to go so long a Circuit as was proposed. I conversed profitably with a godly, zealous Minister from Long-Island, and when I came to New-Haven, I found God strengthening my inner Man.—I wrestled in Prayer, in Company with my dear Fellow-Travellers, and am persuaded the Lord did not let us go without his Blessing. *Oh that we may sit down in the Kingdom of Heaven!*

New-Haven

Friday, October 24. Was refreshed with the Sight of dear Mr. Noble of New-York, who also brought me Letters from Georgia. Blessed be God, the Orphan-House Affairs go on prosperously. The Lord is with my dear Family of a Truth. Declined preaching in the Morning, because it was wet, and the People had no Notice of my Coming, and I had much private Business on my Hands. Perceived my Health grow better. Preach'd in the Afternoon with Power towards the latter End of the Sermon, and observed some deeply affected indeed. It being the Time in which the Assembly met, the Governor, Council, and the Gentlemen of the lower House were present. After Sermon, two young Ministers, who seem'd to have some Experience of divine Things, came to converse with me, and in the Evening I expounded at my Lodgings to a Room full of People. The Power of the Lord was upon me, I spake with much Weight and Freedom, and had sweet Fellowship with my dear Companions afterwards. *Oh! who wou'd but travel for Christ?*

Saturday, October 25. Was again refreshed this Morning by the Sight of Mr. Fedediab Mills, a dear Man of God, Minister at Ripton near Stratford. He wrote to me some Time ago. I felt his Letter, and now also felt the Man. My Soul was much united to him. I could not but think God would do great Things by his Hands. He has had a remarkable Work in his Parish some Time ago, and talked like one that was no Novice in divine Things. With him I dined at the Rev. Mr. C—'s, Rector of New-Haven College, about one third Part as big as that of Cambridge. It has one Rector, three Tutors, and about a hundred Students: But I hear of no remarkable Concern amongst them concerning Religion. I preached twice to the Consolation of God's People, many of which, I have heard, live at New-Haven, and the Countries round about. There were sweet Meltings discernible both Times. I spoke very closely to the Students, and shewed the dreadful Ill-Consequences of an unconverted Ministry. Dear Mr. Mills, when he took his Leave, told me of one Minister in Particular, who had been wrought upon before, but now was gone Home as full as he could hold. *Oh that God may quicken Ministers! Oh that the Lord may make them a flaming Fire! Come Lord Jesus, come quickly,* Amen *and* Amen.

Sunday, October 26. Preach'd both Morning and Evening to much larger Congregations than before, and in the Afternoon observed an especial Presence of God in the Assembly. Many, I believe, were comforted and quickened by the Holy Ghost. The People of God sent me word, that they were much revived, and one came and told me that these Words were lately pressed upon her Heart, *The Winter is gone, the Spring is coming on, the Voice of the Turtle is heard in the Land.* Indeed I believe this will be an acceptable Year of the Lord. Before Evening Service, the following Note was put into my Hand, by one who came to me a Day or two ago, some Miles off, under Distress, and, tho' but weak in Body, could not but follow me "One Self-righteous Pharisee resting in Duties, who hath a rational Belief of his damned Estate, and that he never felt the Pangs of the New-Birth, desires your Prayers to that God that hath said, *Ye must be born again."* After Sermon I waited on the Governor: I observed him to be much affected under the Word. When I came in, he said, "I am glad, Sir, to see you, and heartily glad to hear you." His Heart was so full that he could not speak much. The Tears trickled down his aged Cheeks like Drops of Rain. "He was thankful to God, he said, for such Refreshings in our Way to our Rest. Food does us Good, when we eat it with an Appetite." And indeed, I believe he had fed upon the Word. *The Lord support him, when his Strength faileth him, and bring his grey Heirs with Comfort to the Grave!* In the Evening I expounded at my Lodgings to a great Number of People, and collected upwards of 35*l.* for the Orphans. My Soul was much refreshed to hear how the Children of God were revived under the Word preached. And nothing confirms me more that I have been taught of God, and preach the Truth as it is in Jesus, than to find our Lord's dear old Disciples, feeling the Power of the Word wherever

I go, saying, "It agrees with their Experiences." *My Sheep hear my Voice,* says our Redeemer, *A Stranger will they not hear.* About eight at Night we left New-Haven. The Moon shone bright, and, after we had rode three Miles, we arrived at a House, which, as a faithful Minister told me before, "was full of God." I think, they tell me the Mother and three Daughters were converted Persons. As soon as I came into the House, the Spirit of the Lord came upon me. God gave me to wrestle with him, and my Friends said at departing they were never in such a House before. Oh it was a sweet Time indeed! God made his Power to be felt and known. After I had given a Word of Exhortation, that they would study to adorn the Gospel of our Lord in all Things, we went forward on our Journey, and got to Milford, 10 Miles from New-Haven, about ten at Night. *The Lord's Name be praised from the rising up of the Sun, unto the going down of the same.* Amen *and* Amen.

3

George Whitefield Writes
to the Students at Harvard and Yale

July 1741

To the Students, &c. under convictions at the colleges of Cambridge and New-haven,—in New-England and Connecticut.

Dear Gentlemen,

With unspeakable pleasure have I heard, that there seems to be a general concern among you about the things of GOD. It was no

George Whitefield, *The Works of the Reverend George Whitefield, M.A.* (London, 1771), pp. 296–297.

small grief to me, that I was obliged to say to your college, that "your light was become darkness;" yet are ye now become light in the LORD. I heartily thank GOD, even the Father of our glorious Redeemer, for sending dear Mr. T—— among you. What great things may we not now expect to see in New-England, since it has pleased GOD to work so remarkably among the sons of the prophets? Now we may expect a reformation indeed, since it is beginning at the house of GOD. A dead ministry will always make a dead people. Whereas, if ministers are warmed with the love of GOD themselves, they cannot but be instruments of diffusing that love among others. This, this is the best preparation for the work whereunto you are to be called. Learning without piety, will only make you more capable of promoting the kingdom of satan. Henceforward, therefore, I hope you will enter into your studies not to get a parish, nor to be polite preachers, but to be great saints. This, indeed, is the most compendious way to true learning: for an understanding enlightened by the spirit of GOD, is more susceptible of divine truths, and I am certain will prove most useful to mankind. The more holy you are, the more will GOD delight to honour you. He loves to make use of instruments, which are like himself. I hope the *good old divinity* will now be precious to your souls, and you will think it an honour to tread in the steps of your pious forefathers. They were acquainted with their own hearts.—They know what it was to be tempted themselves, and therefore from their own experience knew how to succqur others. O may you follow them, as they followed CHRIST. Then great, very great will be your reward in heaven. I am sure you can never serve a better Master than JESUS CHRIST, or be engaged in a higher employ than in calling home souls to him. I trust, dear gentlemen, you will not be offended at me for sending you these few lines. I write out of the fulness of my heart. I make mention of you always in my prayers. Forget me not in yours. I am a poor weak worm. I am the chief of sinners, and yet, O stupendous love! the LORD's work still prospers in my unworthy hands.—Fail not to give thanks, as well as to pray for

Your affectionate brother and servant,
in our common LORD,
G. W.

4

Gilbert Tennent to George Whitefield

New York, April 25, 1741

Very Dear Brother,

After cordial Salutation, these may inform you, that through great Mercy I have enjoy'd some Measure of Health, for the most Part of Time. In my Return *homewards,* I have been preaching daily, ordinarily three Times a Day, and sometimes oftner (a few Days in the aforesaid Space excepted) and through *pure Grace* I have met with Success much exceeding my Expectation. In the Town of *Boston* there were many Hun[dreds or] Thousands as some have judged, under Soul-concern. When I left that Place, many Children were deeply affected about their Souls and several had received Consolation. Some aged Persons *in Church Communion* and some open Opposers were convinced; divers of the young and middle-aged were comforted: And several Negroes were hopefully converted. The Shock was rather more general at *Charles-town.* Multitudes were awakened, and several had received great Consolation, especially among the young People, Children and Negroes. At *Cambridge* also in the College and Town, the shaking among the dry Bones was general; and several of the Students have received Consolation. In these Places, I found several Fruits of your Ministry. In *Ipswich,* there was a general Concern among the Inhabitants, so in this Place also I saw some of the Fruits of your Labours. There were also several awakend in *Portsmouth,* in *Greenland,* in *Ipswick, Hamlet, Marble-head,*

Massachusetts Historical Society, *Proceedings,* LIII (1920), 194–196.

Chelsea, Malden, Hampton, New-town, Rosebury, Plimouth, Bristol, Providence, Stoningtown, Geatton [Groton], *New-London, Lime, Guilford, New-haven, Milford, Stratford, New-port.* The shock at *New-port,* was very considerable. Divers Quakers and Children came to me, in distress about their Souls, with others. At *New-haven,* the Concern was general both in College and Town: . . . About thirty Students came on foot ten Miles to hear the Word of God. And at *Milford* the Concern was general. I believe by a Moderate Computation that Divers Thousands have been awakened, *Glory be to God on High!* I have had good Information this Journey, that God has bless'd my poor Labours on *Long Island* in my pass to *New-England.* I thank you, Sir, that you did excite me to this Journey. It was doubtless of God, there have been several Children in several other Places beside these mentioned, Who after Distress, have received Comfort. The Work of God spreads more and more. My Brother *William* has had remarkable Success this Winter at *Burlington.* I hear that there are several religious Societies formed there. Mr. *John Cross* has had remarkable Success at *Stratten* [Staten] *Island,* and many I hear, have been awakened by the Labours of Mr. *Rolinson* in divers places of the *York* Government. Mr. *Mills* has had remarkable Success in *Connecticut,* particularly at *New-haven.* And I hear that Mr. *Blair,* has had remarkable Success in *Pensilvania.* Mr. *Noble* and Family are well. The Lord bless you Dear Brother. I add no more, but Love and remain Yours.

G. *Tennent.*

P.S. *In and about Mr.* Davenport's *Place there is a great Commotion; Multitudes are under Soul-concern: And I hear that he is very warm. From* Horseneck *to* York *beyond* Boston, *there is in most Places a greater or less Degree of Soul-concern.*

5

Ebenezer Pemberton:
"The Knowledge of Christ Recommended"

April 19, 1741

> For I determined not to know any thing among you, save Jesus Christ, and him crucified.

An unquenchable thirst after knowledge was originally im-planted, in the nature of Man, and design'd by our all-wise Creator, for the most excellent and valuable ends.—This tho innocent and commendable in its self, prov'd an unhappy temptation to the first Apostacy, and involv'd the race of mankind in universal ruin. A Criminal Ambition to be wise above the privilege of their natures, allured our first Parents, to violate the law of their creation, and *eat of the fruit of the forbidden tree*—by which they forfeited the divine favour and incurr'd the dreadful penalty of eternal Death. As-piring to become as God's discerning between good and evil, they fell from their exalted station, and rendered themselves viler than the beasts that perish.

But (Blessed be God) there is a knowledge by which we may be delivered, from the ruins of our Apostate state and recover our forfeited felicity.—This is not an acquaintance with the secrets of Nature or the intrigues and policies of Art, but a knowledge *of Christ and him crucified.* . . .

Ebenezer Pemberton, *The Knowledge of Christ Recommended, in a Sermon Preach'd in the Public Hall at Yale-College in New Haven: April 19, 1741* (New London, 1741), pp. 1–2, 16–20.

II. This is the most useful and Necessary knowledge. Men are apt highly to value themselves upon the account of their human knowledge and to look down with contempt upon others, whom they esteem ignorant and unlearn'd: But the wisest Philosopher, the greatest Scholar, if ignorant of Christ and the way of salvation appointed by him; will be finally rejected by God, and with all his attainments lie down in everlasting sorrow.

The wisdom of this world can attain no higher, than to gratify a present inclination, or secure some slight, temporal advantage. But the knowledge of Christ aims at a nobler end—advances the Glory of God, and promotes the universal happiness of man.—The Voice of Nature proclaims our Guilt, fills the mind with anxious fears, and soon convinces us, that we are miserable and mortal sinners. But all the writings of the gentile sages, all the directions of their celebrated moralists are insufficient to recover fallen man, from the ruins of his Apostate state, and restore him to his Original integrity and happiness.—This is the peculiar glory of the Gospel, and can be attain'd only by an experimental knowledge of Christ, and a lively faith in him.

Without this men may be instructed in the Doctrines of Grace and discourse of them with propriety and elegance, but all their knowledge is but specious ignorance, and is esteem'd by God no better than foolishness.—Without this tho men are adorn'd with many amiable qualities, and lead sober, regular, and to all appearance religious lives, yet they remain under the condemning sentence of the Law, and perish at last in a state of unsanctified nature—*For there is no other Name given under heaven by which we can be saved but the name of* Jesus—and no salvation by him, until he is inwardly reveal'd in us by his Spirit.

We may hear the character of Christians, be diligent and devout in our attendance upon the duties of divine worship, but unless our persons are justified thro' the imputation of Christ's perfect righteousness, and our natures are quickned by a principle of new life deriv'd from him; we are no better than—whited Sepulchres—painted Pharisees—and disguis'd hypocrites.—Justly then does the great Doctor of the Gentiles, place so high a value upon this divine, and excellent knowledge—With the highest reason does he determine, *to know nothing but Jesus Christ and him crucified.* And his example is certainly worthy to be diligently imitated by us.

What infinite madness is it then for the guilty Children of men to spend their time and strength in the pursuit of those things, which will leave them, naked, destitute, and miserable; and neglect the knowlege of Christ which will justify, sanctify, and save them. Why O sinner will you waste the lamp of life, in these specious follies & amusements, which belong only to the present world and despise those things, which concern your eternal welfare?—Would you not stand amazed to behold a condemn'd Malefactor, under a sentence of Death, and in continual danger, of being dragg'd out to execution, spend his time in mirth and diversion, or at best in worldly cares and business, without any concern, to prevent the execution of the Law, or prepare for his approaching Death?—And this is the daily madness of tho'tless & inconsiderate sinners. Every Soul in this Assembly, that has not an experimental knowlege of Christ, is under the condemning sentence of the divine Law, and exposed to an infinitely more terrible execution, than any human power can inflict; there remains but a short and uncertain time to fly from the amazing danger and escape the vengeance of eternal fire.—Is it not then worse than brutal stupidity to Neglect the present season and trifle away those flying moments, upon which an eternity depends. Rouse up your selves therefore, My Dear Brethren,—Awake out of this fatal Security—Cry earnestly to God that he would bestow upon you the spirit of *wisdom and revelation, That you may know him—whom to know is Life eternal.*—Resolve to make this your chief study; Your great and principal business. Other knowledge may recommend you to the Applause of men, but this will restore you to the favour of God, and enable you to stand with safety at the awful tribunal of Christ. You may be ignorant of many things, and yet wise for salvation. But if destitute of this divine knowlege you are Sons of death and must dwell in the melancholy regions of eternal darkness. Other knowlege will be shortly unprofitable and Vain—It will afford you but a feeble support against the Assaults of the King of terrors; But an experimental knowlege of Christ, will inlighten the dark valley of the shadow of death, and enable you to meet your last enemy with joy and triumph. If you truly know Christ, tho' ignorant of everything else, you know enough to make you happy in time and thro'out Eternity.—For such as are justified by faith, have peace with God, and are Heirs of immortal Glory.—Neither the reproaches of an accusing Conscience, the demands of a broken Law, nor the flaming sword of divine Justice—Neither former sins or later transgressions, shall ever be able to separate them, from their supreme and eternal felicity.

Nothing now remains but

Thirdly, To Apply this discourse to you my Dear Young friends, the students of this House, and in an especial manner to such of you as are candidates for the service of the sacred ministry.

Your united requests have bro't me into this desk at this time, and for your service this discourse is peculiarly design'd. Suffer me then with a tender concern, for your present usefulness and eternal welfare, earnestly to exhort you, to the diligent practice of the duty recommended in my text.—Resolve with the great Doctor of the Gentiles to know nothing save Christ and him crucified.

Blessed be God there are many of you Enquiring with the Young man in the Gospel, *What shall I do that I may enter into Life Eternal.* This we trust is a token for good—a happy sign that God has mercy in store for future Generations.

In your present Circumstances you will easily find the insufficiency of all human teaching—to deliver you from that depth of misery in which you are involv'd, and to guide your feet in the way to peace & safety. If you have a lively sense of your Guilt and Misery you will soon perceive, That neither the writings of Plato or Seneca, the celebrated Philosophers of Rome and Athens: nor the most accurate delineations of the religion of Nature by the admir'd teachers of morality in the present Age, will afford you a solid foundation of peace and comfort—To a Conscience truly awakened, these will be found *miserable comforters—Physicians of no value!*

Alas what will a knowlege of the secrets of Nature? what will an acquaintance with the Mysteries of Art, or the most eloquent Harangues upon the beauty and excellency of moral Vertue avail me, while I am perishing under the guilt of Sin, and subject to the disgraceful servitude of Satan?—What if I had a genius so sublime, as to contain the whole circle of learning in my capacious mind; a capacity so extensive that I could count the number of the Stars and call them all by their names: Tho I understood all manner of Languages, and could discourse with the tongue of men and Angels, yet if I know not Christ and him crucified—all these will profit me nothing—These splendid attainments which are so highly valued by the learned and polite world, will but render me a richer prey to Satan and lead me with so much more pomp and ceremony to the land of darkness.

Let me then never any more waste my time in the search of that knowlege which will not supply the wants of my immortal Soul, nor spend my strength in seeking after those things which will at last leave me, blind and wretched—Ignorant of my duty and happiness. Let me seek after that knowlege which will restore peace to my troubled mind—that will rectify the disorders of my corrupted nature—that will deliver me, from the tyranny of Satan to whom I am inslaved, and from the terrors of Death of which I am in continual danger.—In fine that will rescue me from that unutterable Misery, which I have deserv'd, and restore me to the Joys of Paradise which I have forfeited.

This O My Brethren is that knowlege which alone is worthy of the study of a rational and immortal Creature. This is that knowlege which is recommended to you in my text. Other knowlege may brighten and adorn the understanding; but this alone will purify the heart. An acquaintance with the Arts and Sciences, may advance your Credit among men, but this alone renders you a Child of God and gives you a title to the Kingdom of heaven. The Study of other things may entertain and amuse You, while you are flourishing in health and prosperity—but this will comfort you when Languishing on a bed of Sickness, and revive and support you in the gloomy hour of approaching Death.

But O! what darkness and horror will surprize the secure and inconsiderate sinner? who has spent his time in the empty speculations of science falsly so called, and the idle amusements of the gay and fashionable world, when he comes to stand upon the awful confines of the grave, and finds himself just stepping into the amazing gulph of eternity. With what sorrow and regret will he reflect, upon those many hours he has wasted upon unprofitable vanities, while he has neglected, the one thing needful, the knowlege of Christ, and the way of Salvation by him? With what anguish and despair will such look up to the mansions of the Blessed, and behold many whom they once despised as Ignorant and unlearned, triumphing in endless Joy and felicity, when they with all their boasted attainments, are thrust down into unutterable darkness and misery.

Allow me my Dear Brethren to go on and say, that not only your own personal welfare, but the prosperity of the Church of Christ is greatly concern'd in your compliance with this Exhortation.

You are the hopes of our Churches and the flourishing of religion in future times depends, upon your having this saving knowlege of Christ. You are many of you design'd for the Service of the Sanctuary, & if you lay the foundation of your preparations for the work of the ministry, in an experimental Acquaintance with Christ—You will doubtless prove extensive blessings in your day, and be the happy Instruments of propagating, pure and undefil'd religion to late posterity.—But if you enter upon this sacred Charge under the influence of Carnal motives—while you are strangers to that Christ, whom you are to preach to others, You will in all probability be the plagues of the Church, and the Unhappy occasion of the damnation of multitudes.

Remember then that the Eyes of God Angels and Men are upon You, to Observe with what temper and disposition—with what views and intentions you engage in the service of the Gospel. Methinks I see the happy Spirits of Your pious Ancestors, who have fought the good fight of faith, and finish'd their course with Joy, look down from the lofty battlements of heaven, to observe your conduct, and see whether you will prove faithful to the cause of Christ, for which they forsook the pleasures of their native land, and encountred with all the difficulties of an howling wilderness. Methinks I hear them calling to you aloud from their exalted seats in Glory, and solemnly adjuring you by all that's sacred and serious—To Choose the God of your Fathers for your God,—to keep the sacred depositum of the Gospel uncorrupted in this day of prevailing degeneracy, and transmit the knowlege of Christ, without any Erroneous mixtures to their Childrens Children for ever.

To propagate the Kingdom of our Great Redeemer and not to promote the designs of a party, was the Blessed Cause in which our Fathers were happily engaged, and for which they underwent numberless hardships and trials. And this should be for ever dear to their posterity, who now stand in their place and stead, and reap the fruits of all their expence and labour.

Let me therefore with the Authority of a Minister of Christ and with the tender affection of a friend zealously concerned for your and the Churches welfare, entreat and perswade you to make this divine knowlege the Great design you have continually in View; and let all your other studies be managed in such a manner as may subserve this noble Intention. This the honour of your profession as Christians, Your Usefulness as Ministers, and the Necessities of the perishing Souls of men, loudly demand from you.—See that you have a saving knowlege of Christ yourselves before you pretend to preach him to others. *For if the blind lead the blind,* what can be expected, but that they both fall into the pit of everlasting darkness and misery?

And when you enter upon the Work of the Ministry, Let *Christ and him crucified* be the favourite subject, of your private meditations and public administrations, without which your sacred performances, how beautifully soever they are contrived, how artfully soever delivered, will be no better than *the sounding brass and tinkling Cymbal.* Remember the Character you are to bear is that of a Minister of Christ, and the Commission you receive, is to preach *his unsearchable Riches* —to proclaim the Glories of the Amiable Jesus—A commission that would dignify an angel, and adorn the Character of the brightest Seraph.—Let his Name therefore triumph in all your discourses, and let it be the height of your ambition to bring Sinners to a saving acquaintance with him.

This was the method made use of by the Apostles in the first ages of the Church, which was own'd and honoured of God, with vast & surprizing success—This was the practice of our Venerable Fathers in the early days of New-England, and they were the happy Instruments in the hands of God of filling his Church with numerous converts, and preparing multitudes for the Kingdom of heaven. And if you imitate these Blessed Examples, and with sacred Courage and Zeal endeavour to promote the practical knowlege of Christ in the world, You will have the same Almighty power to assist, and the same Glorious rewards to Encourage You—Yea if You will unfeignedly give up your Names to this glorious Redeemer, and heartily engage in his Service—You will be standard-bearers in the Camp of Christ, and under the Influence & Conduct of the great Captain of our Salvation, shall lead forth the Armies of Israel to Certain victory and triumph.

Tho' this may expose You to the reproaches of Your friends & acquaintance, tho' you may be called to Oppose the united Endeavours of Earth & Hell. Yet be faithful unto the Death and then you shall receive a Crown of Life. Yet a little while and that Saviour in whose Cause you are engaged, and whose Kingdom you promote, shall appear in the Defence of his despised Interests, and fill the whole Earth with the Glory of his Name.—Yet a little while & *he that shall come, will come and shall not tarry*—Then shall the Wise men & disputers of this world who with all their learnings, remain Ignorant of the Mysteries of Salvation, be found *wandring Stars for whom is reserved blackness of darkness for ever.* While you who have determined to know nothing but Christ and him crucified, and made it the business of Life to make him known unto others, shall shine with Uncommon brightness in the firmament of Glory—While they shall be clothed with everlasting shame & Contempt, You will appear in distinguishing Circumstances of dignity and honour, shall receive the Applause of Your Lord and Judge and Enter into Your Master's Joy—To which, &c. Amen.

The Names of Subscribers and Number of Books

	Books		Books
A.		Eleazar Fitch	4
Thomas Adams M.A.	6	Daniel Farrand	8
Thomas Arthur	6	Joseph Fowler	8
B.		**G.**	
Samuel Buell B.A.	6	David Gardiner M.A.	6
Nehemiah Barker	3	John Grant	6
David Brainard	6	Timothy Griffith	4
David Burr	6	**H.**	
Joshua Belding	6		
Israel Bunnel	7	Nicholas Hallam M.A.	6
Silas Breet	12	Samuel Hopkins B.A.	8
		John Herpin B.A.	10
C.		Joseph Hauley	8
Christopher Christophers		Simon Huntington B.A.	6
M.A.	6	Jabez Huntington B.A.	6
Mr. John Christophers	6	Henry Hausen	3
James Cogswell	4	Elizur Hale	4
Elnathan Chauncey	6	Samuel Huntington	4
Gershom Clark	4	Hezekiah Huntington	12
Ichabod Camp	6	Thomas Hazard	15
Jonathan Copp	6	**I.**	
Mrs. Abigail Caner	4		
		Jared Ingersol	3
D.		**J.**	
Mr. John Dixwell	6		
Aaron Day M.A.	6	Jacob Johnson B.A.	6
Thomas Darling B.A.	6	Jonathan Judd B.A.	6
Edward Darr	8	Reuben Judd B.A.	6
Nathan Dewolf	4	Isaac Jones	3
Timothy Dwight	12	Stephen Johnson	4
		Samuel Johnson	6
E.		**L.**	
Joseph Eliot	3		
		William Livingston B.A.	8
F.		Joseph Lamson B.A.	6
Samuel Fitch	4	Thomas Lewis	6
Samuel Fisk	8	Jonathan Lyman	6

	Books		Books
Jonathan Lee	6	Caleb Smith sen.	6
Joshua Lothrop	6	Caleb Smith jun.	6
Myndert Lansingh	12		

T.

	Books		Books
		William Throope	4

M.

	Books
Timothy Mix M.A.	6
Samuel Mansfield M.A.	6

	Books
Samuel Tracy	6
Agur Tomlinson	6

	Books
Amos Munson B.A.	6
Richard Mansfield B.A.	5
John Moore B.A.	6
Elijah Mason	6

U.

	Books
David Umberfield	6

P.

	Books
James Pierpont M.A.	6
Job Prudden	6
Timothy Prout	8
Alexander Phelps	8

W.

	Books
John Still Winthrop M.A.	6
Enoch Ward M.A.	6
David Wooster M.A.	12
Jeha Whiting B.A.	6
Benjamin Woodbridge B.A.	6
John Worthington B.A.	6
Stephen Williams B.A.	6
Noah Weils B.A.	8

R.

	Books
Simon Ray	10
Asher Rosseter	4
David Rowland	6
Aaron Richards	5
Ebenezer Rosseter	10
Anthony Rutgers	10

	Books
David Webster B.A.	6
Josiah Wolcott	4
Nathan Whiting	5
Solomon Williams	4
Eliphalet Williams	4
Joseph Webb	6
Benjamin Woolsey	9
David Wilcockson	8

S.

	Books
Daniel Southmayd B.A.	10
James Sprout B.A.	8
Nathan Strong	6

Y.

	Books
Thomas Youngs B.A.	12
David Youngs B.A.	6

6

David Brainerd: Memoirs

1732–1741

I Was, I think, from my Youth, something sober, and inclined rather to Melancholy, than the contrary Extreme; but don't remember any Thing of Conviction of Sin, worthy of Remark, 'till I was, I believe, about seven or eight Years of Age; when I became something concern'd for my Soul, and terrified at the Thoughts of Death, and was driven to the Performance of Duties: But it appeared a melancholy Business, and destroyed my Eagerness for Play. And alas! This religious Concern was but short-lived. However, I sometimes attended secret Prayer; and thus lived at Ease in Zion, without God in the World, and without much Concern, as I remember, 'till I was about thirteen Years of Age. But sometime in the Winter 1732, I was something roused out of carnal Security, by I scarce know what Means at first; but was much excited by the prevailing of a mortal Sickness in Haddam: I was frequent, constant and something fervent in Duties, and took Delight in reading, especially Mr. Janeway's *Token for Children*; I felt sometimes much melted in Duties, and took great Delight in the Performance of 'em: And I sometimes hoped, that I was converted, or at least in a good and hopeful Way for Heaven and Happiness, not knowing what Conversion was. The Spirit of God at

Jonathan Edwards (ed.), *An Account of the Life of the Late Reverend Mr. David Brainerd, Minister of the Gospel, Missionary to the Indians, from the Honourable Society in Scotland, for the Propagation of Christian Knowledge, and Pastor of a Church of Christian Indians in New Jersey. . . . Chiefly Taken from His Own Diary, and Other Private Writings, Written for His Own Use: And Now Published* (Boston, 1749), pp. 3–18.

this Time proceeded far with me; I was remarkably dead to the World, and my Thoughts were almost wholly employed about my Soul's Concerns; and I may indeed say, *almost I was persuaded to be a Christian.* I was also exceedingly distressed and melancholy at the Death of my Mother, in March 1732. But afterwards my religious Concern began to decline, and I by Degrees fell back into a considerable Degree of Security; tho' I still attended secret Prayer frequently.

About the 15th of April 1733, I removed from my Father's House to East-Haddam, where I spent four Years, but still *without God in the World;* thou' for the most Part I went a Round of secret Duty. I was not exceedingly addicted to young Company, or Frolicking (as it is called) But this I know, that when I did go into Company, I never returned from a Frolick in my Life, with so good a Conscience as I went with; It always added new Guilt to me, and made me afraid to come to the Throne of Grace, and spoiled those good Frames, I was wont sometimes to please my self with. But alas! all my good Frames were but *Self-Righteousness,* not bottomed on a Desire for the Glory of God.

About the latter End of April 1737, being full 19 years of Age, I removed to Durham, and began to work on my Farm, and so continued the Year out, or near, 'till I was 20 Years old; frequently longing from a natural Inclination, after a liberal Education. When I was about twenty Years of Age, I applied my self to Study; and sometime before, was more than ordinarily excited to and in Duty: But now engaged more than ever in the Duties of Religion. I became very strict, and watchful over my Thoughts, Words, and Actions; and thought I must be sober indeed, because I designed to devote my self to the Ministry; and imagined I did dedicate my self to the Lord.

Some Time in April 1738, I went to Mr. Fiske's, and lived with him, during his Life.[1] And I remember, He advised me wholly to abandon young Company, and associate myself with grave elderly People: which Counsel I followed; and my Manner of Life was now exceeding regular, and full of Religion, such as it was: For I read my Bible more than twice through in less than a Year, I spent much Time every Day in secret Prayer, and other secret Duties; I gave great Attention to the Word preached, and endeavoured to my utmost to retain it: So much concerned was I about Religion, that I agreed with

---

[1] Mr. Fiske was the Pastor of the Church in Haddam. [Jonathan Edwards' note]

---

some young Persons to meet privately on *Sabbath-Evenings* for religious Exercises, and thought my self sincere in these Duties; and after our Meeting was ended, I used to repeat the Discourses of the Day to my self, and recollect what I could, tho' sometimes it was very late in the Night. Again, on *Monday-Mornings,* I used sometimes to recollect the same Sermons. And I had sometimes considerable Movings of Affections in Duties, and much Pleasure, and had many Thoughts of joining to the Church. In short, I had a very good outside, and rested entirely on my Duties, tho' I was not sensible of it.

After Mr. Fiske's Death, I proceeded in my Learning with my Brother; and was still very constant in religious Duties, and often wondered at the Levity of Professors; 'twas a Trouble to me, that they were so careless in religious Matters.—Thus I proceeded a considerable Length on a *self-righteous* Foundation; and should have been entirely lost and undone, had not the meer Mercy of God prevented.

Some Time in the Beginning of Winter, Anno 1738, it pleased God on one Sabbath-day Morning, as I was walking out in some secret Duties (as I remember) to give me on a Sudden such a Sense of my Danger and the Wrath of God, that I stood amazed, and my former good Frames, that I had pleased myself with, all presently vanished; and from the View, that I had of my Sin and Vileness, I was much distressed all that Day, fearing the Vengeance of God would soon overtake me; I was much dejected, and kept much alone, and sometimes begrutched the Birds and Beasts their Happiness, because they were not exposed to eternal Misery, as I evidently saw I was. And thus I lived from Day to Day, being frequently in great Distress: Sometimes there appeared Mountains before me to obstruct my Hopes of Mercy; and the Work of Conversion appeared so great, I thought I should never be the Subject of it: But used, however, to pray and cry to God, and perform other Duties with great Earnestness, and hoped by some Means to make the Case better. And tho' I Hundreds of Times renounced all Pretences of any *Worth* in my Duties (as I thought) even in the Season of the Performance of them, and often confessed to God that I deserved nothing for the very best of them, but eternal Condemnation: Yet still I had a secret latent Hope of *recommending* my self to God by my religious Duties; and when I prayed affectionately, and my Heart seemed in some Measure to melt, I hoped God would be thereby moved to pity me, my Prayers then look'd with some appearance of *Goodness* in 'em, & I seemed to *mourn* for Sin: and then I could in some Measure venture on the Mercy of God in Christ (as I tho't;) Tho' the preponderating Thought and Foundation of my Hope was some Imagination of *Goodness* in, my Heart Meltings, and Flowing of Affections in Duty, and (sometimes) extraordinary Enlargements therein, &c. Tho' at some Times the *Gate* appeared so very strait, that it look'd next to impossible to *enter,* yet at other Times I flattered my self that it was not so very difficult, and hoped I should by Diligence and Watchfulness soon gain the Point. Sometimes after Enlargement in Duty and Considerable Affection, I hoped I had made a good Step towards *Heaven,* and imagined that God was affected as I was, and that he would hear such *sincere Cries* (as I called them) and so sometimes when I withdrew for secret Duties in great Distress, I returned something comfortable; and thus heal'd my self with my Duties.

Some Time in February 1738, 9. I set apart a Day for secret Fasting and Prayer, and spent the Day in almost incessant Cries to God for Mercy, that he would open my Eyes to see the Evil of Sin, and the Way of Life by Jesus Christ. And God was pleased that Day to make considerable Discoveries of my *Heart* to me: But still I *trusted* in all the Duties I performed; tho' there was no Manner of *Goodness* in the Duties I then performed, there being no Manner of Respect to the Glory of God in them, nor any such Principle in my Heart: yet God was pleased to make my Endeavours that Day, a Means to shew me my *Helplessness* in some Measure.

Sometimes I was greatly *encouraged,* and imagin'd that God loved me and was pleased with me, and thought I should soon be fully reconciled to God; while the Whole was founded on meer *Presumption,* arising from Enlargement in Duty, or Flowing of Affections, or some good Resolutions, and the like. And when, at Times, great Distress began to arise, on a Sight of my Vileness and Nakedness, and Inability to deliver my self from a sovereign God, I used to put off the Discovery, as what I could not bear. Once, I remember, a terrible Pang of Distress seized me, and the Thoughts of renouncing my Self, and standing naked before God, stripped of all Goodness, were so dreadful to me, that I was ready to say to 'em as *Felix to Paul, Go thy Way for this Time.* Thus, tho' I daily long'd for greater Conviction of Sin, supposing that I must see more of my dreadful State in order to a Remedy, yet when the Discoveries of my vile hellish Heart were made to me, the Sight was so dreadful, and shewed me so plainly my Exposedness to Damnation, that I could not endure it.—I constantly strove after whatever Qualifications, I imagined others obtained before the Reception of Christ, in order to *recommend* me to his Favour. Sometimes I felt the Power of an *hard* Heart, and supposed it must be soften'd before Christ would accept of me; and when I felt any Meltings of Heart, I hoped now the Work was almost done: And hence, when my Distress still remain'd, I was wont to *murmur* at God's Dealings with me; and thought, when others felt their Hearts softened, God shewed them Mercy: But my Distress remained still.

Sometimes I grew *remiss* and *sluggish,* without any great Convictions of Sin, for a considerable Time together; but after such a Season, *Convictions* sometimes seized me more violently. One Night I remember in particular, when I was walking solitarily Abroad, I had open'd to me such a View of my Sin, that I feared the Ground would cleave asunder under my Feet, and become my Grace, and send my Soul quick into Hell, before I could get Home. And tho' I was forced to go to Bed, lest my Distress should be discovered by others, which I much feared; yet I scarce durst Sleep at all, for I thought it would be a great Wonder if I should be out of Hell in the Morning. And tho' my Distress was sometimes thus great, yet I greatly dreaded the loss of Convictions, and returning back to a State of carnal Security, and to my former Insensibility of impending Wrath; which made me exceeding exact in my Behaviour, lest I should stifle the Motions of God's Spirit. When at any Time I took a View of my Convictions of my own Sinfulness, and thought the Degree of 'em to be considerable, I was wont to trust in my Convictions: But this Confidence, and the Hopes that arose in me from it, of soon making some notable Advances towards Deliverance, would ease my Mind, and I soon became more senseless and remiss: But then again, when I discerned my Convictions to grow languid, and I tho't them about to leave me, this immediately alarmed and distressed me. Sometimes I expected to take a large Step, and get very far towards Conversion, by some particular Opportunity or Means I had in View.

The many Disappointments, and great Distresses and Perplexity I met with, put me into a most *horrible Frame of Contesting* with the Almighty; with an inward Vehemence and Virulence, finding Fault with his Ways of Dealing with Mankind. I found great Fault with the Imputation of *Adam's Sin* to his Posterity: And my wicked Heart often wished for some other Way of Salvation, than by *Jesus Christ*: And being *like the troubled Sea,* and my Thoughts confused, I used to contrive to escape the Wrath of God by some other Means, and had strange Projections, full of Atheism, contriving to disappoint God's Designs and Decrees concerning me, or to escape God's Notice, and hide myself from him: But when, upon Reflection, I saw these Projections were vain, and would not serve me, and that I could contrive nothing for my own Relief, this would throw my Mind into the most horrid Frame, to wish there was *no God,* or to wish there were some other God that could control him, &c. These Thoughts and Desires were the secret Inclinations of my Heart, that were frequently acting before *I was aware;* but alas, they were *mine!* Altho' I was 'affrighted with them, when I came to reflect on them; when I considered of it, it distressed me, to think, that my Heart was so full of Enmity *against God;* and it made me tremble, lest God's Vengeance should suddenly fall upon me. I used before, to imagine my Heart was not so bad, as the Scriptures and some other Books represented. Sometimes I used to take much Pains to work it up into a good Frame, a humble submissive Disposition; and hoped there was then some Goodness in me: But it may be on a sudden, the Thoughts of the Strictness of the Law, or the Sovereignty of God, would so irritate the Corruption of my Heart, that I had so watched over, and hoped I had brought to a good Frame, that it would break over all Bounds, and burst forth on all Sides, like Floods of Waters, when they break down their Damm. But being sensible of the Necessity of a deep *Humiliation* in order to a saving Close with Christ, I used to set my self to work in my own Heart those *Convictions,* that were requisite in such an Humiliation: As, a Conviction, that God would be just, if he cast me off for ever: And that if ever God should bestow Mercy on me, it would be meer Grace, tho' I should be in Distress many Years first, and be never so much engaged in Duty; that God was not in the least obliged to pity me the more for all past Duties, Cries, and Tears, &c. These Things I strove to my utmost to bring my self to a firm belief of, and hearty assent to; and hoped that now I was brought off from my self, and truly humbled and bowed to the divine Sovereignty; and was wont to tell God in my Prayers, that now I had those very Dispositions of Soul that he required, and on which he shewed Mercy to others, and thereupon to beg and plead for Mercy on me: But when I found no Relief, and was still oppressed with Guilt and Fears of Wrath, my Soul was in a Tumult, and my Heart rose against God, as dealing hardly with me. Yet then my Conscience flew in my Face, putting me in Mind of my late Confession to God of his Justice in my Condemnation, &c. And this, giving me a Sight of the Badness of my Heart, threw me again into Distress, and I wished I had watched my Heart more narrowly, to keep it from breaking out against God's Dealings with me, and I even wished I had not pleaded for Mercy on Account of my Humiliation, because thereby I had lost all my seeming Goodness.

Thus, Scores of Times, I vainly imagined my self humbled and prepared for saving Mercy.

While I was in this distressed, bewilder'd, and tumultuous State of Mind, the *Corruption* of my Heart was especially *irritated* with these Things following:

1. The *strictness* of the divine *Law*. For I found it was impossible for me (after my utmost Pains) to answer the Demands of it. I often made new Resolutions, and as often broke them. I imputed the whole to Carelessness, and the Want of being more Watchful, and used to call my self a Fool for my Negligence: But when, upon a stronger Resolution, and greater Endeavours, and close Application of my self to Fasting and Prayer, I found all Attempts fail, then I quarrelled with the Law of God, as unreasonably rigid. I thought, if it extended only to my outward Actions and Behaviours, I could bear with it: But I found it condemned me for my evil Thoughts, and Sins of my Heart, which I could not possibly prevent. I was extreamly loth to give out, and own my utter Helplessness in this Matter: But after repeated Disappointments, thought that, rather than perish, I could *do* a little more still, especially if such and such Circumstances might but attend my Endeavours and Strivings; I hoped, that I should strive more earnestly than ever, if the Matter came to Extremity (tho' I never could find the Time to do my utmost, in the *Manner* I intended). And this Hope of future more favourable Circumstances, and of doing something great hereafter, kept me from utter Despair in my self, and from seeing my self fallen into the Hands of a sovereign God, and dependent on nothing but free and boundless Grace.

2. Another Thing was, that *Faith alone* was the *Condition of Salvation;* and that God would not come down to lower Terms, that he would not promise Life and Salvation upon my sincere and hearty *Prayers* and *Endeavours*. That Word, Mark xvi. 16. *He that believeth not, shall be damned,* cut off all Hope there: And I found, *Faith* was the sovereign *Gift of God;* that I could not get it as of myself, and could not oblige God to bestow it upon me, by any of my Performances. (*Eph.* ii, 1, & 8.) *This,* I was ready to say, is a *hard Saying, who can hear it?* I could not bear, that all I had done should stand for meer nothing, who had been very Consciencious in Duty, and had been exceeding religious a great while, and had (as I thought) done much more than many others that had obtained Mercy. I confess'd indeed the Vileness of my Duties; but then, what made 'em at that Time seem vile, was my wandring Thoughts in them; not because I

was all over defiled like a Devil, and the Principle corrupt from whence they flowed, so that I could not possibly do any Thing that was Good. And therefore I called what I did, by the Name of honest faithful Endeavours; and could not bear it, that God had made no Promises of Salvation to them.

3. Another Thing was, that I could not find out what Faith was; or *what* it was to believe, and *come to Christ.* I read the Calls of Christ, made to the *weary and heavy laden;* but could find no *Way,* that he directed them to come in. I thought I would gladly come, if I knew *how,* tho' the Path of Duty directed to were never so difficult. I read Mr. Stoddard's *Guide to Christ* (which I trust was, in the Hand of God, the happy Means of my Conversion) And my Heart rose against the Author; for tho' he told me my very Heart all along under Convictions, and seem'd to be very beneficial to me in his Directions; yet here he fail'd, He did not tell me any Thing I could do, that would bring me to Christ, but left me as it were with a great Gulf between me and Christ, without any Direction to get through. For I was not yet effectually and experimentally taught, that there could be no Way prescribed, whereby a natural Man could, of his own Strength, obtain that which is supernatural, and which the highest Angel cannot give.

4. Another Thing that I found a great inward Opposition to, was the *Sovereignty* of God. I could not bear, that it should be wholly at God's Pleasure, to save or damn me, just as he would. That Passage, *Rom.* ix. II, —23. was a constant Vexation to me, especially Verse 21. The reading or meditating on this always destroyed my seeming good Frames: When I thought I was almost humbled, and almost resigned to God's Sovereignty, the reading or thinking on this Passage would make my Enmity against the Sovereignty of God appear. And when I came to reflect on my inward Enmity and Blasphemy, that arose on this Occasion, I was the more afraid of God, and driven further from any Hopes of Reconciliation with him; and it gave me such a dreadful View of my self, that I dreaded more than ever to see myself in God's Hands, and at his sovereign Disposal, and it made me more opposite than ever to submit to his Sovereignty; for I thought God designed my Damnation.—

All this Time the *Spirit* of God was powerfully at work with me; and I was inwardly pressed to relinquish all *Self-Confidence,* all Hopes of ever helping my self by any Means whatsoever: And the Conviction of my *lost* Estate was sometimes so clear and manifest before my Eyes, that it was as if it had been declared to me in so many Words, " 'Tis done, 'tis done, 'tis forever impossible to deliver your self." For about three or four Days, my Soul was thus distressed, especially at some Turns, when for a few Moments I seemed to my self lost and undone; but then would shrink back immediately from the Sight, because I dared not venture my self into the Hands of God, as wholly helpless, and at the Disposal of his sovereign Pleasure. I dared not see that important Truth concerning my self, That I was *dead in Trespasses and Sins.* But when I had as it were thrust away these Views of my self at any Time, I felt distressed to have the same Discoveries of myself again; for I greatly feared being given over of God to final Stupidity. When I thought of putting it off to a *more convenient Season,* the Conviction was so close and powerful with Regard to the present Time, that it was the best Time, and probably the only Time, that I dared not put it off. It was the Sight of *Truth* concerning my self, *Truth* respecting my State, as a Creature fallen and alienated from God, and that consequently could make no Demands on God for Mercy, but must subscribe to the absolute Sovereignty of the divine Being; the Sight of the *Truth,* I say, my Soul shrank away from, and trembled to think of beholding. Thus, *he that doth Evil* (as all unregenerate Men continually do) *hates the Light of Truth,* neither cares to *come to it,* because it will *reprove his Deeds,* and shew him his just Deserts. (Job. iii. 20.) And tho', some Time before, I had taken much Pains (as I thought) to submit to the Sovereignty of God, yet I mistook the Thing; and did not once imagine, that seeing and being made experimentally sensible of this Truth, which my Soul now so much dreaded and trembled at a Sense of, was the Frame of Soul that I had been so earnest in pursuit of heretofore: For I had ever hoped, that when I had attained to that *Humiliation,* which I supposed necessary to go before Faith, then it would not be fair for God to *cast me off;* but now I saw it was so far from any Goodness in me, to own my self spiritually dead, and destitute of all Goodness, that, on the contrary, *my Mouth* would be forever *stop'd* by it; and it look'd as dreadful to me, to see my self, and the Relation I stood in to God, as a Sinner and a Criminal, and he a great Judge and Sovereign, as it would be to a poor trembling Creature, to venture off some high Precipice. And hence I put it off for a Minute or two, and tried for better Circumstances to do it in; either I must read a Passage or two, or pray first, or something of the like Nature; or else put off my Submission to God's Sovereignty, with an Objection, that I did not know how to submit: But the Truth was, I could see no Safety in owning my self in the Hands of a Sovereign God, and that I could lay no Claim to any Thing better than Damnation.

But after a considerable Time spent in such like Exercises and Distresses, one Morning, while I was walking in a Solitary Place as usual, I at once saw that all my Contrivances and Projections to effect or procure Deliverance and Salvation for my self, were utterly *in vain:* I was brought quite to a stand, as finding my self totally *lost.* I had thought many Times before, that the Difficulties in my Way were very great: But now I saw, in another and very different Light, that it was forever impossible for me to do any Thing towards helping or delivering my self. I then thought of blaming my self, that I had not done more, and been more engaged, while I had Opportunity (for it seemed now as if the Season of doing was forever over and gone) But I instantly saw, that let me have done what I would, it would no more have tended to my helping myself; than what I had done; that I had made all the Pleas, I ever could have made to all Eternity; and that all my Pleas were vain. The Tumult that had been before in my Mind, was now *quieted;* and I was something eased of that Distress, which I felt, while struggling against a Sight of my self, and of the divine Sovereignty. I had the greatest Certainty, that my State was forever miserable, for all that I could do; and wondered, and was almost astonished, that I had never been sensible of it before.

In the Time while I remain'd in this State, *my Notions* respecting my *Duties,* were quite different from what I had ever entertained in Times past. Before this, the more I did in Duty, the more I thought God was obliged to me; or at least the more hard I thought it would be for God to cast me off; 'tho at the same Time I confessed, and thought I saw, that there was no Goodness or Merit in my Duties; But now the more I did in Prayer or any other Duty, the more I saw I was indebted to God for allowing me to ask for Mercy; For I saw, it was Self-Interest had led me to pray, and that I had never once prayed from any Respect to the Glory of God, Now I saw, there was no necessary Connection between my Prayers and the Bestowment of divine Mercy; that they laid not the least Obligation upon God to bestow his Grace upon me; and that there was no more Vertue or Goodness in them, than there would be in my paddling with my Hand in the Water (which was the Comparison I had then in my Mind) and this because they were not performed from any Love or Regard to God. I saw, that I had been heaping up my Devotions before God, Fasting, Praying &c. pretending, and indeed really thinking, at some Times, that I was aiming at the Glory of God; whereas I never once truly intended it, but only my own Happiness. I saw, that, as I had never done any Thing *for* God, I had no Claim to lay to any Thing *from* him, but Perdition, on Account of my Hypocrisy and Mockery. Oh how different did my Duties now appear from what they used to do! I used to charge them with Sin and Imperfection; But this was only on Account of the Wandrings and vain Thoughts attending them, and not because I had no Regard to God in them; for this I thought I had: But when I saw evidently that I had Regard to nothing but Self-Interest, then they appeared vile Mockery of God, Self-Worship, and a continual Course of Lies; so that I saw now, there was something worse had attended my Duties, than barely a few Wandrings &c. For the whole was nothing but Self-Worship and an horrid Abuse of God.

I continued, as I remember, in this State of Mind, from Friday-Morning 'till the Sabbath-Evening following, July 12, 1739, when I was walking again in the same solitary Place where I was brought to see my self lost and helpless (as was before mention'd) and here, in a mournful melancholy State, was attempting to pray; but found no Heart to engage in that, or any other Duty; my former Concern and Exercise and religious Affections were now gone. I thought, the Spirit of God had quite left me; but still was not distressed: Yet disconsolate, as if there was nothing in Heaven or Earth could make me happy. And having been thus endeavouring to pray (tho' being, as I thought, very stupid and senseless) for near half an Hour, (and by this Time the Sun was about half-an-hour-high, as I remember) then, as I was walking in a dark thick Grove, *unspeakable Glory* seemed to open to the View and Apprehension of my Soul: I don't mean any external Brightness, for I saw no such Thing, nor do I intend any Imagination of a Body of Light, some where away in the third Heavens, or any Thing of that Nature; but it was a new inward Apprehension or View that I had of God, such as I never had before, nor any Thing which had the least Resemblance of it. I stood still, and wonder'd and admired! I knew that I never had seen before any Thing comparable to it for Excellency and Beauty: It was widely different from all the Conceptions, that ever I had had of God, or Things divine. I had no particular Apprehension of any one Person in the Trinity, either the Father, the Son, or the Holy Ghost; but it appeared to be *divine Glory,* that I then beheld: And my Soul *rejoyced with Joy unspeakable,* to see such a God, such a glorious divine Being; and I was inwardly pleased and satisfied, that he should be *God over all* forever and ever. My Soul was so captivated and delighted with the Excellency, Loveliness, Greatness, and other Perfections of God, that I was even swallowed up in *Him;* at least to that Degree, that I had no Thought (as I remember) at first, about my own Salvation, and scarce reflected there was such a Creature as my self.

Thus God, I trust, brought me to a hearty Disposition to *exalt him,* and set him on the Throne, and principally and ultimately to aim at his Honour and Glory, as King of the Universe.

I continued in this State of inward Joy and Peace, yet Astonishment, 'till near Dark, without any sensible Abatement; and then began to think and examine what I had seen; and felt sweetly *composed* in my Mind all the Evening following: I felt myself in a new World, and every Thing about me appeared with a different Aspect from what it was wont to do.

At this Time, the *Way of Salvation* opened to me with such infinite Wisdom, Suitableness and Excellency, that I wondered I should ever think of any other Way of Salvation; was amazed, that I had not drop'd my own Contrivances, and complied with this lovely blessed and excellent Way before. If I could have been saved by my own Duties, or any other Way that I had formerly contrived, my whole Soul would now have refused. I wonder'd, that all the World did not see and comply with this Way of Salvation, intirely by the *Righteousness of Christ.*

The sweet Relish of what I then felt, continued with me for several Days, almost constantly, in a greater or less Degree: I could not but sweetly rejoyce in God, lying down and rising up. The next *Lords-Day* I felt something of the same Kind; tho' not so powerful as before. But, not long after, was again involved in *thick Darkness,* and under great Distress: yet not of the same Kind with my Distress under Convictions. I was guilty, afraid and ashamed to come before God, was exceedingly press'd with a Sense of Guilt: But it was not long before I felt (I trust) true Repentance and Joy in God.

About the latter End of August, I again fell under great Darkness; it seem'd as if the Presence of God was *clean gone forever.* Tho' I was not so much distressed about my spiritual State, as I was at my being shut out from God's Presence, as I then sensible was. But it pleased the Lord to return graciously to me, not long after.

In the Beginning of September I went to *College*[2], and entred there: But with some Degree of Reluctancy, fearing lest I should not be able to lead a Life of strict Religion, in the midst of so many Temp-

---

[2] Yale-College in New-Haven. [Jonathan Edwards' note]

---

tations.—After this, in the Vacancy, before I went to tarry at College, it pleased God to visit my Soul with clearer Manifestations of himself and his Grace. I was spending some Time in Prayer, & Self-Examination; and the Lord by his Grace so shined into my Heart, that I enjoyed full Assurance of his Favour, for that Time; and my Soul was unspeakably refreshed with divine and heavenly Enjoyments. At this Time especially, as well as some others, sundry Passages of God's *Word* open'd to my Soul with divine Clearness, Power and Sweetness, so as to appear exceeding precious, and with clear and certain Evidence of it's being *the Word of God.* I enjoy'd considerable Sweetness in Religion all the Winter following.

In Jan. 1739, 40. The *Measle's* spread much in College; and I having taken the Distemper, went home to *Haddam:* But some Days before I was taken Sick, I seem'd to be greatly deserted, and my Soul mourned the Absence of the *Comforter* exceedingly: It seem'd to me, all Comfort was forever gone; I pray'd and cried to God for Help, yet found no present Comfort or Relief. But thro' divine Goodness, a Night or two before I was taken Ill, while I was walking alone in a very retired Place, and engaged in Meditation and Prayer, I enjoyed a sweet refreshing Visit, as I trust, from above, so that my Soul was raised far above the Fears of *Death;* indeed I rather longed for Death, than feared it. O how much more refreshing this one Season was, than all the Pleasures and Delights that Earth can afford! After a Day or two I was taken with the Measles, and was very Ill indeed, so that I almost despaired of Life: But had no distressing Fears of Death at all. However thro' divine Goodness I soon recovered: Yet, by Reason of hard and close Studies, and being much exposed on Account of my Freshman-ship, I had but little Time for spiritual Duties; my Soul often mourned for Want of more Time and Opportunity to be alone with God. In the Spring and Summer following I had better Advantages for Retirement, and enjoyed more Comfort in Religion: Tho' indeed my Ambition in my Studies greatly wronged the Activity and Vigour of my spiritual Life: Yet this was usually the Case with me, that *in the Multitude of my Thoughts within me, God's Comforts* principally *delighted my Soul:* These were my greatest Consolations Day by Day.

One Day I remember in particular (I think it was in June 1740.) I walked to a considerable Distance from the College in the Fields alone at Noon, and in Prayer found such unspeakable Sweetness and Delight in God, that I thought, if I must continue still in this evil World, I wanted always to be there, to behold God's Glory: My Soul dearly loved all Mankind, and longed exceedingly that they should enjoy what I enjoyed.—It seem'd to be a little Resemblance of Heaven.

On Lord's-Day, July 6. being Sacrament-Day, I found some divine Life and spiritual Refreshment in that holy Ordinance. When I came from the Lord's Table, I wondered how my Fellow-Students could live as I was sensible most did.—Next Lord's-Day July 13. I had some special Sweetness in Religion.—Again Lord's-Day July 20. my Soul was in a sweet and precious Frame.

Sometimes in August following, I became so weakly and dis-ordered, by too close Application to my Studies, that I was advised by my *Tutor* to go Home, and disengage my Mind from Study, as much as I could; for I was grown so Weak, that I began to spit Blood. I took his Advice, and endeavoured to lay aside my Studies. But being brought very low, I look'd Death in the Face more stedfastly; and the Lord was pleased to give me renewedly a sweet Sense and Relish of divine Things; and particularly in October 13, I found divine Help and Consolation in the precious Duties of secret Prayer and Self Examination, and my Soul took Delight in the blessed God.—so like-wise on the 17th of October.

Saturday October 18. in my Morning-Devotions, my Soul was exceedingly melted for and bitterly mourned over my exceeding *Sin-fulness* and *Vileness*. I never before had felt so pungent and deep a Sense of the odious Nature of Sin, as at this Time. My Soul was then unusually carry'd forth in *Love* to God, and had a lively Sense of God's Love to me. And this Love and Hope, at that Time, cast out Fear. Both Morning and Evening I spent some Time in Self-Examina-tion, to find the Truth of Grace, as also my Fitness to approach to God at his Table the next Day; and through infinite Grace, found the holy Spirit influencing my Soul with Love to God, as a *Witness within my self*.

Lord's-Day October 19. In the Morning, I felt my Soul *hungring and thirsting after Righteousness*. In the Fore-Noon, while I was look-ing on the Sacramental Elements, and thinking that *Jesus Christ* could soon be *set forth crucified before me,* my Soul was fill'd with Light and Love, so that I was almost in an Extasy; my Body was so weak I could scarcely stand. I felt at the same Time an exceeding Tenderness and most fervent Love towards all Mankind; so that my Soul and all the Powers of it seemed, as it were, to melt into softness and Sweetness. But in the Season of the Communion there was some Abatement of this sweet Life and Fervour. This Love and Joy cast out Fear; and my Soul longed for perfect Grace and Glory. This sweet Frame continued 'till the Evening, when my Soul was sweetly spiritual in secret Duties.

Monday, October 20. I again found the sweet Assistance of the holy Spirit in secret Duties, both Morning and Evening, and Life and Comfort in Religion through the whole Day.

Tuesday, October 21. I had likewise Experience of the Goodness of God in *shedding abroad his Love in my Heart,* and giving me Delight and Consolation in religious Duties. And all the remaining Part of the Week, my Soul-seemed to be taken up with divine Things. I now so longed after God, and to be freed from Sin, that when I felt myself recovering, and thought I must return to College again, which had proved so hurtful to my spiritual Interest the Year past, I could not but be grieved, and I thought I had much rather have died; for it distress'd me, to think of getting away from God. But before I went, I enjoyed several other sweet and precious Seasons of Communion with God (particularly October 30. and Nov. 4.) wherein my Soul enjoyed unspeakable Comfort.

I returned to College about November 6. and through the Goodness of God felt the Power of Religion almost daily, for the Space of six Weeks.

November 28. In my Evening-Devotion, I enjoyed precious Discoveries of God, and was unspeakably refreshed with that Passage Heb. xii. 22, 23, 24. That my Soul longed to wing away for the Paradise of God; I longed to be conformed to God in all Things.—A Day or two after, I enjoyed much of the *Light of God's Countenance,* most of the Day; and my Soul rested in God.

Tuesday, December 9. I was in a comfortable Frame of Soul most of the Day; but especially in Evening-Devotions, when God was pleased wonderfully to assist and strengthen me; so that I thought nothing should ever move me from the Love of God in Christ Jesus my Lord.—O! *one Hour with God* infinitely exceeds all the Pleasures and Delights of this lower World.

Sometime toward the latter End of January 1740,41. I grew more *cold* and *dull* in Matters of Religion, by Means of my old Temptation, *viz.* Ambition in my Studies.—But thro' divine Goodness, a great and general *Awakening* spread it self over the College, about the latter End of February, in which I was much quickned, and more abundantly engaged in Religion.

1. What was the situation at Yale before Whitefield's visit? Do you get the feeling that it was a den of sinners? What seems to have changed during late 1740 and early 1741? Does the Awakening seem to have affected all of the students equally?

2. Compare Samuel Hopkins and David Brainerd. Do they seem to be representative students? How did the revival change their daily routines?

3. How might Pemberton's sermon have affected a college student in particular? How might he—or his teachers—have reacted to Pemberton's insistence that "The knowledge of Christ . . . is the most useful and necessary knowledge"?

TWO

A Divisive Commencement, September 1741

During the eighteenth century, a college commencement not only dignified the awarding of degrees but also marked the beginning ("commencement") of the academic year. For this reason, it was held during the second week of September, and prominent persons from a wide surrounding area gathered on the occasion to discuss topics of general concern. One of the many notables to attend the 1741 commencement at Yale was the Rev. Daniel Wadsworth (1704–1747), pastor of the first church in Hartford—the oldest and wealthiest church in Connecticut (its communicants included the governor of the colony). A member of the Yale Board of Trustees and a 1726 graduate of the College, Wadsworth felt confused and threatened by the religious revival as early as his first encounter with George Whitefield late in 1740. ("What to think of the man and his itinerant preachings I scarcely know," he had written after hearing Whitefield preach to "a vast concourse of people" on the subject of an ominous Biblical text: "Old things are passed away.") For the last ten years of his life Wadsworth kept a private journal; his entries for September 1741 [#7] record his movements and reactions during this commencement season.

Written early in October, Samuel Johnson's letter to a highly placed English correspondent [#8] describes the same commencement scene. The minister to New Haven's Episcopal church, Johnson (1696–1772) had been raised in Guilford, Connecticut, as a pious Congregationalist; he graduated and then tutored at Yale, and at one time he was even the acting head of the College. Johnson's conversion to the Church of England in 1721 had been notorious enough to alarm the entire New England establishment. In 1754 Johnson became the first president of King's College (now Columbia University) in New York.

Some indication of what Wadsworth and Johnson were talking about can be found in the minute-book of the Yale trustees [#9], who met each year on commencement day to determine the policies and regulations of the College. Another regular event at this time of year was the commencement sermon, delivered in 1741 by the minister from Northampton, Massachusetts, Jonathan Edwards (1703–1758). Like Samuel Johnson, Edwards was a Connecticut native, a Yale graduate (1720, M.A. 1722) and a tutor at the College who had served for a time as its acting head. Unlike Johnson, Edwards was privately and publicly sympathetic to the Awakening. (Some six years earlier, in fact, he had led his own relatively extensive revival in the upper Connecticut valley—the source of his reputation in 1741.) The sermon that Edwards delivered at commencement, published later as "The Distinguishing Marks of the Work of the Spirit of God" [#10], was the first extended examination of the Awakening to be published, and it stands still as a major analytic effort—one of the few enduring documents included in this volume. (Because Edwards enlarged the sermon between delivery and publication, the version printed here is not identical to the one that the assemblage heard on September 10. There is no extant copy of the original sermon.) One of the most original and lucid thinkers that America has produced, Edwards in the next few years composed even more extensive analyses of the revival and the psychology of religion. Fired by his Northampton congregation in 1750 for reasons which can be traced to the revival, he spent his last years preaching to an Indian mission on the Massachusetts frontier; it was there that he wrote his greatest works. At the very end of his life, Edwards was appointed president of what later became Princeton University.

7

September 1741

Sept. 1. This day ye Court Super. sat here [that is, in Hartford] great divisions and Contentions seems to be arising in some Towns.

— 2. This day visiting, discourse &c. prospect of our religious affairs Looks mancholly. ye great awakening &c. seems to be degenerating into Strife and faction.

— 4. This day prayed at Court. discoursed with Capt. Oz. P. abt. our religious affairs a Long time, ye Lord bless him and direct me.

— 6. Lords day I preached . . . and administred ye Sacrament. Laboured under great dullness, difficulty of speaking, inward weakness &c. o Lord bless my weak endeavours.

— 9. Commencement at New-Haven. Davenport and Bellamy preached and Mills at night, great Confusion.

— 10. Much Confusion this day at New-Haven, and at night ye most strange management and a pretence of religion yt ever I saw.

— 11. Went to Stratford in ye afternoon.

— 12. Went to Reading. weary &c.

— 13. preached pr. totum from gal. 6. 15.

— 14. Went to fairfield, nil remarkable

— 15. Came to New-Haven

George L. Walker (ed.), *Diary of Rev. Daniel Wadsworth, Seventh Pastor of the First Church of Christ in Hartford, 1737–1747* (Hartford, 1894), pp. 71–73.

— 16. returned home found my family well, Laus Deo

— 20. Lords day I preached A:M: for Mr. Whitman . . . and P.M: . . . at my own meeting. Mary Pratt owned ye covenant

— 21. Visiting ye sick &c. a time of great distress. 3 persons buried this day

— 22. . . . . Rector Clap here at night

— 24. A day of fasting and prayer on acct. of ye distressing sickness among us. A.M. I preached from Job. 14. 10. & P.M. Mr. Whitman preached from mic. 6. 9.

— 27. Lords day I preached per totum from rom. 14. 17. . . .

— 30. This day went to ye west division preached A:M: from Job 14: 10 & P.M. Mr. Whitman preached Mic. 6. 9. returned home, found my family well Laus Deo. I pray God to direct me in my duty to my poor B. H. O Lord save him from ruin—

The religious stir yt has bin amongst us seems to have had different effects, some I hope are reformed and Converted. others I fear are only turned from one sort of wickedness to another. divisions and Contentions seem to be arising among us. I pray yt god would mercifully Interpose and prevent them if it may consist with his holy will and pleasure, but if not to prepare me for his will and help me to do and suffer wt he has appointed for me.

Itinerant preaching which some have gone into ye practice of, is liked by some and greatly disliked by others; I know not but yt they may have done good in some places, but I think in many places and Especially in this Town they have done a great deal of mischief. I think they have bin very influential of weaning of ye religious impressions yt were on ye minds of our people, and Turning ym to disputes, debates and quarrels, and wt will be ye event God only knows. The principle Itinerant preachers among us are Jed: Mills, Pomroy & Wheelock, some others young ministers are getting into yt way. Steady christians & ye most Judicious among ministers and people so far as I can Learn generally dislike these new things set afoot by these Itinerant preachers.

8

Samuel Johnson to George Berkeley

October 3, 1741

My Lord:—

This comes to your Lordship upon occasion of our recommending to the Society, Mr. Richard Caner (brother to my good neighbor Mr. H. Caner, Missionary to Fairfield, of whom you may possibly retain some remembrance), who well deserves the Society's notice. On this occasion I have the pleasure to inform your Lordship that upon the occasion of our new Rector, Mr. Clap, and his application to the business of the College, we have the satisfaction to see classical as well as mathematical learning improve among us; there having been a better appearance the last May than what I gave your Lordship an account of before; for this gentleman proves a solid, rational, good man, and much freer from bigotry than his predecessor.

But this new enthusiasm, in consequence of Whitefield's preaching through the country and his disciples', has got great footing in the College, we well as throughout the country. Many of the scholars have been possessed of it, and two of this year's candidates were denied their degrees for their disorderly and restless endeavors to propagate it. Indeed Whitefield's disciples have in this country much improved upon the foundations which he laid; so that we have now prevailing among us the most odd and unaccountable enthusiasm that

Herbert and Carol Schneiders (eds.), *Samuel Johnson, President of King's College: His Career and Writings* (2 vols., New York, 1929), Vol. I, pp. 102–103.

perhaps ever obtained in any age or nation. For not only the minds of many people are at once struck with prodigious distresses upon their hearing the hideous outcries of our itinerant preachers, but even their bodies are frequently in a moment affected with the strangest convulsions and involuntary agitations and cramps, which also have sometimes happened to those who came as mere spectators, and are no friends to their new methods, and even without their minds being at all affected. The Church, indeed, has not, as yet, much suffered, but rather gained by these commotions, which no men of sense of either denomination have at all given in to, but it has required great care and pains in our clergy to prevent the mischief. How far God may permit this madness of the people to proceed, He only knows. But I hope that neither religion nor learning will in the whole event of things much suffer by it.

I humbly beg an interest in your Lordship's prayers and blessing, and remain,

Etc.

S. J.

9

Proceedings of the Yale Trustees

September 9, 1741

At a Meeting of the Trustees of Yale-College in New-Haven in the Library Wednesday September 9th 1741. where were present of the Trustees

Franklin B. Dexter (ed.), *Documentary History of Yale University* . . . *1701–1745* (New Haven: 1916); from the original minutes in the Yale Archives.

The Revd
{
Mr Thomas Clapp Rector, chosen Moderator
Mr Samuel Whitman
Mr Jared Eliot
Mr Jonathan Marsh
Mr Samuel Cooke, chosen Scribe
Mr Samuel Whittelsey
Mr Joseph Noyes
Mr Anthony Stoddard.
}

Voted, that the Revd Mr Rector Clapp on behalf of this Body acquaint the Revd Dr Berkley with the Proffits accruing to this College, for the Encouragement of our Students, from his generous Donation of the Estate at Rhode-Island & offer our repeated Thanks on the Occasion.

Voted, that the Revd Mr Rector Clapp, Mr Jared Eliot, Mr Samuel Whittelsey and Mr Joseph Noyes be a Comtee to ascertain the Price of Commons for the ensuing Year, and provide for the College any Tutor, Steward or Butler for the sd Year, if any unforeseen Providence Shall render such a Provision necessary in the Intervall betwixt & the next Commencement; and to direct our Steward, as in Prudence they judge meet, as to the Preparation of the Commencement Dinner.

Voted, that Mr Thomas Balch be admitted to a Master's Degree.

Voted, that the Revd Mr Whittelsey & Mr Noyes be a Comtee to view & provide for what Repairs may be thought needfull to be made of the Rector's House & Fences, & to draw out of the Treasury Money needfull for that purpose, & return an Account to this Board the next Commencement.

Voted, that the Revd Mr Rector Clapp, Mr Samuel Cooke & Mr Anthony Stoddard be a Comtee to address the General Assembly on Behalf of the Trustees with a Petition for the Renewall of the Annuity lately allowed the College.

Voted, that if any Student of this College shall directly or indirectly say, that the Rector, either of the Trustees or Tutors are Hypocrites, carnall or unconverted Men, he Shall for the first Offence make a publick Confession in the Hall, & for the Second Offence be expell'd.

Ordered that the Steward Shall provide the Commons for the Schollars as follows vizt

For Breakfast

One Loaf of Bread for 4, which (the Dough) Shall weigh one Pound.

For Dinner for 4

One Loaf of Bread as aforesd; 2-½ pounds of Beef, Veal or Mutton or 1-¾ pounds of Salt Pork about twice a Week in the Summer Time; one Quart of Beer; 2 penny Worth of Sauce.

For Supper for 4

2 Quarts of Milk & one Loaf of Bread, when Milk can conveniently be had, and when it cannot then an Apple-Pye which shall be made of 1-¾ lb Dough, ¼ lb Hogs fat, 2 oz Sugar & ½ peck of Apples.

And the Comtee appointed to State the Price of the Commons Shall State the Commodities aforesd at the currant Market Price & allow the Steward 50 pr Cent. Advance for his Care & Trouble.

Teste Samuel Cooke Scribe
Yale College in New-Haven

10

Jonathan Edwards:
Distinguishing Marks of a
Work of the Spirit of God

September 10, 1741

John iv.—Beloved, believe not every spirit, but try the spirits whether they are of God: because many false prophets are gone out into the world.

In the apostolic age, there was the greatest outpouring of the Spirit of God that ever was; both as to his extraordinary influences and gifts, and his ordinary operations, in convincing, converting, enlightening, and sanctifying the souls of men. But as the influences of the true Spirit abounded, so counterfeits did also abound: the devil was abundant in mimicking, both the ordinary and extraordinary influences of the Spirit of God, as is manifest by innumerable passages of the apostles' writings. This made it very necessary that the church of Christ should be furnished with some certain rules, distinguishing and clear marks, by which she might proceed safely in judging of the

Jonathan Edwards, *The Distinguishing Marks of a Work of the Spirit of God. Applied to That Uncommon Operation That Has Lately Appeared in the Minds of Many of the People of This Land; with a Particular Consideration of the Extraordinary Circumstances with Which This Work Is Attended. A Discourse Delivered at New-Haven, September 10th, 1741, Being the Day after Commencement; and Now Published at the Earnest Desire of many Ministers and Other Gentlemen That Heard It; with Great Enlargements* (Boston, 1741). This very long sermon has been edited down by about 15% of its published length. The omitted passages are short—anywhere from a few sentences to a page—and consist generally of Biblical examples.

true from the false without danger of being imposed upon. The giving of such rules is the plain design of this chapter, where we have this matter more expressly and fully treated of than anywhere else in the Bible. The apostle, of set purpose, undertakes to supply the church of God with such marks of the true Spirit as may be plain and safe, and well accommodated to use and practice; and that the subject might be clearly and sufficiently handled, he insists upon it throughout the chapter, which makes it wonderful that what is here said is no more taken notice of in this extraordinary day, when there is such an uncommon and extensive operation on the minds of people, such a variety of opinions concerning it, and so much talk about the work of the Spirit.

The apostle's discourse on this subject is introduced by an occasional mention of the indwelling of the Spirit, as the sure evidence of an interest in Christ: "And he that keepeth his commandments dwelleth in him, and he in him; and hereby we know that he abideth in us, by the Spirit which he hath given us." Whence we may infer, that the design of the apostle is not only to give marks whereby to distinguish the true Spirit from the false, in his extraordinary gifts of prophecy and miracles, but also in his ordinary influences on the minds of his people, in order to their union to Christ, and being built up in him; which is also manifest from the marks themselves that are given, which we shall hereafter notice.

The words of the text are an introduction to this discourse of the distinguishing signs of the true and false Spirit.—Before the apostle proceeds to lay down the signs, he exhorteth Christians, first, against an over credulousness, and a forwardness to admit every specious appearance as the work of a true Spirit: "Beloved, believe not every spirit, but try the spirits whether they are of God." And, second, he shows, that there were many counterfeits, "because many false prophets were gone out into the world." These did not only pretend to have the Spirit of God in his extraordinary gifts of inspiration, but also to be the great friends and favorites of heaven to be eminently holy persons, and to have much of the ordinary saving, sanctifying influences of the Spirit of God on their hearts. Hence we are to look upon these words as a direction to examine and try their pretences to the Spirit of God, in both these respects.

My design therefore at this time is to show what are the true, certain, and distinguishing evidences of a work of the Spirit of God, by which we may safely proceed in judging of any operation we find in ourselves, or see in others. And here I would observe, that we are to take the *Scriptures* as our guide in such cases. This is the great and standing rule which God has given to his church, in order to guide them in things relating to the great concerns of their souls; and it is an infallible and sufficient rule. There are undoubtedly sufficient marks given to guide the church of God in this great affair of judging of spirits, without which it would lie open to woful delusion, and would be remedilessly exposed to be imposed on and devoured by its enemies. And we need not be afraid to trust these rules. Doubtless that Spirit who indited the Scriptures knew how to give us good rules, by which to distinguish his operations from all that is falsely pretended to be from him. And this, as I observed before, the Spirit of God has here done of set purpose, and done it more particularly and fully than any where else: so that in my present discourse I shall go nowhere else for rules or marks for the trial of spirits, but shall confine myself to those that I find in this chapter. But before I proceed particularly to speak to these, I would prepare my way by, FIRST, observing *negatively,* in some instances, what are *not signs* or evidences of a work of the Spirit of God.

Section I.

Negative Signs; or, What are no signs by which we are to judge of a work—and especially, What are no evidences that a work is not from the Spirit of God.

I. Nothing can be certainly concluded from this, That a work is carried on in a way very unusual and extraordinary; provided the variety or difference be such, as may still be comprehended within the limits of Scripture rules. What the church has been used to, is not a rule by which we are to judge; because there may be new and extraordinary works of God, and he has heretofore evidently wrought in an extraordinary manner. He has brought to pass new things, strange works; and has wrought in such a manner as to surprise both men and angels. And as God has done thus in times past, so we have no reason to think but that he will do so still. The prophecies of Scripture give us reason to think that God has things to accomplish, which have never yet been seen. No deviation from what has hitherto been usual, let it be never so great, is an argument that a work is not from the Spirit of God, if it be no deviation from his prescribed rule. The Holy Spirit is sovereign in his operation; and we know that he uses a great variety; and we cannot tell how great a variety he may use, within the compass of the rules he himself has fixed. We ought not to limit God where he has not limited himself.

Therefore it is not reasonable to determine that a work is not from God's Holy Spirit because of the extraordinary degree in which the minds of persons are influenced. If they seem to have an extraordinary conviction of the dreadful nature of sin, and a very uncommon sense of the misery of a Christless condition—or extraordinary views of the certainty and glory of divine things,—and are proportionably moved with very extraordinary affections of fear and sorrow, desire, love, or joy: or if the apparent change be very sudden, and the work be carried on with very unusual swiftness—and the persons affected are very numerous, and many of them are very young, with other unusual circumstances, not infringing upon Scripture marks of a work of the Spirit—these things are no argument that the work is not of the Spirit of God.—The extraordinary and unusual degree of influence, and power of operation, if in its nature it be agreeable to the rules and marks given in Scripture, is rather an argument in its favor; for by how much higher the degree which in its nature is agreeable to the rule, so much the more is there of conformity to the rule; and so much the more evident that conformity. When things are in small degrees, though they be really agreeable to the rule, it is not so easily seen whether their nature agrees with the rule.

There is a great aptness in persons to doubt of things that are strange; especially elderly persons, to think that to be right which they have never been used to in their day, and have not heard of in the days of their fathers. But if it be a good argument that a work is not from the Spirit of God, that it is very unusual, then it was so in the apostles' days. The work of the Spirit then, was carried on in a manner that, in very many respects, was altogether new; such as never had been seen or heard since the world stood. The work was then carried on with more visible and remarkable power than ever; nor had there been seen before such mighty and wonderful effects of the Spirit of God in sudden changes, and such great engagedness and zeal in great multitudes—such a sudden alteration in towns, cities, and countries; such a swift progress, and vast extent of the work—

and many other extraordinary circumstances might be mentioned. The great unusualness of the work surprised the Jews; they knew not what to make of it, but could not believe it to be the work of God: many looked upon the persons that were the subjects of it as bereft of reason; as you may see in Acts ii. 13, xxvi. 24, and 1 Cor. iv. 10.

And we have reason from Scripture prophecy to suppose, that at the commencement of that last and greatest outpouring of the Spirit of God, that is to be in the latter ages of the world, the manner of the work will be very extraordinary, and such as never has yet been seen; so that there shall be occasion then to say, as in Isa, lxvi. 8, "Who hath heard such a thing? Who hath seen such things? Shall the earth be made to bring forth in one day? Shall a nation be born at once? for as soon as Zion travailed, she brought forth her children." It may be reasonably expected that the extraordinary manner of the work then, will bear some proportion to the very extraordinary events, and that glorious change in the state of the world, which God will bring to pass by it.

II. A work is not to be judged of by any effects on the bodies of men; such as tears, trembling, groans, loud outcries, agonies of body, or the failing of bodily strength. The influence persons are under, is not to be judged of one way or other, by such effects on the body; and the reason is, because the Scripture nowhere gives us any such rule. We cannot conclude that persons are under the influence of the true Spirit because we see such effects upon their bodies, because this is not given as a mark of the true Spirit; nor on the other hand, have we any reason to conclude, from any such outward appearances, that persons are not under the influence of the Spirit of God, because there is no rule of Scripture given us to judge of spirits by, that does either expressly or indirectly exclude such effects on the body, nor does reason exclude them. It is easily accounted for from the consideration of the nature of divine and eternal things, and the nature of man, and the laws of the union between soul and body, how a right influence, a true and proper sense of things, should have such effects on the body, even those that are of the most extraordinary kind, such as taking away the bodily strength, or throwing the body into great agonies, and extorting loud outcries. There are none of us but do suppose, and would have been ready at any time to say it, that the misery of hell is doubtless so dreadful, and eternity so vast, that if a person should have a clear apprehension of that misery as it is, it would be more than his feeble frame could bear, and especially if at the same time he saw himself in great danger of it, and to be utterly uncertain whether he should be delivered from it, yea, and to have no security from it one day or hour. If we consider human nature, we must not wonder, that when persons have a great sense of that which is so amazingly dreadful, and also have a great view of their own wickedness and God's anger, that things seem to them to forebode speedy and immediate destruction. We see the nature of man to be such that when he is in danger of some terrible calamity to which he is greatly exposed, he is ready upon every occasion to think, that *now* it is coming.—When persons' hearts are full of fear, in time of war, they are ready to tremble at the shaking of a leaf, and to expect the enemy every minute, and to say within themselves, *now* I shall be slain. If we should suppose that a person saw himself hanging over a great pit, full of fierce and glowing flames, by a thread that he knew to be very weak, and not sufficient to bear his weight, and knew that multitudes had been in such circumstances before, and that most of them had fallen and perished, and saw nothing within reach, that he could take hold of to save him, what distress would he be in! How ready to think that *now* the thread was breaking, that now, *this minute,* he should be swallowed up in those dreadful flames! And would not he be ready to cry out in such circumstances? How much more those that see themselves in this manner hanging over an infinitely more dreadful pit, or held over it in the hand of God, who at the same time they see to be exceedingly provoked! No wonder that the wrath of God, when manifested but a little to the soul, overbears human strength.

So it may easily be accounted for, that a true sense of the glorious excellency of the Lord Jesus Christ, and of his wonderful dying love, and the exercise of a truly spiritual love and joy, should be such as very much to overcome the bodily strength. We are all ready to own, that no man can see God and live, and that it is but a very small part of that apprehension of the glory and love of Christ which the saints enjoy in heaven, that our present frame can bear; therefore it is not at all strange that God should sometimes give his saints such foretastes of heaven, as to diminish their bodily strength. If it was not unaccountable that the queen of Sheba fainted, and had her bodily strength taken away, when she came to see the glory of Solomon, much less is it unaccountable that she who is the antitype of the queen of Sheba, viz., the Church, that is brought, as it were, from the utmost ends of the earth, from being an alien and stranger, far off, in a state of sin and misery, should faint when she comes to see the glory of Christ, who is the antitype of Solomon; and especially will be so in that prosperous, peaceful, glorious kingdom, which he will set up in the world in its latter age. . . .

It is a weak objection, that the impressions of enthusiasts have a great effect on their bodies. That the Quakers used to tremble, is no argument that Saul, afterwards Paul, and the jailer, did not tremble from real convictions of conscience. Indeed all such objections from effects on the body, let them be greater or less, seem to be exceeding frivolous; they who argue thence, proceed in the dark, they know not what ground they go upon, nor by what rule they judge. The root and course of things is to be looked at, and the nature of the operations and affections are to be inquired into, and examined by the rule of God's word, and not the motions of the blood and animal spirits.

III. It is no argument that an operation on the minds of people is not the work of the Spirit of God, that it occasions a great deal of noise about religion. For though true religion be of a contrary nature to that of the Pharisees—which was ostentatious, and delighted to set itself forth to the view of men for their applause—yet such is human nature, that it is morally impossible there should be a great concern, strong affection, and a general engagedness of mind amongst a people without causing a notable, visible, and open commotion and alteration amongst that people.—Surely, it is no argument that the minds of persons are not under the influence of God's Spirit, that they are very much moved: for indeed spiritual and eternal things are so great, and of such infinite concern, that there is a great absurdity in men's being but moderately moved and affected by them; and surely it is no argument that they are not moved by the Spirit of God, that they are affected with these things in some measure as they deserve, or in some proportion to their importance. And when was there ever any such thing since the world stood, as a people in general being greatly affected in any affair whatsoever, without noise or stir? The nature of man will not allow it. . . .

IV. It is no argument that an operation on the minds of a people, is not the work of the Spirit of God, that many who are the subjects of it, have great impressions made on their imaginations. That persons have many impressions on their imaginations, does not prove that they have nothing else. It is easy to be accounted for, that there should be much of this nature amongst a people, where a great multitude of all kinds of constitutions have their minds engaged with intense thought and strong affections about invisible things; yea, it would be strange if there should not. Such is our nature, that we cannot think of things invisible, without a degree of imagination. I dare appeal to any man, of the greatest powers of mind, whether he is able to fix his thoughts on God, or Christ, or the things of another world, without imaginary ideas attending his meditations? And the more engaged the mind is, and the more intense the contemplation and affection, still the more lively and strong the imaginary idea will ordinarily be; especially when attended with surprise. And this is the case when the mental prospect is very new, and takes strong hold of the passions, as fear or joy; and when the change of the state and views of the mind is sudden, from a contrary extreme, as from that which was extremely dreadful, to that which is extremely ravishing and delightful. And it is no wonder that many persons do not well distinguish between that which is imaginary and that which is intellectual and spiritual; and that they are apt to lay too much weight on the imaginary part, and are most ready to speak of that in the account they give of their experiences, especially persons of less understanding and of distinguishing capacity.

As God has given us such a faculty as the imagination, and so made us that we cannot think of things spiritual and invisible, without some exercise of this faculty; so, it appears to me, that such is our state and nature, that this faculty is really subservient and helpful to the other faculties of the mind, when a proper use is made of it; though oftentimes, when the imagination is too strong, and the other faculties weak, it overbears, and disturbs them in their exercise. It appears to me manifest, in many instances with which I have been acquainted, that God has really made use of this faculty to truly divine purposes; especially in some that are more ignorant. God seems to condescend to their circumstances, and deal with them as babes; as of old he instructed his church, whilst in a state of ignorance and minority, by types and outward representations. I can see nothing unreasonable in such a position. Let others who have much occasion to deal with souls in spiritual concerns, judge whether experience does not confirm it.

It is no argument that a work is not of the Spirit of God, that some who are the subjects of it have been in a kind of ecstasy, wherein they have been carried beyond themselves, and have had their minds transported into a train of strong and pleasing imaginations, and a kind of visions, as though they were rapt up even to heaven, and there saw glorious sights. I have been acquainted with some such instances, and I see no need of bringing in the help of the devil into the account that we give of these things, nor yet of supposing them to be of the same nature with the visions of the prophets, or St. Paul's rapture into paradise. Human nature, under these intense exercises and affections, is all that need be brought into the account. If it may be well accounted for, that persons under a true sense of a glorious and wonderful greatness and excellency of divine things, and soul-ravishing views of the beauty and love of Christ, should have the strength of nature overpowered, as I have already shown that it may; then I think it is not at all strange, that amongst great numbers that are thus affected and overborne, there should be some persons of particular constitutions that should have their imaginations thus affected. The effect is no other than what bears a proportion and analogy to other effects of the strong exercise of their minds. It is no wonder, when the thoughts are so fixed, and the affections so strong—and the whole soul so engaged, ravished, and swallowed up—that all other parts of the body are so affected, as to be deprived of their strength, and the whole frame ready to dissolve. Is it any wonder that, in such a case, the brain in particular (especially in some constitutions), which we know is most especially affected by intense contemplations and exercises of mind, should be so affected, that its strength and spirits should for a season be diverted, and taken off from impressions made on the organs of external sense, and be wholly employed in a train of pleasing delightful imaginations, corresponding with the present frame of the mind? Some are ready to interpret such things wrong, and to lay too much weight on them, as prophetical visions, divine revelations, and sometimes significations from heaven of what shall come to pass; which the issue, in some instances I have known, has shown to be otherwise. But yet, it appears to me that such things are evidently sometimes from the Spirit of God, though indirectly; that is, their extraordinary frame of mind, and that strong and lively sense of divine things which is the occasion of them, is from his Spirit; and also as the mind continues in its holy frame, and retains a divine sense of the excellency of spiritual things even in its rapture; which holy frame and sense is from the Spirit of God, though the imaginations that attend it are but accidental, and therefore there is commonly something or other in them that is confused, improper, and false.

V. It is no sign that a work is not from the Spirit of God, that example is a great means of it. It is surely no argument that an effect is not from God, that means are used in producing it; for we know that it is God's manner to make use of means in carrying on his work in the world, and it is no more an argument against the divinity of an effect, that this means is made use of, than if it was by any other means. It is agreeable to Scripture that persons should be influenced by one another's good example. The Scripture directs us to set good examples to that end. . . .

And as it is a *Scriptural* way of carrying on God's work, by example, so it is a *reasonable* way. It is no argument that men are not influenced by reason, that they are influenced by example. This way of persons holding forth truth to one another, has a tendency to enlighten the mind, and to convince reason. None will deny but that for persons to signify things one to another by words, may rationally be supposed to tend to enlighten each other's minds. But the same thing may be signified by actions, and signified much more fully and effectually. Words are of no use any otherwise than as they convey our own ideas to others; but actions, in some cases, may do it much more fully. There is a language in actions; and in some cases, much more clear and convincing than in words. It is therefore no argument against the goodness of the effect, that persons are greatly affected by seeing others so; yea, though the impression be made only by seeing the tokens of great and extraordinary affection in others in their behavior, taking for granted what they are affected with, without hearing them say one word. There may be language sufficient in such a case in their behavior only, to convey their minds to others, and to signify to them their sense of things more than can possibly be done by words only. If a person should see another under extreme bodily torment, he might receive much clearer ideas, and more convincing evidence of what he suffered by his actions in his misery, than he could do only by the words of an unaffected indifferent relater. In like manner he might receive a greater idea of any thing that is excellent and very delightful, from the behavior of one that is in actual enjoyment, than by the dull narration of one which is inexperienced and insensible himself. I desire that this matter may be examined by the strictest reason.—Is it not manifest, that effects produced in persons' minds are rational, since not only weak and ignorant people are much influenced by example, but also those that make the greatest boast of strength of reason, are more influenced by reason held forth in this way, than almost any other way. Indeed the religious affections of many when raised by this means, as by hearing the word preached, or any other means, may prove flashy, and soon vanish, as Christ represents the stony-ground hearers; but the affections of some thus moved by example, are abiding, and prove to be of saving issue.

There never yet was a time of remarkable pouring out of the Spirit, and great revival of religion, but that example had a main hand. So it was at the Reformation, and in the apostles' days, in Jerusalem and Samaria, and Ephesus, and other parts of the world, as will be most manifest to any one that attends to the accounts we have in the Acts of the Apostles. As in those days one person was moved by another, so one city or town was influenced by the example of another: 1 Thess. i. 7, 8, "So that ye were ensamples to all that believe in Macedonia and Achaia, for from you sounded out the word of the Lord, not only in Macedonia and Achaia, but also in every place your faith to God-ward is spread abroad."

It is no valid objection against examples being so much used, that the Scripture speaks of the word as the principal means of carrying on God's work; for the word of God is the principal means, nevertheless, by which other means operate and are made effectual. Even the sacraments have no effect but by the word; and so it is that example becomes effectual; for all that is visible to the eye is unintelligible and vain, without the word of God to instruct and guide the mind. . . .

VI. It is no sign that a work is not from the Spirit of God, that many, who seem to be the subjects of it, are guilty of great imprudences and irregularities in their conduct. We are to consider that the end for which God pours out his Spirit, is to make men holy, and not to make them politicians. It is no wonder that, in a mixed multitude of all sorts—wise and unwise, young and old, of weak and strong natural abilities, under strong impressions of mind—there are many who behave themselves imprudently. There are but few that know how to conduct themselves under vehement affections of any kind, whether of a temporal or spiritual nature; to do so requires a great deal of discretion, strength, and steadiness of mind. A thousand imprudences will not prove a work to be not of the Spirit of God; yea, if there be not only imprudences, but many things prevailing that are irregular, and really contrary to the rules of God's holy word. That it should be thus may be well accounted for from the exceeding weakness of human nature, together with the remaining darkness and corruption of those that are yet the subjects of the saving influences of God's Spirit, and have a real zeal for God.

We have a remarkable instance, in the New Testament, of a people that partook largely of that great effusion of the Spirit in the apostles' days, among whom there nevertheless abounded imprudences and great irregularities; viz., the church at Corinth. There is scarcely any church more celebrated in the New Testament for being blessed with large measures of the Spirit of God, both in his ordinary influences, in convincing and converting sinners, and also in his extraordinary and miraculous gifts; yet what manifold imprudences, great and sinful irregularities, and strange confusion did they run into, at the Lord's supper, and in the exercise of church discipline! To which may be added, their indecent manner of attending other parts of public worship, their jarring and contention about their teachers, and even the exercise of their extraordinary gifts of prophecy, speaking with tongues, and the like, wherein they spake and acted by the immediate inspiration of the Spirit of God.

And if we see great imprudences, and even sinful irregularities, in some who are great instruments to carry on the work, it will not prove it not to be the work of God. The apostle Peter himself, who was a great, eminently holy, and inspired apostle—and one of the chief instruments of setting up the Christian church in the world— when he was actually engaged in this work, was guilty of a great and sinful error in his conduct; of which the apostle Paul speaks, Gal. ii. 11–13: "But when Peter was come to Antioch, I withstood him to the face, because he was to be blamed; for before that certain came from James, he did eat with the Gentiles, but when they were come, he withdrew, and separated himself, fearing them that were of the circumcision; and the other Jews dissembled likewise with him; insomuch, that Barnabas also was carried away with their dissimulation." If a great pillar of the Christian church—one of the chief of those who are the very foundations on which, next to Christ, the whole church is said to be built—was guilty of such an irregularity; is it any wonder if other lesser instruments, who have not that extraordinary conduct of the divine Spirit he had, should be guilty of many irregularities?

And in particular, it is no evidence that a work is not of God, if many who are either the subjects or the instruments of it, are guilty of too great forwardness to censure others as unconverted. For this may be through mistakes they have embraced concerning the marks by which they are to judge of the hypocrisy and carnality of others; or from not duly apprehending the latitude the Spirit of God uses in the methods of his operations; or, from want of making due allowance for that infirmity and corruption that may be left in the hearts of the saints; as well as through want of a due sense of their own blindness and weakness, and remaining corruption, whereby spiritual pride may have a secret vent this way, under some disguise, and not be discovered.—If we allow that truly pious men may have a great deal of remaining blindness and corruption, and may be liable to mistakes about the marks of hypocrisy, as undoubtedly all will allow, then it is not unaccountable that they should sometimes run into such errors as these. It is as easy, and upon some accounts more easy to be accounted for, why the remaining corruption of good men should sometimes have an unobserved vent this way than most other ways; and without doubt (however lamentable) many holy men have erred in this way.

Lukewarmness in religion is abominable, and zeal an excellent grace, yet above all other Christian virtues, this needs to be strictly watched and searched; for it is that with which corruption, and particularly pride and human passion, is exceedingly apt to mix unobserved. And it is observable, that there never was a time of great reformation, to cause a revival of zeal in the church of God, but that it has been attended, in some notable instances, with irregularity, and a running out some way or other into an undue severity. Thus in the apostles' days, a great deal of zeal was spent about unclean meats, with heat of spirit in Christians one against another, both parties condemning and censuring one another, as not true Christians; when the apostle had charity for both, as influenced by a spirit of real piety: "He that eats," says he, "to the Lord he eats, and giveth God thanks; and he that eateth not, to the Lord he eateth not, and giveth God thanks." So in the church of Corinth, they had got into a way of extolling some ministers, and censuring others, and were puffed up one against another; but yet these things were no sign that the work then so wonderfully carried on, was not the work of God. And after this, when religion was still greatly flourishing in the world, and a Spirit of eminent holiness and zeal prevailed in the Christian church, the zeal of Christians ran out into a very improper and undue severity, in the exercise of church discipline towards delinquents. In some cases they would by no means admit them into their charity and communion though they appeared never so humble and penitent. And in the days of Constantine the Great, the zeal of Christians against heathenism ran out into a degree of persecution. So in that glorious revival of religion, at the reformation, zeal in many instances appeared in a very improper severity, and even a degree of persecution; yea, in some of the most eminent reformers; as in the great Calvin in particular. And many in those days of the flourishing of vital religion, were guilty of severely censuring others that differed from them in opinion in some points of divinity.

VII. Nor are many errors in judgment, and some delusions of Satan intermixed with the work, any argument that the work in general is not of the Spirit of God. However great a spiritual influence may be, it is not to be expected that the Spirit of God should be given now in the same manner as to the apostles, infallibly to guide them in points of Christian doctrine, so that what they taught might be relied on as a rule to the Christian church. And if many delusions of Satan appear, at the same time that a great religious concern prevails, it is not an argument that the work in general is not the work of God, any more than it was an argument in Egypt, that there were no true miracles wrought there, by the hand of God, because Jannes and Jambres wrought false miracles at the same time by the hand of the devil. Yea, the same persons may be the subjects of much of the influences of the Spirit of God, and yet in some things be led away by the delusions of Satan, and this be no more of paradox than many other things that are true of real saints, in the present state, where grace dwells with so much corruption, and the new man and the old man subsist together in the same person; and the kingdom of God and the kingdom of the devil remain for a while together in the same heart. Many godly persons have undoubtedly in this and other ages, exposed themselves to woful delusions, by an aptness to lay too much weight on impulses and impressions, as if they were immediately revelations from God, to signify something future, or to direct them where to go, and what to do.

VIII. If some, who were thought to be wrought upon, fall away into gross errors, or scandalous practices, it is no argument that the work in general is not the work of the Spirit of God. That there are some counterfeits, is no argument that nothing is true: such things are always expected in a time of reformation. If we look into church history, we shall find no instance of any great revival of religion, but what has been attended with many such things. Instances of this nature in the apostles' days were innumerable; some fell away into gross heresies, others into vile practices, though they seemed to be the subjects of a work of the Spirit—and were accepted for a while amongst those that were truly so, as their brethren and companions —and were not suspected till they went out from them. And some of these were teachers and officers—and eminent persons in the Christian church—whom God had endowed with miraculous gifts of the Holy Ghost; as appears by the beginning of the 6th chapter of the Hebrews. An instance of these was Judas, who was one of the twelve apostles, and had long been constantly united to, and intimately conversant with, a company of truly experienced disciples, without being discovered or suspected till he discovered himself by his scandalous practice. He had been treated by Jesus himself, in all external things, as if he had truly been a disciple, even investing him with the character of apostle, sending him forth to preach the gospel, and enduing him with miraculous gifts of the Spirit. For though Christ knew him, yet he did not then clothe himself with the character of omniscient Judge, and searcher of hearts, but acted the part of a minister of the visible church (for he was his Father's minister;) and therefore rejected him not, till he had discovered himself by his scandalous practice; thereby giving an example to guides and rulers of the visible church, not to take it upon them to act the part of searcher of hearts, but to be influenced in their administrations by what is visible and open. There were some instances then of such apostates, as were esteemed eminently full of the grace of God's Spirit. An instance of this nature probably was Nicolas, one of the seven deacons, who was looked upon by the Christians in Jerusalem, in the time of that extraordinary pouring out of the Spirit, as a man full of the Holy Ghost, and was chosen out of the multitudes of Christians to that office, for that reason; as you may see in Acts vi. 3, 5; yet he afterwards fell away and became the head of a sect of vile heretics, of gross practices, called from his name the sect of the Nicolaitans, Rev. ii. 6, and 15.

So in the time of the reformation from popery, how great was the number of those who for a while seemed to join with the reformers, yet fell away into the grossest and most absurd errors, and abominable practices. And it is particularly observable, that in times of great pouring out of the Spirit to revive religion in the world, a number of those who for a while seemed to partake in it, have fallen off into whimsical and extravagant errors, and gross enthusiasm, boasting of high degrees of spirituality and perfection, censuring and condemning others as carnal. Thus it was with the Gnostics in the apostles' times; and thus it was with several sects at the Reformation, as Anthony Burgess observes in his book called Spiritual Refinings, Part I. Serm. 23. p. 132: "The first worthy reformers, and glorious instruments of God, found a bitter conflict herein, so that they were exercised not only with formalists, and traditionary papists on the one side, but men that pretended themselves to be more enlightened than the reformers were, on the other side: hence they called those that did adhere to the Scripture, and would try revelations by it, Literists and Vowelists; as men acquainted with the words and vowels of the Scripture, having nothing of the Spirit of God: and wheresoever in any town, the true doctrine of the gospel brake forth to the displacing of popery, presently such opinions arose like tares that came up among the good wheat; whereby great divisions were raised, and the reformation made abominable and odious to the world; as if that had been the sun to give heat and warmth to those worms and serpents to crawl out of the ground. Hence they inveighed against Luther, and said he had only promulgated a carnal gospel."—Some of the leaders of those wild enthusiasts had been for a while highly esteemed by the first reformers, and peculiarly dear to them.—Thus also in England, at the time when vital religion much prevailed in the days of king Charles I. the interregnum, and Oliver Cromwell, such things as these abounded. And so in New England, in her purest days, when vital piety flourished, such kind of things as these broke out. Therefore the devil's sowing of such tares is no proof that a true work of the Spirit of God is not gloriously carried on.

IX. It is no argument that a work is not from the Spirit of God, that it seems to be promoted by ministers insisting very much on the terrors of God's holy law, and that with a great deal of pathos and earnestness. If there be really a hell of such dreadful and never-ending torments, as is generally supposed, of which multitudes are in great danger—and into which the greater part of men in Christian countries do actually from generation to generation fall, for want of a sense of its terribleness, and so for want of taking due care to avoid it—then why is it not proper for those who have the care of souls to take great pains to make men sensible of it? Why should they not be told as much of the truth as can be? If I am in danger of going to hell, I should be glad to know as much as possibly I can of the dreadfulness of it. If I am very prone to neglect due care to avoid it, he does me the best kindness, who does most to represent to me the truth of the case, that sets forth my misery and danger in the liveliest manner.

I appeal to every one whether this is not the very course they would take in case of exposedness to any great temporal calamity? If any of you who are heads of families saw one of your children in a house all on fire, and in imminent danger of being soon consumed in the flames, yet seemed to be very insensible of its danger, and neglected to escape after you had often called to it—would you go on to speak to it only in a cold and indifferent manner? Would not you cry aloud, and call earnestly to it, and represent the danger it was in, and its own folly in delaying, in the most lively manner of which you was capable? Would not nature itself teach this, and oblige you to it? If you should continue to speak to it only in a cold manner, as you are wont to do in ordinary conversation about indifferent matters, would not those about you begin to think you were bereft of reason yourself? This is not the way of mankind in temporal affairs of great moment, that require earnest heed and great haste, and about which they are greatly concerned. They are not wont to speak to others of their danger, and warn them but a little or in a cold and indifferent manner. Nature teaches men otherwise. If we who have the care of souls, knew what hell was, had seen the state of the damned, or by any other means had become sensible how dreadful their case was—and at the same time knew that the greater part of men went thither, and saw our hearers not sensible of their danger—it would be morally impossible for us to avoid most earnestly setting before them the dreadfulness of that misery, and their great exposedness to it and even to cry aloud to them.

When ministers preach of hell, and warn sinners to avoid it, in a cold manner—though they may say in words that it is infinitely terrible—they contradict themselves. For actions, as I observed before, have a language as well as words. If a preacher's words represent the sinner's state as infinitely dreadful, while his behavior and manner of speaking contradict it—showing that the preacher does not think so—he defeats his own purpose; for the language of his actions, in such a case, is much more effectual than the bare signification of his words. Not that I think that the law only should be preached: ministers may preach other things too little. The gospel is to be preached as well as the law, and the law is to be preached only to make way for the gospel, and in order that it may be preached more effectually. The main work of ministers is to preach the gospel: "Christ is the end of the law for righteousness." So that a minister would miss it very much if he should insist so much on the terrors of the law, as to forget his Lord, and neglect to preach the gospel; but yet the law is very much to be insisted on, and the preaching of the gospel is like to be in vain without it.

And certainly such earnestness and affection in speaking is beautiful, as becomes the nature and importance of the subject. Not but that there may be such a thing as an indecent boisterousness in a preacher, something besides what naturally arises from the nature of his subject, and in which the matter and manner do not well agree together. Some talk of it as an unreasonable thing to fright persons to heaven; but I think it is a reasonable thing to endeavor to fright persons away from hell. They stand upon its brink, and are just ready to fall into it, and are senseless of their danger. Is it not a reasonable thing to fright a person out of a house on fire? The word *fright* is commonly used for sudden, causeless fear, or groundless surprise; but surely a just fear, for which there is good reason, is not to be spoken against under any such name.

Section II.

What are distinguishing Scripture evidences of a work of the Spirit of God.

Having shown, in some instances, what are not evidences that a work wrought among a people, is not a work of the Spirit of God, I now proceed, in the second place, as was proposed, to show positively, what are the sure, distinguishing Scripture evidences and marks of a work of the Spirit of God, by which we may proceed in judging of any operation we find in ourselves, or see among a people, without danger of being misled.—And in this, as I said before, I shall confine myself wholly to those marks which are given us by the apostle in the chapter wherein is my text, where this matter is particularly handled, and more plainly and fully than anywhere else in the Bible. And in speaking to these marks, I shall take them in the order in which I find them in the chapter.

I. When the operation is such as to raise their esteem of that Jesus who was born of the Virgin, and was crucified without the gates of Jerusalem; and seems more to confirm and establish their minds in the truth of what the gospel declares to us of his being the Son of God, and the Saviour of men; it is a sure sign that it is from the Spirit of God. . . .

So that if the spirit that is at work among a people is plainly observed to work so as to convince them of Christ, and lead them to him—to confirm their minds in the belief of the history of Christ as he appeared in the flesh—and that he is the Son of God, and was sent of God to save sinners; that he is the only Saviour, and that they stand in great need of him; and if he seems to beget in them higher and more honorable thoughts of him than they used to have, and to incline their affections more to him; it is a sure sign that it is the true and right Spirit; however incapable we may be to determine, whether that conviction and affection be in that manner, or to that degree, as to be saving or not.

But the words of the apostle are remarkable; the person to whom the Spirit gives testimony, and for whom he raises their esteem, must be that Jesus who appeared in the flesh, and not another Christ in his stead; nor any mystical, fantastical Christ; such as the light within. This the spirit of Quakers extols, while it diminishes their esteem of and dependence upon an outward Christ—or Jesus as he came in the flesh—and leads them off from him; but the spirit that gives testimony for that Jesus, and leads to him, can be no other than the Spirit of God.

The devil has the most bitter and implacable enmity against that person, especially in his character of the Saviour of men; he mortally hates the story and doctrine of his redemption; he never would go about to beget in men more honorable thoughts of him, and lay greater weight on his instructions and commands. The Spirit that inclines men's hearts to the seed of the woman, is not the spirit of the serpent that has such an irreconcilable enmity against him. He that heightens men's esteem of the glorious Michael, that prince of the angels, is not spirit of the dragon that is at war with him.

II. When the spirit that is at work operates against the interests of Satan's kingdom, which lies in encouraging and establishing sin, and cherishing men's worldly lusts; this is a sure sign that it is a true, and not a false spirit. This sign we have given us in the 4th and 5th verses: "Ye are of God, little children, and have overcome them; because greater is he that is in you, than he that is in the world. They are of the world, therefore speak they of the world, and the world heareth them." Here is a plain antithesis: it is evident that the apostle is still comparing those that are influenced by the two opposite kinds of spirits, the true and the false, and showing the difference; the one is of God, and overcomes the spirit of the world; the other is of the world, and speaks and savors of the things of the world. The spirit of the devil is here called, "he that is in the world." Christ says, "My kingdom is not of this world." But it is otherwise with Satan's kingdom; he is "the god of this world."

What the apostle means by *the world,* or "the things that are of the world," we learn by his own words, in the 2d chapter of this epistle, 15th and 16th verses: "Love not the world, neither the things that are in the world: if any man love the world, the love of the Father is not in him: for all that is in the world, the lust of the flesh, and the lust of the eyes, and the pride of life, is not of the Father, but is of the world." So that by the world the apostle evidently means every thing that appertains to the interest of sin, and comprehends all the corruptions and lusts of men, and all those acts and objects by which they are gratified.

So that we may safely determine, from what the apostle says, that the spirit that is at work amongst a people, after such a manner as to lessen men's esteem of the pleasures, profits, and honors of the world, and to take off their hearts from an eager pursuit after these things; and to engage them in a deep concern about a future state and eternal happiness which the gospel reveals, and puts them upon earnestly seeking the kingdom of God and his righteousness; and the spirit that convinces them of the dreadfulness of sin, the guilt it brings, and the misery to which it exposes, must needs be the Spirit of God.

It is not to be supposed that Satan would convince men of sin, and awaken the conscience; it can no way serve his end to make that candle of the Lord shine the brighter, and to open the mouth of that viceregent of God in the soul. It is for his interest, whatever he does, to lull conscience asleep, and keep it quiet. To have that, with its eyes and mouth open in the soul, will tend to clog and hinder all his designs of darkness, and evermore to disturb his affairs, to cross his interest, and disquiet him, so that he can manage nothing to his mind without molestation. Would the devil, when he is about to establish men in sin, take such a course, in the first place, to en-lighten and awaken the conscience to see the dreadfulness of sin, and make them exceedingly afraid of it, and sensible of their misery by reason of their past sins, and their great need of deliverance from their guilt? Would he make them more careful, inquisitive, and watch-ful to discern what is sinful, and to avoid future sins; and so more afraid of the devil's temptations, and more careful to guard against them? What do those men do with their reason, that suppose that the Spirit that operates thus, is the spirit of the devil?

Possibly some may say, that the devil may even awaken men's consciences to deceive them, and make them think they have been the subjects of a saving work of the Spirit of God, while they are in-deed still in the gall of bitterness. But to this it may be replied, that the man who has an awakened conscience, is the least likely to be deceived of any man in the world; it is the drowsy, insensible, stupid conscience that is most easily blinded. The more sensible conscience is in a diseased soul, the less easily is it quieted without a real healing.

The more sensible conscience is made of the dreadfulness of sin, and of the greatness of a man's own guilt, the less likely is he to rest in his own righteousness, or to be pacified with nothing but shadows. A man that has been thoroughly terrified with a sense of his own danger and misery, is not easily flattered and made to believe himself safe, without any good grounds. To awaken conscience, and convince it of the evil of sin, cannot tend to establish it, but certainly tends to make way for sin and Satan's being cut out. Therefore this is a good argument that the Spirit that operates thus, cannot be the spirit of the devil; except we suppose that Christ knew not how to argue, who told the Pharisees—who supposed that the Spirit by which he wrought was the spirit of the devil—*that Satan would not cast out Satan,* Matt. xii. 25, 26. And, therefore, if we see persons made sensible of the dreadful nature of sin, and of the displeasure of God against it; of their own miserable condition as they are in themselves, by reason of sin, and earnestly concerned for their eternal salvation, and sensible of their need of God's pity and help, and engaged to seek it in the use of the means that God has appointed, we may certainly conclude that it is from the Spirit of God, whatever effects this concern has on their bodies; though it cause them to cry out aloud, or to shriek, or to faint; or though it throw them into convulsions, or whatever other way the blood and spirits are moved.

The influence of the Spirit of God is yet more abundantly manifest, if persons have their hearts *drawn off* from the world and weaned from the objects of their worldly lusts, and taken off from worldly pursuits, by the sense they have of the excellency of divine things, and the affection they have to those spiritual enjoyments of another world, that are promised in the gospel.

III. The spirit that operates in such a manner, as to cause in men a greater regard to the Holy Scriptures, and establishes them more in their truth and divinity, is certainly the Spirit of God. This rule the apostle gives us in the 6th verse: "We are of God; he that knoweth God heareth us; he that is not of God heareth not us: hereby know we the spirit of truth, and the spirit of error." *We are of God;* that is, "we the apostles are sent forth of God, and appointed by him to teach the world, and to deliver those doctrines and instructions, which are to be their rule; *he that knoweth God, heareth us,*" &c.—The apostle's argument here equally reaches all that in the same sense are *of God;* that is, all those that God has appointed and inspired to deliver to his church its rule of faith and pratice; all the prophets and apostles, whose doctrine God has made the foundation on which he has built his church, as in Eph. ii. 20; in a word, all the penmen of the Holy Scriptures. The devil never would attempt to beget in persons a regard to that divine word which God has given to be the great and standing rule for the direction of his church in all religious matters, and all concerns of their souls, in all ages. A spirit of delusion will not incline persons to seek direction at the mouth of God. To the law and to the testimony, is never the cry of those evil spirits that have no light in them; for it is God's own direction to discover their delusions. Isa. viii. 19, 20, "And when they shall say unto you, Seek unto them that have familiar spirits, and unto wizards that peep and that mutter: should not a people seek unto their God? for the living to the dead? To the law and to the testimony; if they speak not according to this word, it is because there is no light in them." The devil does not say the same as Abraham did, "They have Moses and the prophets, let them hear them:" nor the same that the voice from heaven did concerning Christ, "Hear ye him." Would the spirit of error, in order to deceive men, beget in them a high opinion of the infallible rule, and incline them to think much of it, and be very conversant with it? Would the prince of darkness, in order to promote his kingdom of darkness, lead men to the sun? The devil has ever shown a mortal spite and hatred towards that holy book the Bible: he has done all in his power to extinquish that light; and to draw men off from it: he knows it to be that light by which his kingdom of darkness is to be overthrown. He has had for many ages experience of its power to defeat his purposes, and baffle his designs: it is his constant plague. It is the main weapon which Michael uses in his war with him: it is the sword of the Spirit, that pierces him and conquers him. It is that great and strong sword, with which God punishes Leviathan, that crooked serpent. It is that sharp sword that we read of, Rev. xix. 15, that proceeds out of the mouth of him that sat on the horse, with which he smites his enemies. Every text is a dart to torment the old serpent. He has felt the stinging smart thousands of times; therefore he is engaged against the Bible, and hates every word in it: and we may be sure that he never will attempt to raise persons' esteem of it, or affection to it. And accordingly we see it common in enthusiasts, that they depreciate this written rule, and set up the light within or some other rule above it.

IV. Another rule to judge of spirits may be drawn from those compellations given to the opposite spirits, in the last words of the 6th verse, "The spirit of truth and the spirit of error." These words exhibit the two opposite characters of the Spirit of God, and other spirits that counterfeit his operations. And therefore, if by observing the manner of the operation of a spirit that is at work among a people, we see that it operates as a spirit of truth, leading persons to truth, convincing them of those things that are true, we may safely determine that it is a right and true spirit. For instance, if we observe that the spirit at work makes men more sensible than they used to be, that there is a God, and that he is a great and a sin-hating God: that life is short, and very uncertain; and that there is another world; that they have immortal souls, and must give account of themselves to God, that they are exceeding sinful by nature and practice; that they are helpless in themselves; and confirms them in other things that are agreeable to some sound doctrine; the spirit that works thus, operates as a spirit of truth; he represents things as they truly are. He brings men to the light; for whatever makes truth manifest is light; as the Apostle Paul observes, Eph. v. 13, "But all things that are reproved (or discovered, as it is in the margin) are made manifest by the light; for whatsoever doth make manifest is light." And therefore we may conclude, that it is not the spirit of darkness that doth thus discover and make manifest the truth. Christ tells us that Satan is a liar, and the father of liars; and his kindom is a kingdom of darkness. It is upheld and promoted only by darkness and error. Satan has all his power and dominion by darkness. Hence we read of the power of darkness, Luke xxii. 53, and Col. i, 13. And devils are called "the rulers of the darkness of this world." Whatever spirit removes our darkness, and brings us to the light, undeceives us, and, by convincing us of the truth, doth us a kindness. If I am brought to a sight of truth, and am made sensible of things as they really are, my duty is immediately to thank God for it, without standing first to inquire by what means I have such a benefit.

V. If the spirit that is at work among a people operates as a spirit of love to God and man, it is a sure sign that it is the Spirit of God. . . . Therefore, when the spirit that is at work amongst the people, tends this way, and brings many of them to high and exalting thoughts of the Divine Being, and his glorious perfections; and works in them an admiring, delightful sense of the excellency of Jesus Christ; representing him as the chief among ten thousand, and altogether lovely, and makes him precious to the soul; winning and drawing the heart with those motives and incitements to love, of which the apostle speaks in that passage of Scripture we are upon, viz., the wonderful free love of God in giving his only-begotten Son to die for us, and the wonderful dying love of Christ to us, who had no love to him, but were his enemies, must needs be the Spirit of God, as verses

9, 10: "In this was manifested the love of God towards us, because God sent his only-begotten Son into the world, that we might live through him. Herein is love; not that we loved God, but that he loved us, and sent his Son to be the propitiation for our sins." And ver. 16, "And we have known, and believed, the love that God hath to us." And ver. 19, "We love him because he first loved us." The spirit that excites to love on these motives, and makes the attributes of God as revealed in the gospel, and manifested in Christ, delightful objects of contemplation; and makes the soul to long after God and Christ—after their presence and communion, acquaintance with them, and conformity to them—and to live so as to please and honor them; the spirit that quells contentions among men, and gives a spirit of peace and good-will, excites to acts of outward kindness, and earnest desires of the salvation of souls, and causes a delight in those that appear as the children of God, and followers of Christ; I say, when a spirit operates after this manner among a people, there is the highest kind of evidence of the influence of a true and divine spirit.

Indeed there is a counterfeit love, that often appears among those who are led by a spirit of delusion. There is commonly in the wildest enthusiasts a kind of union and affection, arising from self-love, occasioned by their agreeing in those things wherein they greatly differ from all others, and from which they are objects of the ridicule of all the rest of mankind. This naturally will cause them so much the more to prize those peculiarities that make them the objects of others' contempt. Thus the ancient Gnostics, and the wild fanatics that appeared at the beginning of the Reformation, boasted of their great love one to another; one sect of them, in particular, calling themselves the *family of love*. But this is quite another thing than that Christian love I have just described: it is only the working of a natural self-love, and no true benevolence, any more than the union and friendship which may be among a company of pirates, that are at war with all the rest of the world. There is enough said in this passage of the nature of a truly Christian love, thoroughly to distinguish it from all such counterfeits. It is love that arises from apprehension of the wonderful riches of the free grace and sovereignty of God's love to us, in Christ Jesus; being attended with a sense of our own utter unworthiness, as in ourselves the enemies and haters of God and Christ, and with a renunciation of all our own excellency and right-eousness. See verses 9, 10, 11, and 19. The surest character of true divine supernatural love—distinguishing it from counterfeits that arise from a natural self-love—is, that the Christian virtue of *humility* shines in it; that which above all others renounces, abases, and annihilates what we term *self*. Christian love, or true charity, is a humble love. 1 Cor. xiii. 4, 5, "Charity vaunteth not itself, is not puffed up, doth not behave itself unseemly, seeketh not her own, is not easily provoked." When, therefore, we see love in persons attended with a sense of their own littleness, vileness, weakness, and utter insufficiency; and so with self-diffidence, self-emptiness, self-renunciation, and poverty of spirit; these are the manifest tokens of the Spirit of God. He that thus dwells in love, dwells in God, and God in him. What the apostle speaks of as a great evidence of the true spirit, is God's love or Christ's love; as ver. 12, "His love is perfected in us." What kind of love that is, we may see best in what appeared in Christ's example. The love that appeared in that Lamb of God, was not only a love to friends, but to enemies, and a love attended with a meek and humble spirit. "Learn of me," says he, "for I am meek and lowly in heart." Love and humility are two things the most contrary to the spirit of the devil, of any thing in the world; for the character of that evil spirit, above all things, consists in pride and malice.

Thus I have spoken particularly to the several marks the apostle gives us of a work of the true Spirit. There are some of these things which the devil *would not* do if he could: thus he would not awaken the conscience, and make men sensible of their miserable state by reason of sin, and sensible of their great need of a Saviour; and he would not confirm men in the belief that Jesus is the Son of God, and the Saviour of sinners, or raise men's value and esteem of him: he would not beget in men's minds an opinion of the necessity, usefulness, and truth of the Holy Scriptures, or incline them to make much use of them; nor would he show men the truth, in things that concern their souls' interest; to undeceive them, and lead them out of darkness into light, and give them a view of things as they really are. And there are other things that the devil *neither can nor will* do; he will not give men a spirit of divine love, or Christian humility and poverty of spirit; nor *could* he if he would. He cannot give those things he has not himself: these things are as contrary as possible to his nature. And therefore when there is an extraordinary influence or operation appearing on the minds of a people, if these things are found in it, we are safe in determining that it is the work of God, whatever other circumstances it may be attended with, whatever instruments are used, whatever methods are taken to promote it; whatever means a sovereign God, whose judgments are a great deep, employs to carry it on; and whatever motion there may be of the animal spirits, whatever effects may be wrought on men's bodies. These marks, that the apostle has given us, are sufficient to stand alone, and support themselves. They plainly show *the finger of God,* and are sufficient to outweigh a thousand such little objections, as many make from oddities, irregularities, errors in conduct, and the delusions and scandals of some professors. . . .

Having thus fulfilled what I first proposed, in considering what are the certain, distinguishing marks, by which we may safely proceed in judging of any work that falls under our observation, whether it be the work of the Spirit of God or no; I now proceed to the Application.

Section III.

Practical Inferences.

I. From what has been said, I will venture to draw this inference, *viz., that the extraordinary influence that has lately appeared causing an uncommon concern and engagedness of mind about the things of religion, is undoubtedly, in the general, from the Spirit of God.* There are but two things that need to be known in order to such a work's being judged of, *viz., facts* and *rules.* The *rules* of the word of God we have had laid before us; and as to *facts,* there are but two ways that we can come at them, so as to be in a capacity to compare them with the rules, either by our own observation, or by information from others who have had opportunity to observe them.

As to this work, there are many things concerning it that are notorious, and which, unless the apostle John was out in his rules, are sufficient to determine it to be in general the work of God. The Spirit that is at work, takes off persons' minds from the vanities of the world, and engages them in a deep concern about eternal happiness, and puts them upon earnestly seeking their salvation, and convinces them of the dreadfulness of sin, and of their own guilty and miserable state as they are by nature. It awakens men's consciences, and makes them sensible of the dreadfulness of God's anger, and causes in them a great desire and earnest care and endeavor to obtain his favor.

It puts them upon a more diligent improvement of the means of grace which God has appointed; accompanied with a greater regard to the word of God, a desire of hearing and reading it, and of being more conversant with it than they used to be. And it is notoriously manifest, that the spirit that is at work, in general, operates as a spirit of truth, making persons more sensible of what is really true in those things that concern their eternal salvation: as, that they must die, and that life is very short and uncertain; that there is a great sin-hating God, to whom they are accountable, and who will fix them in an eternal state in another world; and that they stand in great need of a Saviour. It makes persons more sensible of the value of Jesus who was crucified, and their need of him; and that it puts them upon earnestly seeking an interest in him. It cannot be but that these things should be apparent to people in general through the land; for these things are not done in a corner; the work has not been confined to a few towns, in some remoter parts, but has been carried on in many places all over the land, and in most of the principal, the populous, and public places in it. Christ in this respect has wrought amongst us, in the same manner that he wrought his miracles in Judea. It has now been continued for a considerable time; so that there has been a great opportunity to observe the manner of the work. And all such as have been very conversant with the subjects of it, see a great deal more, that, by the rules of the apostle, does clearly and certainly show it to be the work of God.

And here I would observe, that the nature and tendency of a spirit that is at work, may be determined with much greater certainty, and less danger of being imposed upon, when it is observed in a great multitude of people of all sorts, and in various places, than when it is only seen in a few, in some particular place, that have been much conversant one with another. A few particular persons may agree to put a cheat upon others, by a false pretence, and professing things of which they never were conscious. But when the work is spread over great parts of a country, in places distant from one another, among people of all sorts and of all ages, and in multitudes possessed of a sound mind, good understanding, and known integrity; there would be the greatest absurdity in supposing, from all the observation that can be made by all that is heard from and seen in them—for many months together, and by those who are most intimate with them in these affairs, and have long been acquainted with them—that yet it cannot be determined what kind of influence the operation they are under has upon people's minds. Can it not be determined whether it tends to awaken their consciences, or to stupify them; whether it inclines them more to seek their salvation, or neglect it; whether it seems to confirm them in a belief of the Scriptures, or to lead them to deism; whether it makes them have more regard for the great truths of religion, or less?

And here it is to be observed, that for persons to profess that they are so convinced of certain divine truths, as to esteem and love them in a *saving manner;* and for them to profess, that they are *more convinced* or confirmed in the truth of them, than they used to be, and find that they have a greater regard to them than they had before, are two very different things. Persons of honesty and common sense, have much greater right to demand credit to be given to the latter profession, than to the former. Indeed in the former, it is less likely that a people in general should be deceived, than some particular persons. But whether persons' convictions, and the alteration in their dispositions and affections, be in a degree and manner that is saving, is beside the present question. If there be such effects on people's judgments, dispositions, and affections, as have been spoken of, whether they be in a degree and manner that is saving or no, it is nevertheless a sign of the influence of the Spirit of God. Scripture rules serve to distinguish the common influences of the Spirit of God, as well as those that are saving, from the influence of other causes.

And as, by the providence of God, I have for some months past been much amongst those who have been the subjects of the work in question; and particularly, have been in the way of seeing and observing those extraordinary things with which many persons have been offended;—such as persons' crying out aloud, shrieking, being put into great agonies of body, &c.— and have seen the manner and issue of such operations, and the fruits of them, for several months together; many of them being persons with whom I have been intimately acquainted in soul concerns, before and since; so I look upon myself called on this occasion to give my testimony, that—so far as the nature and tendency of such a work is capable of falling under the observation of a by-stander, to whom those that have been the subjects of it have endeavored to open their hearts, or can be come at by diligent and particular inquiry—this work has all those marks that have been pointed out. And this has been the case in very many instances, in *every article;* and in many others, all those marks have appeared in a very *great degree.*

The subjects of these uncommon appearances, have been of two sorts; either those who have been in great distress from an apprehension of their sin and misery; or those who have been overcome with a sweet sense of the greatness, wonderfulness, and excellency of divine things. Of the multitude of those of the former sort, that I have had opportunity to observe, there have been very few, but their distress has arisen apparently from real proper conviction, and being in a degree sensible of that which was the truth. And though I do not suppose, when such things were observed to be common, that persons have laid themselves under those violent restraints to avoid outward manifestations of their distress, that perhaps they otherwise would have done; yet there have been very few in whom there has been any appearance of feigning or affecting such manifestations, and very many for whom it would have been undoubtedly utterly impossible for them to avoid them. Generally, in these agonies they have appeared to be in the perfect exercise of their reason; and those of them who could speak, have been well able to give an account of the circumstances of their mind, and the cause of their distress, at the time, and were able to remember, and give an account of it afterwards. I have known a very few instances of those, who, in their great extremity, have for a short space been deprived, in some measure, of the use of reason; and among the many hundreds, and it may be thousands, that have lately been brought to such agonies, I never yet knew one lastingly deprived of their reason. In some that I have known, melancholy has evidently been mixed; and when it is so, the difference is very apparent; their distresses are of another kind, and operate quite after another manner, than when their distress is from mere conviction. It is not truth only that distresses them, but many vain shadows and notions that will not give place either to Scripture or reason. Some in their great distress have not been well able to give an account of themselves, or to declare the sense they have of things, or to explain the manner and cause of their trouble to others, that yet I have had no reason to think were not under proper convictions, and in whom there has been manifested a good issue. But this will not be at all wondered at, by those who have had much to do with souls under spiritual difficulties: some things of which they are sensible, are altogether new to them; their ideas and inward sensations are new, and what they therefore know not how to express in words. Some who, on first inquiry, said they knew not what was the matter with them, have on being particularly examined and interrogated, been able to represent their case, though of themselves they could not find expressions and forms of speech to do it.

Some suppose, that terrors producing such effects are only a fright. But certainly there ought to be a distinction made between a very great fear, or extreme distress arising from an apprehension of some dreadful truth—a cause fully proportionable to such an effect—and a needless, causeless fright. The latter is of two kinds; either, first, when persons are terrified with that which is not the truth (of which I have seen very few instances unless in case of melancholy); or, secondly, when they are in a fright from some terrible outward appearance and noise, and a general notion thence arising. These apprehend, that there is something or other terrible, they know not what; without having in their minds any particular truth whatever. Of such a kind of fright I have seen very little appearance, among either old or young.

Those who are in such extremity, commonly express a great sense of their exceeding wickedness, the multitude and aggravations of their actual sins; their dreadful pollution, enmity, and perverseness; their obstinacy and hardness of heart; a sense of their great guilt in the sight of God; and the dreadfulness of the punishment due to sin. Very often they have a lively idea of the horrible pit of eternal misery; and at the same time it appears to them, that the great God who has them in his hands, is exceedingly angry, and his wrath appears amazingly terrible to them. God appears to them so much provoked, and his great wrath so increased; that they are apprehensive of great danger, and that he will not bear with them any longer; but will now forthwith cut them off, and send them down to the dreadful pit they have in view; at the same time seeing no refuge. They see more and more of the vanity of every thing they used to trust to, and with which they flattered themselves, till they are brought wholly to despair in all, and to see that they are at the disposal of the mere will of that God who is so angry with them. Very many, in the midst of their extremity, have been brought to an extraordinary sense of their fully deserving that wrath, and the destruction which was then before their eyes. They feared every moment, that it would be executed upon them; they have been greatly convinced that this would be altogether just, and that God is indeed absolutely sovereign. Very often, some text of Scripture expressing God's sovereignty, has been set home upon their minds, whereby they have been calmed. They have been brought, as it were, to lie at God's feet; and after great agonies, a little before light has arisen, they have been composed and quiet, in submission to a just and sovereign God; but their bodily strength much spent. Sometimes their lives, to appearance, were almost gone; and then light has appeared, and a glorious Redeemer, with his wonderful, all-sufficient grace, has been represented to them often, in some sweet invitation of Scripture. Sometimes the light comes in suddenly, sometimes more gradually, filling their souls with love, admiration, joy, and self-abasement; drawing forth their hearts after the excellent lovely Redeemer, and longings to lie in the dust before him; and that others might behold, embrace, and be delivered by him. They had longings to live to his glory; but were sensible that they can do nothing of themselves, appearing vile in their own eyes, and having much jealousy over their own hearts. And all the appearances of a real change of heart have followed; and grace has acted, from time to time, after the same manner that it used to act in those that were converted formerly, with the like difficulties, temptations, buffetings, and comforts; excepting that in many, the light and comfort have been in higher degrees than ordinary. Many very young children have been thus wrought upon. There have been some instances very much like those (Mark i. 26, and chap. ix. 26,) of whom we read, that "when the devil had cried with a loud voice, and rent them sore, he came out of them." And probably those instances were designed for a type of such things as these. Some have several turns of great agonies, before they are delivered; and others have been in such distress, which has passed off, and no deliverance at all has followed.

Some object against it as great confusion, when there is a number together in such circumstances making a noise; and say, God cannot be the author of it; because he is the God of order, not of confusion. But let it be considered, what is the proper notion of confusion, but the breaking that order of things, whereby they are properly disposed, and duly directed to their end, so that the order and due connection of means being broken, they fail of their end. Now the conviction of sinners for their conversion is the obtaining of the end of religious means. Not but that I think the persons thus extraordinarily moved, should endeavor to refrain from such outward manifestations, what they well can, and should refrain to their utmost, at the time of their solemn worship. But if God is pleased to convince the consciences of persons, so that they cannot avoid great outward manifestations, even to interrupting and breaking off those public means they were attending, I do not think this is confusion, or an unhappy interruption, any more than if a company should meet on the field to pray for rain, and should be broken off from their exercise by a plentiful shower. Would to God that all the public assemblies in the land were broken off from their public exercises with such confusion as this the next Sabbath day! We need not be sorry for breaking the order of means, by obtaining the end to which that order is directed. He who is going to fetch a treasure, need not be sorry that he is stopped, by meeting the treasure in the midst of his journey.

Besides those who are overcome with conviction and distress, I have seen many of late, who have had their bodily strength taken away with a sense of the glorious excellency of the Redeemer, and the wonders of his dying love; with a very uncommon sense of their own littleness and exceeding vileness attending it, with all expressions and appearances of the greatest abasement and abhorrence of themselves. Not only new converts, but many who were, as we hope, formerly converted, have had their love and joy attended with a flood of tears, and a great appearance of contrition and humiliation, especially for their having lived no more to God's glory since their conversion. These have had a far greater sight of their vileness, and the evil of their hearts, than ever they had; with an exceeding earnestness of desire to live better for the time to come, but attended with greater self-diffidence than ever; and many have been overcome with pity to the souls of others, and longing for their salvation.—And many other things I might mention, in this extraordinary work, answering to every one of those marks which have been insisted on. So that if the apostle John knew how to give signs of a work of the true Spirit, this is such a work.

Providence has cast my lot in a place where the work of God has *formerly* been carried on. I had the happiness to be settled in that place two years with the venerable Stoddard; and was then acquainted with a number who, during that season, were wrought upon under his ministry. I have been intimately acquainted with the experiences of many others who were wrought upon under his ministry, before that period, in a manner agreeable to the doctrine of all orthodox divines. And of late, a work has been carried on there, with very much of uncommon operations; but it is evidently the same work that was carried on there, in different periods, though attended with some new circumstances. And certainly we must throw by all talk of conversion and Christian experience; and not only so, but we must throw by our Bibles, and give up revealed religion; if this be not in general the work of God. Not that I suppose the degree of the Spirit's influence is to be determined by the degree of effect on men's bodies; or, that those are always the best experiences which have the greatest influence on the body.

And as to the imprudencies, irregularities, and mixture of delusion that has been observed; it is not at all to be wondered at, that a reformation, after a long continued and almost universal deadness, should at first, when the revival is new, be attended with such things. In the first creation God did not make a complete world at once; but there was a great deal of imperfection, darkness, and mixture of chaos and confusion, after God first said, "Let there be light," before the whole stood forth in perfect form. When God at first began his great work for the deliverance of his people, after their long-continued bondage in Egypt, there were false wonders mixed with the true for a while; which hardened the unbelieving Egyptians, and made them to doubt of the divinity of the whole work. When the children of Israel first went to bring up the ark of God, after it had been neglected, and had been long absent, they sought not the Lord after the due order, 1 Chron. xv. 13. At the time when the sons of God came to present themselves before the Lord, Satan came also among them. And Solomon's ships, when they brought gold, and silver, and pearls, also brought apes and peacocks. When day-light first appears after a night of darkness, we must expect to have darkness mixed with light for a while, and not have perfect day and the sun risen at once. The fruits of the earth are first green before they are ripe, and come to their proper perfection gradually; and so, Christ tells us, is the kingdom of God. Mark iv. 26, 27, 28, "So is the kingdom of God; as if a man should cast seed into the ground, and should sleep, and rise night and day; and the seed should spring and grow up, he knoweth not how: for the earth bringeth forth fruit of herself; first the blade, then the ear, after that the full corn in the ear."

The imprudencies and errors that have attended this work, are the less to be wondered at, if it be considered, that chiefly young persons have been the subjects of it, who have less steadiness and experience, and being in the heat of youth, are much more ready to run to extremes. Satan will keep men secure as long as he can; but when he can do that no longer, he often endeavors to drive them to extremes, and so to dishonor God, and wound religion in that way. And doubtless it has been one occasion of much misconduct, that in many places, people see plainly that their ministers have an ill opinion of the work; and therefore, with just reason, durst not apply themselves to them as their guides in it; and so are without guides.— No wonder then that when a people are as sheep without a shepherd, they wander out of the way. A people in such circumstances, stand in great and continual need of guides, and their guides stand in continual need of much more wisdom than they have of their own. And if a people have ministers that favor the work, and rejoice in it, yet it is not to be expected that either the people or ministers should know so well how to conduct themselves in such an extraordinary state of things—while it is new, and what they never had any experience of before, and time to see their tendency, consequences, and issue. The happy influence of experience is very manifest at this day, in the people among whom God has settled my abode. The work which has been carried on there this year, has been much purer than that which was wrought there six years before: it has seemed to be more purely spiritual; free from natural and corrupt mixtures, and any thing savoring of enthusiastic wildness and extravagance. It has wrought more by deep humiliation and abasement before God and men; and they have been much freer from imprudencies and irregularities. And particularly there has been a remarkable difference in this respect, that whereas many before, in their comforts and rejoicings, did too much forget their distance from God, and were ready in their conversation together of the things of God, and of their own experiences, to talk with too much lightness; but now they seem to have no disposition that way, but rejoice with a more solemn, reverential, humble joy, as God directs, Psal. ii. 11. Not because the joy is not as great, and in many instances much greater. Many among us who were wrought upon in that former season, have now had much greater communications from heaven than they had then. Their rejoicing operates in another manner; it abases them, breaks their heart, and brings them into the dust. When they speak of their joys, it is not with laughter, but a flood of tears. Thus those who laughed before, weep now, and yet by their united testimony, their joy is vastly purer and sweeter than that which before did more raise their animal spirits. They are now more like Jacob, when God appeared to him at Bethel, when he saw the ladder that reached to heaven, and said, "How dreadful is this place!" And like Moses, when God showed him his glory on the mount, when he made haste and "bowed himself unto the earth."

II. Let us all be hence warned, *by no means to oppose, or do any thing in the least to clog or hinder, the work; but, on the contrary, do our utmost to promote it.* Now Christ is come down from heaven in a remarkable and wonderful work of his Spirit, it becomes all his professed disciples to acknowledge him, and give him honor.

The example of the Jews in Christ's and the apostles' times, is enough to beget in those who do not acknowledge this work, a great jealousy of themselves, and to make them exceeding cautious of what they say or do. Christ then was in the world, and the world knew him not: he came to his own professing people, and his own received him not. That coming of Christ had been much spoken of in the prophecies of Scripture which they had in their hands, and it had been long expected; and yet because Christ came in a manner they did not expect, and which was not agreeable to their carnal reason, they would not own him. Nay, they opposed him, counted him a madman, and pronounced the spirit that he wrought by to be the spirit of the devil. They stood and wondered at the great things done, and knew not what to make of them; but yet they met with so many stumbling-blocks, that they finally could not acknowledge him. And when the Spirit of God came to be poured out so wonderfully in the apostles' days, they looked upon it as confusion and distraction. They were *astonished* by what they saw and heard, but not *convinced*. And especially was the work of God then rejected by those that were most conceited of their own understanding and knowledge, agreeable to Isa. xxix. 14: "Therefore, behold, I will proceed to do a marvellous work amongst this people, even a marvellous work and a wonder; for the wisdom of their wise men shall perish, and the understanding of their prudent men shall be hid." And many who had been in reputation for religion and piety, had a great spite against the work, because they saw it tended to diminish their honor, and to reproach their formality and lukewarmness. Some, upon these accounts, maliciously and openly opposed and reproached the work of the Spirit of God, and called it the work of the devil, against inward conviction, and so were guilty of the unpardonable sin against the Holy Ghost.

There is another, a spiritual coming of Christ, to set up his kingdom in the world, that is as much spoken of in Scripture prophecy as that first coming, and which has long been expected by the church of God. We have reason to think, from what is said of this, that it will be, in many respects, parallel with the other. And certainly, that low state into which the visible church of God has lately been sunk is very parallel with the state of the Jewish church, when Christ came; and therefore no wonder at all, that when Christ comes, his work should appear a strange work to most; yea, it would be a wonder if it should be otherwise. Whether the present work be the beginning of that great and frequently predicted coming of Christ to set up his kingdom, or not, it is evident, from what has been said, that it is a work of the same Spirit, and of the same nature. And there is no reason to doubt, but that the conduct of persons who continue long to refuse acknowledging Christ in the work—especially those who are set to be teachers in his church—will be in like manner provoking to God, as it was in the Jews of old, while refusing to acknowledge Christ; notwithstanding what they may plead of the great stumbling-blocks that are in the way, and the cause they have to doubt of the work. . . .

It is not to be supposed that the great Jehovah has bowed the heavens, and appeared here now for so long a time, in such a glorious work of his power and grace—in so extensive a manner in the most public places of the land, and in almost all parts of it—without giving such evidences of his presence, that great numbers, and even many teachers in his church, can remain guiltless in his sight, without ever receiving and acknowledging him, and giving him honour, and appearing to rejoice in his gracious presence; or without so much as once giving him thanks for so glorious and blessed a work of his grace, wherein his goodness does more appear, than if he had bestowed on us all the temporal blessings that the world affords. A long-continued silence in such a case is undoubtedly provoking to God; especially in ministers. It is a secret kind of opposition, that really tends to hinder the work. Such silent ministers stand in the way of the work of God, as Christ said of old, "He that is not with us is against us." Those who stand wondering at this strange work, not knowing what to make of it, and refusing to receive it—and ready it may be sometimes to speak contemptibly of it, as was the case with the Jews of old—would do well to consider, and to tremble at St. Paul's words to them, Acts xiii. 40, 41: "Beware therefore, lest that come upon you which is spoken of in the prophets, Behold, ye despisers, and wonder, and perish; for I work a work in your days, which you shall in no wise believe, though a man declare it unto you." Those who cannot believe the work to be true, because of the extraordinary degree and manner of it, should consider how it was with the unbelieving lord in Samaria, who said, "Behold, if the Lord should make windows in heaven, might this thing be?" To whom Elisha said, "Behold, thou shall see it with thine eyes, but shalt not eat thereof." Let all to whom this work is a cloud and darkness—as the pillar of cloud and fire was to the Egyptians—take heed that it be not their destruction, while it gives light to God's Israel.

I would entreat those who quiet themselves, that they proceed on a principle of prudence, and are waiting to see the issue of things —and what fruits those that are the subjects of this work will bring forth in their lives and conversations—to consider, whether this will justify a long refraining from acknowledging Christ when he appears so wonderfully and graciously present in the land. It is probable that many of those who are thus waiting, know not for what they are waiting. If they wait to see a work of God without difficulties and stumbling-blocks, it will be like the fool's waiting at the river side to have the water all run by. A work of God without stumbling-blocks is never to be expected. "It must needs be that offences come." There never yet was any great manifestation that God made of himself to the world, without many difficulties attending it. It is with the works of God, as with this word: they seem at first full of things that are strange, inconsistent, and difficult to the carnal unbelieving hearts of men. Christ and his work always was, and always will be, a stone of stumbling, and rock of offence, a gin and a snare to many. . . .

It is probable that the stumbling-blocks that now attend this work, will in some respects be increased, and not diminished. We probably shall see more instances of apostasy and gross iniquity among professors. And if one kind of stumbling-blocks are removed, it is to be expected that others will come. It is with Christ's works as it was with his parables; things that are difficult to men's dark minds are ordered of purpose, for the trial of their dispositions and spiritual sense; and that those of corrupt minds and of an unbelieving, perverse, cavilling spirit, "seeing might see and not understand." Those who are now waiting to see the issue of this work, think they shall be better able to determine by and by; but probably many of them are mistaken. The Jews that saw Christ's miracles, waited to see better evidences of his being the Messiah; they wanted a sign from heaven; but they waited in vain; their stumbling-blocks did not diminish, but increase. They found no end to them, and so were more and more hardened in unbelief. Many have been praying for that glorious reformation spoken of in Scripture, who knew not what they have been praying for (as it was with the Jews when they prayed for the coming of Christ), and who, if it should come, would not acknowledge or receive it.

This pretended prudence, in persons waiting so long before they acknowledged this work, will probably in the end prove the greatest imprudence. Hereby they will fail of any share of so great a blessing, and will miss the most precious opportunity of obtaining divine light, grace, and comfort, heavenly and eternal benefits, that God ever gave in New England. While the glorious fountain is set open in so wonderful a manner, and multitudes flock to it and receive a rich supply for the wants of their souls, they stand at a distance, doubting, wondering, and receiving nothing, and are like to continue thus till the precious season is past.—It is indeed to be wondered at, that those who have doubted of the work, which has been attended with such uncommon external appearances, should be easy in their doubts, without taking thorough pains to inform themselves, by going where such things have been to be seen, narrowly observing and diligently inquiring into them; not contenting themselves with observing two or three instances, nor resting till they were fully informed by their own observation. I do not doubt but that if this course had been taken, it would have convinced all whose minds are not shut up against conviction. How greatly have they erred, who only from the uncertain reproofs of others, have ventured to speak slightly of these things! That caution of an unbelieving Jew might teach them more prudence, Acts v. 38, 39: "Refrain from these men, and let them alone; for if this counsel or this work be of men, it will come to nought; but if it be of God, ye cannot overthrow it; lest haply ye be found to fight against God." Whether what has been said in this discourse be enough to produce conviction, that this is the work of God, or not; yet I hope that for the future, they will at least hearken to the caution of Gamaliel, now mentioned; so as not to oppose it, or say any thing which has even an indirect tendency to bring it into discredit, lest they should be found opposers of the Holy Ghost. There is no kind of sins so hurtful and dangerous to the souls of men, as those committed against the Holy Ghost. We had better speak against God the Father, or the Son, than to speak against the Holy Spirit in his gracious operations on the hearts of men. Nothing will so much tend forever to prevent our having any benefit of his operations on our own souls.

If there be any who still resolutely go on to speak comtemptibly of these things, I would beg of them to take heed that they be not guilty of the unpardonable sin. When the Holy Spirit is much poured out, and men's lusts, lukewarmness, and hypocrisy are reproached by its powerful operations, then is the most likely time of any, for this sin to be committed. If the work goes on, it is well if among the many that show an enmity against it, some be not guilty of this sin, if none have been already. Those who maliciously oppose and reproach this work, and call it the work of the devil, want but one thing of the unpardonable sin, and that is, doing it against inward conviction. And though some are so prudent, as not openly to oppose and reproach this work, yet it is to be feared—at this day, when the Lord is going forth so gloriously against his enemies—that many who are silent and inactive, especially ministers, will bring that curse of the angel of the Lord upon themselves, Judg. v. 23: "Curse ye Meroz, said the angel of the Lord, curse ye bitterly the inhabitants thereof: because they came not to the help of the Lord, to the help of the Lord against the mighty."

Since the great God has come down from heaven, and manifested himself in so wonderful a manner in this land, it is vain for any of us to expect any other than to be greatly affected by it in our spiritual state and circumstances, respecting the favor of God, one way or other. Those who do not become more happy by it, will become far more guilty and miserable. It is always so; such a season as proves an acceptable year, and a time of great favor to them who accept and improve it, proves a day of vengeance to others, Jsa. lix. 2. When God sends forth his *word,* it shall not return to him void; much less his *Spirit.* When Christ was upon earth in Judea, many slighted and rejected him; but it proved in the issue to be no matter of indifference to them. God made all that people to feel that Christ had been among them; those who did not feel it to their comfort, felt it to their great sorrow. When God only sent the prophet Ezekiel to the children of Israel, he declared that whether they would hear or whether they would forbear, yet they should know that there had been a prophet among them; how much more may we suppose that when God has appeared so wonderfully in this land, that he will make every one to know that the great Jehovah had been in New England. —I come now, in the last place,

III. To apply myself to those who are the friends of this work, who have been partakers of it, and are zealous to promote it. Let me earnestly exhort such to give diligent heed to themselves to avoid all errors and misconduct, and whatever may darken and obscure the work; and to give no occasion to those who stand ready to reproach it. The apostle was careful to cut off occasion from those that desired occasion. The same apostle exhorts Titus, to maintain a strict care and watch over himself, that both his preaching and behavior might be such as "could not be condemned; that he who was of the contrary part might be ashamed, having no evil thing to say of them," Tit. ii. 7, 8. We had need to be wise as serpents and harmless as doves. It is of no small consequence that we should at this day behave ourselves innocently and prudently. We must expect that the great enemy of this work will especially try his utmost with us; and he will especially triumph if he can prevail in any thing to blind and mislead us. He knows it will do more to further his purpose and interest than if he had prevailed against a hundred others. We had need to watch and pray, for we are but little children; this roaring lion is too strong for us, and this old serpent too subtle for us.

Humility and self-diffidence, and an entire dependence on our Lord Jesus Christ, will be our best defence. Let us therefore maintain the strictest watch against spiritual pride, or being lifted up with extraordinary experiences and comforts, and the high favors of heaven, that any of us may have received. We had need, after such favors, in a special manner to keep a strict and jealous eye upon our own hearts, lest there should arise self-exalting reflections upon what we have received, and high thoughts of ourselves, as being now some of the most eminent of saints and peculiar favorites of heaven, and that the secret of the Lord is especially with us. Let us not presume, that we above all are fit to be advanced as the great instructors and censors of this evil generation; and, in a high conceit of our own wisdom and discerning, assume to ourselves the airs of prophets, or extraordinary ambassadors of heaven. When we have great discoveries of God made to our souls, we should not shine bright in our own eyes. Moses, when he had been conversing with God in the mount, though his face shone so as to dazzle the eyes of Aaron and the people, yet he did not shine in his own eyes; "he wist not that his face shone." Let none think themselves out of danger of this spiritual pride, even in their best frames. God saw that the apostle Paul (though probably the most eminent saint that ever lived) was not out of danger of it, no not when he had just been conversing with God in the third heaven: see 2 Cor. xii. 7. Pride is the worst viper in the heart; it is the first sin that ever entered into the universe, lies lowest of all in the foundation of the whole building of sin, and is the most secret, deceitful, and unsearchable in its ways of working, of any lusts whatever. It is ready to mix with every thing; and nothing is so hateful to God, contrary to the spirit of the gospel, or of so dangerous consequence; and there is no one sin that does so much let in the devil into the hearts of the saints, and expose them to his delusions. I have seen it in many instances, and that in eminent saints. The devil has come in at this door presently after some eminent experience and extraordinary communion with God, and has wofully deluded and led them astray, till God has mercifully opened their eyes and delivered them; and they themselves have afterwards been made sensible that it was pride that betrayed them.

Some of the true friends of the work of God's Spirit have erred in giving too much heed to impulses and strong impressions on their minds, as though they were immediate significations from heaven to them, of something that should come to pass, or something that it was the mind and will of God that they should do, which was not signified or revealed anywhere in the Bible without those impulses. These impressions, if they are truly from the Spirit of God, are of a quite different nature from his gracious influences on the hearts of the saints: they are of the nature of the extraordinary *gifts* of the Spirit, and are properly inspiration, such as the prophets and apostles and others had of old; which the apostle distinguishes from the *grace* of the Spirit, 1 Cor. xiii.

One reason why some have been ready to lay weight on such impulses, is an opinion they have had, that the glory of the approaching happy days of the church would partly consist in restoring those *extraordinary gifts* of the Spirit. This opinion, I believe, arises partly through want of duly considering and comparing the nature and value of those two kinds of influences of the Spirit, viz., those that are ordinary and gracious, and those that are extraordinary and miraculous. The former are by far the most excellent and glorious; as the apostle largely shows, 1 Cor. xii. 31, &c. Speaking of the extraordinary gifts of the Spirit, he says, "But covet earnestly the best gifts; and yet I show you a more excellent way;" i.e., a more excellent way of the influence of the Spirit. And then he goes on, in the next chapter, to show what that more excellent way is, even the grace of that Spirit, which summarily consists in charity, or divine love. And throughout that chapter he shows the great preference of that above inspiration. God communicates his own nature to the soul in saving *grace* in the heart, more than in all miraculous *gifts*. The blessed image of God consists in *that* and not in *these*. The excellency, happiness, and glory of the soul, immediately consists in the former. That is a root which bears infinitely more excellent fruit. Salvation and the eternal enjoyment of God is promised to divine grace, but not to inspiration. A man may have those extraordinary gifts, and yet be abominable to God, and go to hell. The spiritual and eternal life of the soul consists in the grace of the Spirit, which God bestows only on his favorites and dear children. He has sometimes thrown out the other as it were to dogs and swine, as he did to Balaam, Saul, and Judas; and some who in the primitive times of the Christian church, committed the unpardonable sin, Heb. vi. Many wicked men at the day of judgment will plead, "Have we not prophesied in thy name, and in thy name cast out devils, and in thy name done many wonderful works." The greatest privilege of the prophets and apostles, was not their being inspired and working miracles, but their eminent holiness. The grace that was in their hearts, was a thousand times more their dignity and honor, than their miraculous gifts. The things in which we find David comforting himself, are not his being a king, or a prophet, but the holy influences of the Spirit of God in his heart, communicating to him divine light, love, and joy. The apostle Paul abounded in visions, revelations, and miraculous gifts, above all the apostles; but yet he esteems all things but loss for the excellency of the spiritual knowledge of Christ. It was not the gifts but the grace of the apostles, that was the proper evidence of their names being written in heaven; in which Christ directs them to rejoice, much more than in the devils being subject to them. To have grace in the heart, is a higher privilege than the blessed Virgin herself had, in having the body of the second person in the Trinity conceived in her womb, by the power of the Highest overshadowing her: Luke xi. 27, 28, "And it came to pass as he spake these things, a certain woman of the company lift up her voice, and said unto him, Blessed is the womb that bare thee, and the paps that thou hast sucked! But he said, Yea, rather blessed are they that hear the word of God, and keep it." See also to the same purpose, Matt. xii. 47, &c.—The influence of the Holy Spirit, or divine charity in the heart, is the greatest privilege and glory of the highest archangel in heaven; yea, this is the very thing by which the creature has fellowship with God himself, with the Father and the Son, in their beauty and happiness. Hereby the saints are made partakers of the divine nature, and have Christ's joy fulfilled in themselves. . . .

I do not expect a restoration of these miraculous gifts in the approaching glorious times of the church, nor do I desire it. It appears to me, that it would add nothing to the glory of those times, but rather diminish from it. For my part, I had rather enjoy the sweet influences of the Spirit, showing Christ's spiritual divine beauty, infinite grace, and dying love, drawing forth the holy exercises of faith, divine love, sweet complacence, and humble joy in God, one quarter of an hour, than to have prophetical visions and revelations the whole year. It appears to me much more probable that God should give immediate revelations to his saints in the dark times of prophecy, than now in the approach of the most glorious and perfect state of his church on earth. It does not appear to me that there is any need of those extraordinary gifts to introduce this happy state, and set up the kingdom of God through the world; I have seen so much of the power of God in a more excellent way, as to convince me that God can easily do it without.

I would therefore entreat the people of God to be very cautious how they give heed to such things. I have seen them fail in very many instances, and know by experience that impressions being made with great power, and upon the minds of true, yea eminent, saints—even in the midst of extraordinary exercises of grace, and sweet communion with God, and attended with texts of Scripture strongly impressed on the mind—are no sure signs of their being revelations from heaven. I have known such impressions fail, in some instances, attended with all these circumstances. They who leave the sure word of prophecy—which God has given us as a light shining in a dark place—to follow such impressions and impulses, leave the guidance of the polar star, to follow a *Jack with a lantern*. No wonder therefore that sometimes they are led into woful extravagances.

Moreover, seeing inspiration is not to be expected, *let us not despise human learning.* They who assert that human learning is of little or no use in the work of the ministry, do not well consider what they say; if they did, they would not say it. By human learning I mean, and suppose others mean, the improvement of common knowledge by human and outward means. And therefore to say, that human learning is of no use, is as much as to say that the education of a child, or that the common knowledge which a grown man has more than a little child, is of no use. At this rate, a child of four years old is as fit for a teacher in the church of God, with the same degree of grace—and capable of doing as much to advance the kingdom of Christ, by his instruction—as a very knowing man of thirty years of age. If adult persons have greater ability and advantage to do service, because they have more knowledge than a little child, then doubtless if they have more human knowledge still, with the same degree of grace, they would have still greater ability and advantage to service. An increase of knowledge, without doubt, increases a man's advantage either to do good or hurt, according as he is disposed. It is too manifest to be denied, that God made great use of human learning in the apostle Paul, as he also did in Moses and Solomon.

And if knowledge, obtained by human means, is not to be despised, then it will follow that the means of obtaining it are not to be neglected, viz., *study;* and that this is of great use in order to a preparation for publicly instructing others. And, though having the heart full of the powerful influences of the Spirit of God, may at some time enable persons to speak profitably, yea, very excellently, without study; yet this will not warrant us needlessly to cast ourselves down from the pinnacle of the temple, depending upon it that the angel of the Lord will bear us up, and keep us from dashing our foot against a stone, when there is another way to go down, though it be not so quick. And I would pray that *method* in public discourses, which tends greatly to help both the understanding and memory, may not be wholly neglected.

Another thing I would beg the dear children of God more fully to consider of is, how far, and upon what grounds, the rules of the Holy Scriptures will truly justify their passing censures upon other professing Christians, as hypocrites, and ignorant of real religion. We all know that there is a judging and censuring of some sort or other, that the Scripture very often and very strictly forbids. I desire that those rules of Scripture may be looked into, and thoroughly weighed; and that it may be considered whether our taking it upon us to discern the state of others, and to pass sentence upon them as wicked men, though professing Christians, and of a good visible conversation, be not really forbidden by Christ in the New Testament. If it be, then doubtless the disciples of Christ ought to avoid this practice, however sufficient they may think themselves for it, or however needful or of good tendency they may think it. It is plain that the sort of judgment which God claims as his prerogative, whatever that be, is forbidden. We know that a certain judging of the hearts of the children of men, is often spoken of as the great prerogative of God, and which belongs only to him, as in 1 Kings viii. 39: "Forgive, and do, and give unto every man according to his ways, whose heart thou knowest: for thou, even thou only, knowest the hearts of all the children of men." And if we examine, we shall find that the judging of hearts which is spoken of as God's prerogative, relates not only to the aims and dispositions of men's hearts in particular actions, but chiefly to the state of their hearts as the professors of religion, and with regard to that profession. . . .

Again, whatsoever kind of judging is the proper work and business of the day of judgment, is what we are forbidden, as in 1 Cor. iv. 5: "Therefore judge nothing before the time, until the Lord come; who both will bring to light the hidden things of darkness, and will make manifest the counsels of the heart; and then shall every man have praise of God." But to distinguish hypocrites, that have the form of godliness and the visible conversation of godly men from true saints, or to separate the sheep from the goats, is the proper business of the day of judgment; yea, it is represented as the main business and end of that day. They, therefore, do greatly err who take it upon them positively to determine who are sincere, and who are not; to draw the dividing line between true saints and hypocrites, and to separate between sheep and goats, setting the one on the right hand and the other on the left; and to distinguish and gather out the tares from amongst the wheat. . . .

I know there is a great aptness in men who suppose they have had some experience of the power of religion, to think themselves sufficient to discern and determine the state of others by a little conversation with them; and experience has taught me that this is an error. I once did not imagine that the heart of man had been so unsearchable as it is. I am less charitable, and less uncharitable than once I was. I find more things in wicked men that may counterfeit, and make a fair show of piety; and more ways that the remaining corruption of the godly may make them appear like carnal men, formalists, and dead hypocrites, than once I knew of. The longer I live, the less I wonder that God challenges it as his prerogative to try the hearts of the children of men, and directs that this business should be let alone till harvest. I desire to adore the wisdom of God, and his goodness to me and my fellow-creatures, that he has not committed this great business into the hands of such a poor, weak, and dim-sighted creature; one of so much blindness, pride, partiality, prejudice, and deceitfulness of heart; but has committed it into the hands of one infinitely fitter for it, and has made it his prerogative. . . .

To suppose that men have ability and right to determine the state of the souls of visible Christians, and so to make an open separation between saints and hypocrites, that true saints may be of one visible company, and hypocrites of another, separated by a partition that men make, carries in it an inconsistency: for it supposes that God has given men power to make another visible church, within his visible church; for by visible Christians or visible saints is meant, persons who have a right to be received as such in the eye of a public charity. None can have a right to exclude any one of this visible church but in the way of that regular ecclesiastical proceeding, which God has established in his visible church.—I beg of those who have a true zeal for promoting this work of God, well to consider these things. I am persuaded, that as many of them as have much to do with souls, if they do not hearken to me now, will be of the same mind when they have had more experience.

And another thing that I would entreat the zealous friends of this glorious work of God to avoid, is managing the controversy with opposers with too much heat, and appearance of an angry zeal; and particularly insisting very much in public prayer and preaching, on the persecution of opposers. If their persecution were ten times so great as it is, methinks it would not be best to say so much about it. If it becomes Christians to be like lambs, not apt to complain and cry when they are hurt; it becomes them to be dumb and not to open their mouth, after the example of our dear Redeemer; and not to be like swine, that are apt to scream aloud when they are touched. We should not be ready presently to think and speak of fire from heaven, when the Samaritans oppose us, and will not receive us into their villages. God's zealous ministers would do well to think of the direction the apostle Paul gave to a zealous minister, 2 Tim. ii. 24–26: "And the servant of the Lord must not strive, but be gentle unto all men, apt to teach, patient, in meekness instructing those that oppose themselves; if God peradventure will give them repentance, to the acknowledging of the truth; and that they may recover themselves out of the snare of the devil, who are taken captive by him at his will."

I would humbly recommend to those that love the Lord Jesus Christ, and would advance his kingdom, a good attendance to that excellent rule of prudence which Christ has left us, Matt. ix. 16, 17: "No man putteth a piece of new cloth into an old garment; for that which is put in to fill it up, taketh from the garment, and the rent is made worse. Neither do men put new wine into old bottles; else the bottles break and the wine runneth out, and the bottles perish. But they put new wine into new bottles, and both are preserved." I am afraid the wine is now running out in some part of this land, for want of attending to this rule. For though I believe we have confined ourselves too much to a certain stated method and form in the management of our religious affairs; which has had a tendency to cause all our religion to degenerate into mere formality; yet whatever has the appearance of a great innovation—that tends much to shock and surprise people's minds, and to set them a talking and disputing—tends greatly to hinder the progress of the power of religion. It raises the opposition of some, diverts the minds of others, and perplexes many with doubts and scruples. It causes people to swerve from their great business, and turn aside to vain jangling. Therefore that which is very much beside the common practice, unless it be a thing in its own nature of considerable importance, had better be avoided. Herein we shall follow the example of one who had the greatest success in propagating the power of religion: 1 Cor. ix. 20–23, "Unto the Jews I became as a Jew, that I might gain the Jews; to them that are under the law, as under the law, that I might gain them that are under the law; to them that are without law, as without law, (being not without law to God, but under the law to Christ,) that I might gain them that are without law. To the weak became I as weak, that I might gain the weak. I am made all things to all men, that I might by all means save some. And this I do for the gospel's sake, that I might be partaker thereof with you."

Study Questions

1. Why do Daniel Wadsworth and Samuel Johnson object to the revival? Compare their position in society with that of Samuel Hopkins and David Brainerd. What kinds of people seem to be taking each side?

2. Does Jonathan Edwards defend everything about the revival? Does he confront the objections of men like Wadsworth and Johnson? How do you think the different people in his audience reacted to his sermon? Would anybody you have already met have been completely satisfied with it? (Compare, for example, his ideas about formal education and study with those of Ebenezer Pemberton, or his statements about judging other men with those of George Whitefield.)

Study Questions

THREE

Schism in the Church, September 1741–May 1742

Until 1753 Yale College did not run religious services of its own; instead, the student body was required to attend the town church in New Haven, pastored at this time by a 1709 Yale graduate and ex-tutor, Joseph Noyes (1688–1761). Noyes's undisguised hostility to the revival and what many felt to be the deadness of his preaching —after hearing him lecture on a winter morning one freshman wrote that "this day has been a very cold day in so much that many scholars went from meeting before the meeting was over"—caused both student and nonstudent members of his congregation to become profoundly dissatisfied with the man. What precipitated their dissatisfaction into out-and-out schism was the appearance in New Haven of an itinerant minister who was the complete opposite of Noyes in every respect except his social origin. This was James Davenport (1710–1757), a Yale graduate (1732) and a member of one of Connecticut's most distinguished families—his grandfather had been a founder of New Haven and the first incumbent of the very pulpit that Joseph Noyes presently occupied. A minister on Long Island since 1738, Davenport had met George Whitefield in Philadelphia just before the beginning of the Great Awakening, and soon afterward he had heard the preaching of Gilbert Tennent. At the urging of New Light (pro-revival) ministers in Connecticut, Davenport began a tour of his native colony in July 1741. The effect of his visit is indicated in Connecticut Governor Talcott's letter [#11] to a correspondent in Saybrook who had written him shortly after Davenport's arrival there.

Davenport reached New Haven, where he had lived for several years after his graduation, sometime in August; he remained based there for more than a month, preaching and arguing continually before he finally sailed back to Long Island. He was in New Haven for commencement; in fact, much of the "great confusion" which marked this occasion was provoked by Davenport. To one hostile observer of the commencement, the Episcopalian Samuel Johnson, the scene of Davenport "raving among the people" resembled nothing so much as "a visit to Bedlam—for we heard no prayers nor anything that could be called preaching, any more than the ravings of a man distracted."

It was not long before Davenport had a direct confrontation with Joseph Noyes. The incident is described by the Rector of Yale, Thomas Clap (1703–1767), in his letter to a Boston newspaper [#12]. Davenport's accusations hardly fell on deaf ears, though, because only two months later, on November 18, 1741, a statement of complaints levied against Noyes was signed by 112 area residents. On December 28, some of these people—all of them communicants at Noyes' church—presented a memorial to the whole congregation [#13] in which they indicated their desire to secede from the congregation and form a church of their own. (There were no student signatures on this memorial, but they were absent only because the students remained members of their home-town churches while attending college. They were not technically members of Noyes' church.) After some complicated maneuvering on both sides, 61 persons offered the New Haven County Court a petition requesting legal recognition as dissenters under a 1708 Connecticut statute (the Toleration Act) which had been passed to insure freedom of worship for persons who belonged to sects other than the officially established Congregational church. Their request was an unusual one in that the 61 petitioners had no intention of joining another sect; all they wanted was to attend a Congregational church pastored by someone more to their taste than Noyes—but under the laws and customs of the age, such a change was not possible as long as they lived within the bounds of an existing parish. Only after the Great Awakening did it become possible for people to form new churches for reasons other than those caused by a natural increase in population.

On January 29, 1742, the Court granted the separation. Over the next few months Noyes and his supporters in the New Haven church, recognizing the extent to which disaffection had set in, took the steps described by Rector Clap in his letter to a colleague in New Jersey, a widely respected man who was himself a supporter of the revival [#14]. But Noyes' attempt at mediation proved only half-hearted, and at the beginning of May a council of New Light ministers from outside the New Haven area approved formation of the new church. On May 7, 1742, three of these ministers—Samuel Cooke of Stratfield (now Bridgeport), and Joseph Bellamy and John Graham, both of Woodbury—participated in the ceremonies at which the church was created [#15]. The separation was quickly condemned as illegitimate by the New Haven association of ministers, which to a man supported Noyes and Clap. It was nine years before the Association permitted the new church to employ a regular minister. In June 1742, meanwhile, Noyes finally made a serious effort to mollify the dissidents by taking on a co-pastor more acceptable to them, but this plan too fell through (see #28 and #31).

11

Governor Talcott to Colonel Lynde

Hartford, September 4, 1741

Sr: I received youres without Date, Inclosing an account of Mr. Davenport's Coming to Saybrook, with the questions put to him and his answers,—am Surprised that Mr. Davenport, a minister of ye Gospell, should in so imperious and unwarrientable a manner take upon him to condemn any, and Especielly our most Emenently pious and Industrious Ministers, to be Carnall, &c., which I look upon as usurping the authority of the Most High.—It is said, I will give to him a white Stone, &c. And his advice to people not to hearken to their Ministers by him condemned, but to go 10 or 20 miles &c.,—and that

Connecticut Historical Society, *Collections,* V (1896) [The Talcott Papers], pp. 372–373.

they had better sett upon private meetings amongst themselves &c.,— all which is a violation and open contempt of ye Laws of this Coloney, and so aparently tends to the breach of the peace of our Religious Sosiaties and subvention of all good orders in Church and State: that every stedie, Rationall Christian I should think, would see it and prudently avoide such men, that so their pernisious proceedings might come to an End. And I think youre ministers will doe well to keep their pulpits from all such men, least they be partakers with them in their Evill Deeds,—and that youre Civill authority will do well to take all necesarie Care that peace and good order be maintained amongst you, and I hope they will observe and conduct themselves with ye Necessery care, prudence and Courage in their stations as the day Requires; and that ye Civill authority, the Ministers and people, will all use their Joynt Intrest, by advice, Influence and authority, to Incourage what is vertuous and praiseworthy, and to Suppress every disorderly and Vile practice, and what so Ever tends to the hurt and Reproach of Religion.

Perhaps the least difficult and Most safe Method of dealing with so boysterous a person as your letter mentions might (at this day) be, to send him by boat or otherwise out of this Government, that he may go to his own people &c. And being (I hope) a sinceer well-wisher to peace, vertue and true Religion, shall say no more at present but that I am, Sr, (with due regards to ye Revd Mr. Hart)

youre obliged humble Servant, J. Talcott.
To Collo. Samll. Lynde, Esqr.

12

Thomas Clap to the Boston *Post-Boy*

New-Haven, September 21, 1741

Sundry of the Brethren of the Church in New-Haven, being offended at Mr. Davenport's publickly condemning their Pastor, the Rev. Mr. Noyes, as an *unconverted* Man; calling him a *Wolf in Sheep's Cloathing,* with many other the like opprobrious Expressions, being met together at the House of the Rev. Mr. Noyes, desir'd Mr. Davenport to give the Reasons, why he has thus reproach'd and scandalis'd their *Pastor:* Which he did as follows, viz,

1. That a Woman told him, that she came to Mr. Noyes's under *Conviction,* and said that she was the greatest Sinner in the World; and that Mr. Noyes endeavoured to abate her Convictions: To which Mr. Noyes replied,

"That he did not remember the Instance; but supposed it might be thus, viz. That he might tell her, that she was a very great Sinner, and that she ought to be sensible of it, and more sensible of her *own* Sins than of any *other* Person's in the World; but that he did not suppose she was really the greatest Sinner in the World. Upon this, Mr. Davenport declar'd, that Mr. Noyes's saying so, was an Evidence to him that he was an *unconverted* Man; and afterward, in explaining himself upon the Word *Evidence* said, that it gave him Reason to believe it was so.

2. Another Reason was, because Mr. Noyes assumed an Honour

Boston *Post-Boy,* October 5, 1741; quoted in Charles Chauncy, *Seasonable Thoughts on the Recent Revival of Religion* (Boston, 1743), pp. 158–161.

---

to himself, in the Ministry, which did not belong to him, because a Woman told him that, some Years ago, she came to Mr. Noyes, and brought a *Relation* wherein she mentioned the Names of several Ministers, whom she supposed had been instrument of her *Conversion,* and Mr. Noyes ask'd her if he had not also done something towards her Conversion, and ask'd her why his Name was not mentioned: Mr. Davenport also added, that several other Persons had told him, that Mr. Noyes dislik'd their *Relations* because there were so many Names in them besides his. To which Mr. Noyes replied.

That he did not remember any such Thing, and was confident that it was a Misrepresentation.

3. Another Reason was, that Mr. Noyes was not a Friend to this *Work* going on among them; and that he did not countenance *Itinerant* Preachers; and that several Persons had told him that they came to *Meeting* with their Affections rais'd, and that Mr. Noyes's *Preaching* dedned and discouraged them, and tended to stifle their Convictions. To which Mr. Noyes reply'd,

That his *Preaching* and *Conduct* in *these Things* were publickly known, and that every one was capable of Judging without his saying any Thing upon them.

4. That Mr. Noyes, in private Conversation with Mr. Davenport, had said to this Effect, that he had been deeply sensible of the Vileness and Corruption of his own Nature; and that every one that turned his Thoughts inward might easily have such a Sense: and that Mr. Noyes, seem'd to suppose that it was an easy Thing; that Mr. Davenport thence concluded, that he had never experienced it himself. To which Mr. Noyes replied,

That he, at that Time, utterly refus'd to give Mr. Davenport any Account of his Experiences; but that they had some Discourse upon some *doctrinal* Points, but he could not think that Mr. Davenport could reasonably understand him, to mean or intend, that every natural Man had a Sense of the Vileness and Corruption of his Nature, or that it was an easy Thing to have it. Several Things were said upon this Head which could not easily be minuted down; but on the whole, there seemed to be a Misunderstanding between them.

Upon the whole Mr. Davenport declared, that *these Reasons* were sufficient to justify him in *censuring* and *condemning* Mr. Noyes as he had done: Then, he said he would make a Sort of Acknowledgment; and, without any Notice given, while divers in the Room were talking loud, and others smoking, and some with their Hats on, he began a *Prayer;* but there being so much Noise in the Room, he was hardly heard at first: Many kept on talking, others cry'd out stop him; the Revd. Mr. Noyes spoke once or twice, and said, Mr. Davenport, I forbid your praying in my House without my Leave; but he persisted, and went on in the midst of the greatest Noise, Confusion and Consternation, and declar'd Mr. Noyes an *unconverted Man, and his People to be as Sheep without a Shepherd,* and prayed, that what he had now said might be a Means of *his* and *their Conversions:* Or else, *according to thy Will let them be confounded;* and after *that Manner* went on near a Quarter of an Hour. And when he had done, Mr. Noyes—forbid him ever going into his Pulpit any more; and some declar'd to Mr. Davenport, that his praying in that Manner was a taking the Name of GOD in vain: And so the Assembly broke up in great Consternation.

This is the Truth according to the best of our Remembrance; and the Substance of the Conference was minuted down at the Time of it, and publickly read to Mr. Davenport, and the rest immediately after.

Thomas Clap	}	*Rector* of Yale-College.
John Punderson		
John Munson		
Theoph. Munson	}	Subscribers.
Andrew Tuttle		
Samuel Mix		

13

New Haven Church Members: Memorial to the Congregation

December 28, 1741

"To the First Society in the town of New Haven:—Whereas we, the subscribers, have, by long and sorrowful experience, found, that the preaching and conduct of the Rev. Mr. Noyes has been in great measure unprofitable to us, and that we have also reason to think that he differs from us in some points of faith, we desire, (not as we hope out of any prejudice to the persons of Mr. Noyes and our brethren and friends of the society, to whom we heartily wish all good,) that they would allow us, and others that may incline to join with us, to draw off from them in charity, wishing to be a distinct society, that we may put ourselves under the best advantage to worship God, under such means, as he in his good providence may allow and we hope will bless, for our spiritual good and edification."

[Signed:]

Gideon Andrews, Caleb Tuttle, Joseph Mix, Caleb Bradley, Joseph Burroughs, David Austin, Jacob Turner, Caleb Andrews, Enos Tuttle, Obadiah Munson, Stephen Johnson, Samuel Cook, Timothy Mix, Samuel Horton, Thomas Punderson, Junr., Joseph Sackett, Hez. Beecher, Jos. Mix, Junr., Enos Thompson, John Bull, Caleb Hotchkiss, Junr., Benjamin Woodin, Caleb Bull,

Samuel W. S. Dutton, *The History of the North Church in New Haven, from Its Formation in May, 1742, During the Great Awakening* (New Haven, 1842), p. 7.

Timothy Jones, Benjamin Wilmott, Daniel Turner, Stephen Austin, Thomas Wilmott, Abraham Thompson, Mercy Alling, David Punderson, Enos Alling, Jabez Sherman, Amos Tuttle, Thomas Leek, Ezekiel Sanford, Timothy Alling, Amos Peck.

14

Thomas Clap to Jonathan Dickinson

New Haven, May 3, 1742

For the Revd Mr. Jonathan Dickenson of Elizabeth-Town

Rev. and Dear Sir

The State [of] Religion among us continues very Difficult, some Ministers declaring that the generality of others have no more Religion than Turks or Mahometans, and that it is Impossible to hold any Communion with them. Accordingly there are about 10 or a dozen Ministers in the Government who are for making an open Separation. They have had one Separate Convention last Feb. and intend to have another in May at Weathersfield. It is to this End they endeavour to keep up a Separation at New-Haven, and to make one in the College. And to encourage the Scholars hereunto the ministers of that Party tell them, that if they will Separate from the College they will License them to Preach without any Regard to a degree. And it is said that at their next Convention they Intend to License one to preach who has been Expelled for plain Breeches of the Laws of

From the original in the Charles Roberts Autograph Collection, Haverford College.

Christianity as well as those of College. The people in the first Society in N. Haven have lately sent for the Revd Mr. Russell of Middletown and Mr. Edwards of North Hampton to advise them under the Present Difficulties and they have advised them to Settle a Colleague with Mr. Noyes and advise that Mr. Burr be obtained if possible. The standing part of the Society are universally pleased with the Advice and it is the opinion of every one that the generality of the separate party will come in, in a little time, but 4 or 5 of the Heads and leaders of the party who are engaged in the general Scheme of a Separation violently oppose a Union, but it is universally tho[ugh]t that if Mr. Burr comes, it will not be in their power to keep the lesser people of their party from uniting. And his coming will Doubtless save this Town and College from many disorders and Confusions which otherwise they will be likely to fall into. Mr. Edwards says he believes that Mr. Burr is the most likely to accommodate all Difficulties. You will doubtless be very loath to part with so agreeable & valuable a neighbor, but I make no doubt but that you will be willing to forego something of your own private Interest for the sake of a greater Public Good, especially the Good of the College wherein the whole County [country] is concerned. Mr. Edwards has wrote largely to Mr. Burr upon it, and Mr. Tutor Whittelsey, the bearer will inform you more fully of the state of things. I am very glad that there is a Prospect of a Union in your Synod. I am Sir

Your most Humble Servant
Thomas Clap

15

Convenant of the New Haven Separate Church

May 7, 1742

Whereas, in addition to other grievances too tedious and un-necessary here to enumerate, of which we would not willingly per-petuate the memory, a considerable part of the first church in New-Haven have lately, viz. on the 25th day of January last, under the conduct of their present pastor, voted a conformity to the Saybrook platform, and in consequence of it, (to show more plainly the design of said vote) at the same time, by their vote, carried to the standing consociation of this county a complaint against sundry members of said church, thereby owning a juridical and decisive authority in the said stated consociation, contrary to the known, fundamental princi-ple and practice of said church, time out of mind, which has always denied any juridical or decisive authority under Christ, vested in any particular persons or class, over any particular congregational church confederated as this:

We the subscribers, members of said church, firmly adhering to the congregational principles and privileges on which the said church was founded, and hath stood unshaken from the beginning, through successive generations, until the 25th day of January last, being by the said innovations hereunto necessitated, apprehend ourselves called of God, in company, to vindicate our ancient rightful powers and privileges, and to put ourselves into a proper capacity for the enjoy-

---

Benjamin Trumbull, *A Complete History of Connecticut, Civil and Ec-clesiastical* (2 volumes, New Haven, 1818), Vol. II, pp. 342–344.

---

ment thereof, upon the ancient footing. And for that purpose, do now, under the conduct of divine providence, humbly sought, by fasting and prayer, assume a church state of the gospel, on the ancient basis of that church, whereof we stood members, in fact, as well as of right, until the unhappy period above mentioned, wherein the pastor and a number of the brethren with him, went off from the ancient foundation as aforesaid.

And we, with all affection invite others, the members of said church, who do or may see just cause of grievance at the said innovations, to join with us in asserting our ancient rightful powers and privileges broken in upon.

We solemnly declare our belief of the christian religion, as contained in the sacred scriptures, and with such a view thereof, as the confession of faith has exhibited, which is hereto annexed, fully agreeing, in substance, with the confession of faith owned by said church, time out of mind, heartily resolving to conform our lives unto the rule thereof, that holy religion, as long as we live in this world.

We solemnly renew a religious dedication of ourselves to the Lord Jehovah, who is the Father, the Son and the Holy Spirit; and avouch him this day to be our God, our Father, our Saviour and Leader; and receive him as our portion forever.

We give up ourselves anew unto the blessed Jesus, who is the Lord Jehovah, and adhere to him, as the head of his people in the covenant of grace, and rely on him as our prophet, priest and king, to bring us unto eternal blessedness.

We renewedly acknowledge our everlasting and indispensable obligations to glorify our God, in all the duties of a godly, sober and righteous life; and very particularly in the duties of a church state, as a body of people associated for an obedience to Him, in all ordinances of the gospel; and we thereupon depend on His gracious assistance for our faithful discharge of the duties thus incumbent on us.

We desire and intend, and (with dependence on His promised and powerful grace) we engage anew to walk together as a church of our Lord Jesus Christ, in the faith and order of the gospel, so far as we shall have the same revealed unto us, conscientiously attending the public worship of God, the sacraments of the New Testament, the discipline of His kingdom, and all His holy institutions in common with one another, and watchfully avoiding sinful stumbling blocks and contentions, as becometh a people, whom the Lord hath bound up together in the bundle of life. At the same time, we do also present our offspring with us unto the Lord, purposing, with His help, to do our part in the methods of religious education, that they may be the Lord's.

And all this we do, flying to the blood of the everlasting covenant for the pardon of our many errors, praying that the glorious Lord who is the great Shepherd, would prepare and strengthen us for every good work, to do His will, working in us that which will be well pleasing to Him, to whom be glory for ever and ever, Amen.

Study Questions

1. To what extent is James Davenport responsible for Noyes's problems with his church? To what extent is Noyes himself responsible? To what extent are these problems beyond the responsibility of either man?

2. What can you infer from this section about the relationship between the College and the New Haven community? How large a part of the community is deeply committed to the revival? How much local backing can the New Light students expect if they rebel against Clap's leadership? What form might such a rebellion take?

3. What is Clap worried about as he writes to Jonathan Dickinson? How does he expect that bringing "Mr. Burr" to New Haven might help?

FOUR

Official
Countermeasures,
October 1741–May 1742

By the early fall of 1741 New Haven and Yale College were rapidly becoming the major locus of religious and social tension in Connecticut. Polarized between a student body that generally greeted the revival and its itinerant preachers with tremendous enthusiasm and a ministerial and administrative leadership that was in large measure hostile to them, the community was torn by dissension and the College was scarcely able to function. It was no surprise, then, that an initiative for controlling the Great Awakening in the colony arose from this quarter. As soon as the Connecticut colonial legislature met for its regular semi-annual session in October 1741, Rector Clap and several of his colleagues in the New Haven association of ministers presented the body with a petition [#16] requesting its support for a "General Consociation" or gathering of the churches, to include all the ministers in the colony along with lay representatives from each congregation. (Under Connecticut's so-called Saybrook Platform of 1708, each county in the colony had been organized into "Associations" of ministers and "Consociations" of churches. These organizations held significant power over policies and personnel within their jurisdictions, but this jurisdiction technically included only those churches in the colony that had voted, as most but by no means all of them had, to accept the Saybrook Platform. The New Haven county association of ministers, for example, was restricted in its ability to control the schism in Joseph Noyes' church by the fact that this church did not accept the Saybrook Platform until January 1742 —and then only by a disputed election in which Noyes had barred his opponents from participating.)

The colonial Assembly agreed to support Clap's request for a General Consociation [#17]. Before it was held, the New Haven association prepared a list of resolutions for presentation at the meeting [excerpted in #18]. The so-called "Guilford Resolves" [#19] form the official policy statement adopted by the General Consociation late in November.

By this time, the colonial legislature itself had adjourned its October session. When it met again, in May 1742, the representatives were greeted with a long opening address delivered by the Rev. Isaac Stiles (1697–1760), pastor of the church in North Haven and a close friend of Joseph Noyes. This sermon, "A Prospect of the City of Jerusalem", was the first public attack on the Great Awakening delivered in New England—the negative equivalent, in a sense, of Jonathan Edwards' commencement address the previous September. After listening to Stiles, the General Assembly sat through a speech by the newly elected governor, Jonathan Law [#20]. (Governor Talcott had died at the end of 1740.) When it finally got down to business, the legislature found in its hands a copy of the Guilford Resolves, presented [#21] by a committee of ministers who awaited some official response. The lobbying brought quick results: before it adjourned, the Assembly passed "An Act for Regulating Abuses and Correcting Disorders in Ecclesiastical Affairs" [#22]. This "anti-itinerancy law," as it became known, was quickly employed to arrest James Davenport and deport him from the colony—a procedure soon repeated on several occasions. Those against whom the law was later invoked included, among others, the future president of Princeton, Samuel Finley.

16

The New Haven Ministerial Association Petitions the General Assembly

October 8, 1741

To the Honbl the General Assembly now Sitting at New-Haven, Octr 8th 1741

Whereas there has been a Serious and Religious Concern upon the Minds of many People in this Government, which if under due Regulations might be Improved to good Ends and Purposes; and whereas several Persons under Religious Pretenses have taken up several new Practices which tend to hinder those good Ends and Effects and to make Divisions and Confusions in our Churches, and several of them seem now to be upon the Point of Dividing and Running into great Disorders very much to the Dishonour of Religion and the Hindrance of true Vital Piety;

And whereas it has been several times Proposed and discoursed upon by many Ministers in this Colony that it would be very Convenient and Expedient in order to Maintain a good Harmony and Agreement among the Ministers and Churches, and to Prevent and Heal Divisions, to have a General Consociation of the Churches in this Colony, consisting of Three Ministers and Three Messengers from each perticular Consociation in the several Counties to be Convened at Guilford on the 24th day of November next; and whereas the

---

From the original in the Connecticut Archives: *Ecclesiastic Affairs,* VII, 243 (Connecticut State Library, Hartford).

Charge of such a Convention would be [too] considerable to be born by the Particular Members;

We the Subscribers humbly move to this Honble Assembly to Consider, Whether, if they think such a Convention be Advisable, they would be pleased to order that the Charges thereof be defrayed out of the Public Treasury. And that they would be Pleased to Desire some person to give notice of it to the Moderator of the several Consociations accordingly.

> Thomas Clap, Jared Eliot, Joseph Noyes,
> Samuel Whittelsey, Jacob Heminway,
> Samuel Hall

In the Upper House: the above Address read and Ordered to be Transmitted to the lower House.

> Test [attested] George Wyllys Secrety

In ye Lower house: ye Above Address Read and Approved, and ordered yt a bill in form be Drawn,

> Testt Jno Fowler Clerk

17

The General Assembly
of Connecticut Responds to the Petition

October 1741

Whereas several of the reverend ministers in this Colony have informed this Court, that it is proposed by many ministers in this Colony, in order to maintain a good harmony and agreement among

Charles J. Hoadly (ed.), *The Public Records of the Colony of Connecticut,* Vol. VIII (Hartford, 1874), pp. 438–439.

the ministers and churches, and to prevent and heal divisions in the land, to have a General Consociation of the churches in this Colony, consisting of three ministers and three messengers from each particular consociation, to be convened at Guilford on the 24th day of November next; and proposing to this Assembly to be at the charge and expence thereof:

Whereupon this Assembly, considering the unhappy misunderstandings and divisions subsisting in this Colony, whereby the peace of our churches is much threatened; and this Assembly hoping that such a general convention may issue in the accommodation of divisions, settling peace, love and charity, and promoting the true interest of vital religion, for which there seems to be so general a concern among the people of this land: Therefore, if the particular consociations aforesaid think proper to, and do accordingly send their several delegates as aforesaid, and they meet as is above proposed, resolved, that the charge and expence for entertainment of such a general convention at Guilford shall be born by this government. And this Assembly appoints Colonel Samuel Hill to make the necessary provision for the support of the members of said general consociation, during their continuance at Guilford aforesaid, for the purpose aforesaid, and lay the accounts thereof before this Assembly in May next.

18

Resolution of the New Haven Association

November 1741

Resolved, that for a minister to enter into another minister's parish, and preach, or administer the seals of the covenant, without

Benjamin Trumbull, *A Complete History of Connecticut,* Vol. II, p. 196.

the consent of, or in opposition to the settled minister of the parish, is disorderly: notwithstanding, if a considerable number of the people in the parish, are desirous to hear another minister preach, provided the same be orthodox, and sound in the faith, and not notoriously faulty in censuring other persons, or guilty of any other scandal, we think it ordinarily advisable for the minister of the parish to gratify them, by giving his consent, upon their suitable application to him for it, unless neighboring ministers should advise him to the contrary.

19

The Guilford Resolves

November 24, 1741

Vote of the General Consociation

At a General Consociation Conven'd at Guilford, Novr 24th 1741

The Revd Messrs Samuel Whitman, William Burnham and Benjamin Colton were chosen a Committee to Present the Thanks of this Consociation to the Honble the General Assembly in May next for their Goodness in Countenanceing and defraying ye charge of this present Convention.

Test Samuel Whittelsey Scribe

Resolves of the General Consociation

The Resolves of the General Conso[ciation, convened at Guilford,] Novbr 24th 1741

This General Consociation having Sought to God by Prayer for his Direction & Guidance and freely Confer'd and Debated came unanimously to the following Resolves

It appears that there has for Some time past been a great and remarkable Work of God carried on in this Land and in this Government, that great Numbers of Persons chiefly of the lower and younger Sort have been awakened in an uncommon Manner to be concern'd for their Eternal Salvation, and Inquiring what they Shall Do to be Saved, And it is to be hoped, that a great many Souls have been brought Savingly to believe in Jesus Christ unto Eternal Life.

At Such a time it becomes the Ministers & People of the Lord Jesus Christ to Testify their Thankfulness & Praise to him for his wonderfull Mercy to a Sinfull People, who having been long highly favour'd with Distinguishing previlidges and having abused them are yet favour'd with Such a Glorious and Mercifull out pouring of his Holy Spirit.

As is natural to Expect in this corrupt and Dark St[ate of the] world, there are diverse [human weaknesses, imperfections and impru]dences, which have attended this great and [work, both in some] of the Instruments, who have appeared most Zealous to pr[omote it] and in Some, who we hope are wrought upon Sincerely to beli[eve in] the lord Jesus Christ, as well as in those under awakening and concern and there are also diverse Stratigems and Devices of Satan & Endeavours of his to deceive unwary Souls and to Impose on them and thereby throw a Blemish and Reproch on the work of God.

There ought to be great Care taken by People in the Choice of Ministers, that they get men of Learning, Wisdom and of Piety and

Connecticut Historical Society, *Collections,* XI (1907) [The Law Papers], pp. 5–10.

ought to attend only on the Ministry of Such as are approv'd or allow'd by the Constitution of the Colony.

Ministers and Associations ought to be Carefull to licence Recommend or put into the ministry, none but Such as are men of learning wisdom and Prudence and as far as they can Discern men of true Piety and Experimental acquaintance with Jesus Christ.

When Persons of this Character (according to a Judgment of Charity) are introduced into the Ministry by the Regular Choice of the People and Regular Ordination by the h[ands of] the Pr[esby]ter as hath been Practised in the Chu[rches of New England, they are lawful ministers of Christ e]ven if after all they Should Really [be] Uncon[verted] men

If any person Should apprehend this was the State of any Minister or other Public Person, tis not lawfull either Publickly to Declare Such a Judgment or privately to Insinuate the Same or Peremptorily to pronounce this concerning any one of them, nor undertake by open Censures and Seperations to Remove them and Reform the Church.

That Heresie, False Doctrine grossly Such Scandalous Sin and the unjust Imposition of Such Terms of Communion as Christ hath not made are the only just grounds of open Seperation, and that not till proper Steps are taken in order to A Regular Conviction.

And in Case of Seperation or Seperations not so Qualified We advise the Several and Respective Consociations, within whose Circuit they may happen to take Cognizance of the Same and proceed therein according to the Constitution.

We know of no way to Determine of the Conversion of any [other p]erson, but from his Christian Profession, life and Conver[sation, on a particular informa]tion of his Experience of a work [of God on his heart], and to pretend to Judge thereof by any [part]ictular impression made upon a persons mind concerning another is unsafe and dangerous having no warrant in the word of God.

We are all agreed that the holy Scriptures are the only Rule of Faith and manners, and whatever inward impressions any person may pretend to as a Direction to Duty or Judgment which is not by and according to the word of God is an unsafe and fallacious ground of action and Judgment in Religion and Duty.

We approve of the Established Constitution in this Government both as to Doctrine and Discipline and purpose to abide by it and act in Conformity to it

That for A Minister to Enter into another Ministers Parish and

Preach or Administer the Seals of the Covenant without the Consent of or in Opposition to the Setled Minister of ye parish is disorderly

Not with Standing if a considerable Number of People in a Parish are desireous to hear another Minister Preach pro[vided] the [Same] be orthodox and Sound in the Faith & not notoriously [faulty in censuring other] Persons or Guilty of any other Scandle we think it Ordinarily advisa[ble for the minister of the parish] to Gratifie them by giving his Consent upon the[ir s]uitable [appli]cation to him for it unless Neighbouring Ministers Should advis[e] him to the Contrary.

That no Perticular Association or Consociation Shall Intermeddle or take upon them to act out of their own limits or precincts in the Affairs of another Association or Consociation without their Consent as to the Examination of Candidates or any other matter tending to disorder and Confusion

That in Voluntary meetings for Religious Exercises Endeavours be used that they may not Interfeer with the Stated Worship of families or with Civil order to the offence of any

We are Sorry to find that Some Persons are gone So far as to withdraw and Separate themselves from the Communion of the Churches, where they belong, having taken up an Opinion that their ministers are unconverted, whereby we think muc[h] uncharitableness is Encouraged, and hard thoughts and E[vil mur]murings among Profesing Christ[ians, which it is to be wished] might be Remedied by Gentle mea[ns, with the meekness and gentle]ness of Christ and we would Propose

1. That Such places and as many others as See Cause would keep a Day of fasting and prayer to Seek wisdom and Light from God to teach them their Duty and that he would not Suffer Satan to get an Advantage against them, nor by any other means Suffer the good work of his Grace to be hindred but would Powfully carry it on among them.

2. We would Earnestly Advise ye Ministers of Christ and all Serious Christians to be united in Advising those who are under mistakes and prejudices to avoid Such Seperations & Divisions and to wait patiently on God for light and Direction And that all would be of a patient and forgiving Spirit bearing one anothers Burthens and So fulfill the Law of Christ.

And further to carry on this good work, which is Begun in the land, and to Remove & Prevent whatever may hinder it, We would Recommend it to the Several Associations to meet t[ogether] to unite their prayers to God for [this purpose, in their next stated meeting, or sooner if] they please and in their Assistance and Advice to one another that as far as possible they all may be One as Christ and the Father are One in promoting the great Designs of the Redemption of Christ

That the Thanks of this General Consociation be in Some proper method presented to the Honorable the General Assembly in May next for their goodness in Countenancing and Defraying the Charge of this Present Convention, and that the Committee Appointed to present the Thanks of this Consociation to the General Assembly do also Inform by an Attested Copy the Said General Assembly of the Doings of this General Consociation.

All the foregoing Articles and Perticulars were unanimously Resolv'd by this General Consociation and Concluded with Prayer.

Test Samuel Whittelsey Scribe

A true Copy of ye Original on file

Examind pr Samuel Whittelsey Scribe

20

Governor Law's Address
to the General Assembly

May 1742

Gentlemen of ye Council and House of Representatives

It becomes us to lay aside all private Views and sinister Reports and I trust we all come here with a single Design to promote the pub-

Connecticut Historical Society, *Collections,* XVI (1916) [The Walcott Papers], pp. 455–458.

lick good of the people who sent us and at whose Expence we come, and yrin to advance ye Interest of the British Crown, by ye authority wrof under god we are formd into one body Corporate, that as we are one body, we may have but one mind and in our publick Capacity may we with one heart wisely consult ye good of ye whole with as much Industry and truth as we would our own personal Interest in our private Capacities.

Its unreasonable to expect that in a Body aggregate every individual Member should have the same way of thinking in every thing, yet if we can content our selves with the Results and Determinations of ye Majority by wch we are authorizd to act, we shall comply with our own Make and Constitution, but if we are otherwise minded we contradict our beings and would destroy even that wch gives us our very Existence. A Stepp or two lower would sink us into Anarchy and Confusion, and every Stepp higher would advance towards Monarchy. How happy then should we esteem our Constitution, and chearfully submitt our selves to ye Rules of it, the natural Consequence wrof would be peace and we might hope the god of peace would be with us and bless us.

It will be necessary for us to remember that we stand here in civil Capacities as State's or comonwealth's men and consider what is ye proper work and business for us to enter upon.

I think it will be a mistake in us if we think we come here in the Quality of Divines to settle abstruse Points in Divinity and it has eve'r been of ill Consequence to a State wn different sentiments in matters of Religion have been permitted to break in upon and perplex ye Civil State to ye making Parties and Divisions in it, by means wrof the good of the whole is neglected and the Administration tends only to the good of a Party. Kings indeed should be nursing ffathers to the Church of god, and there are things of a civil nature, without which humane Societies civil or sacred cant be subsisted. proper Measures therefore should be consulted by civil powers for that part of religious Affairs which are of a civil nature wthout imposing on mens Consciences, that peace and good Order may be kept and maintained. and if any thing of this nature be found in our civil Establishments that dos exceed or come short of these Limitts it may require the Care and Attention of this Assembly to rectify it. is there any thing amiss let it be repeald is any thing wanting to support our Constitution let it be supplyd

The true christian Rule is To be subject to ye higher Powers when yr Comands are not contrary to ye laws of God. but ye Romish erroneous Tenet is that there are no higher Powers yn yr own to be subject to, and assume the Supremacy to ymselves.

To disobey Magistrates is a Doctrine destructive to all civil powers and cant be cloakd under a consciencious pretence.

We come here cloathd with civil powers and ought to keep our selves within our proper Limitts and prudently concert measures for the best good of ye body of the people whom we represent.

That Moses and Aaron go hand in hand doubtless is expedient for ye good and Tranquility of our people, and if we compare the civil with our ecclesiastical Constitution we shall find a perfect Harmony between them, in our civil there is required a Majority of ye Upper house as well as in ye lower, in our lower Courts of ye Court as well as a Concurrence of the Countrey of Jury In our ecclesiastical Courts, a Concurrence of the Major part of ye Ministers as well as of the major parts of ye whole, of ye churches by yr Messengers and Elders. possibly this may be wanting among our Ecclesiasticks That no Appeal from our ecclesiastick Courts in ye Consociation to ye Delegates from ye several Consociations is not provided for as in civil Affairs ye last Resort is to this Assembly in some suitable form

Suffer not our ecclesiastick Constitution so agreable to our civil Polity be sappd and undermined for want of suitable Precautions. let not ye Indulgencies given to men of other Professions be used by men whom you imploy to sett aside all ye Care and Charge of this Assembly in settling suitable Bounds of Parishes.

How we may protect our Coasts, Ports and Borders from the Insults of our open and profest Enemies and from all secret Attempts and maintain peace and good Order among our selves requires your serious Meditation

The Battery begun in our principal Port is not prepard for our Defence as it might and ought to be. our Neighbour Provinces are making Preparations for yr Defence as men under Apprehensions of danger. why should we indulge our selves in Security

The unhappy Circumstances of our Colledge which for want of supporting due Order and Regulation has dispersd ye Students at an unusual Season should be rectifyd before yr Return least it suffer a fatal Dissolution. good and wholesom laws and orders ought to be made by ye Govrs of ye Colledge and then duely executed, for youth there to be trained up in Disobedience to them will lay a foundation for Sedition and Disregard to all humane laws

A Door seems to be opend att which men of ye most corrupt Principles may enter and mislead and corrupt unwary people and its much to be feard the popish faction have yr Emissaries among us under Disguise as well as in other parts of ye Kings Dominions

The further Attack Mr. Mason is making upon us must be guarded against

Mr Secry shall lay before you the several Accounts that have occurrd since our last Sessions and have come to my hands

God grant our Counsells may not be divided but directed. Its a time of much difficulty and Distress in ye world notwithstanding ye many favours that may be shewn in it.

Your close Application to ye business of this Assembly I need not urge upon you Gentlemen.

21

Committee of the General Consociation: Presentation

May 1742

To the Honourable the General Assembly of the Collony of Connecticut, Convened at Hartford May 13, 1742.

May it please your Honours

The General Consociation Convened at Guilford Novbr 24, 1741 having deputed us to lay before this Honourable Assembly their resolves, with the thanks of this Convention for your great goodness in calling of them there, and defraying the charg of it.

And we cannot but observe with pleasure your great Wisdom & paternal care of these churches and tender concern for their good

Connecticut Historical Society, *Collections,* XI (1907) [The Law Papers], pp. 41–42.

order, peace and Edification therein appearing: and humbly offer the resolves of this Consociation, and with a gratefull sense of your abundant goodness the Thanks of the Convention to this Assembly— and shall ever pray that you may have the presence of god with you in all your Consultations: and that these Churches may have peace and vital piety may be yet more and more revived in them—and remain

> Your humble and obedient
> Rev. Samuel Whitman
> Rev. William Burnham
> Rev. Benjamin Colton

22

General Assembly: The Anti-Itineracy Act

May 1742

An Act for regulating Abuses and correcting Disorders in Ecclesiastical Affairs

Whereas this Assembly did, by their act made in the seventh year of the reign of her late Majesty Queen Anne, establish and confirm a confession of faith, and an agreement for ecclesiastical discipline, made at Saybrook, *anno Dom.* 1708, by the reverend elders and the messengers delegated by the churches in this Colony for that purpose, under which establishment his Majesty's subjects inhabiting in this Colony have enjoyed great peace and quietness, till of late

Charles J. Hoadly (ed.), *Public Records of Connecticut,* Vol. VIII, pp. 454–457.

sundry persons have been guilty of disorderly and irregular practices: whereupon this Assembly, in October last, did direct to the calling of a general consociation, to sit at Guilford in November last, which said consociation was convened accordingly; at which convention it was endeavoured to prevent the growing disorders amongst the ministers that have been ordained or licenced by the associations in this government to preach, and likewise to prevent divisions and disorder among the churches and ecclesiastical societies settled by order of this Assembly: Notwithstanding which, divers of the ministers, ordained as aforesaid, and others licenced to preach by some of the associations allowed by law, have taken upon them, without any lawful call, to go into parishes immediately under the care of other ministers, and there to preach to and teach the people; and also sundry persons, some of whom are very illiterate, and have no ecclesiastical character or any authority whatsoever to preach or teach, have taken upon them publickly to teach and exhort the people in matters of religion, both as to doctrine and practice; which practices have a tendency to make divisions and contentions among the people in this Colony, and to destroy the ecclesiastical constitution established by the laws of this government, and likewise to hinder the growth and increase of vital piety and godliness in these churches, and also to introduce unqualified persons into the ministry, and more especially where one association doth intermeddle with the affairs that by the platform and agreement abovesaid, made at Saybrook aforesaid, are properly within the province and jurisdiction of another association, as to the licencing persons to preach, and ordaining ministers: Therefore,

1. *Be it enacted by the Governor, Council and Representatives, in General Court assembled, and by the authority of the same,* That if any ordained minister, or other person licenced as aforesaid to preach, shall enter into any parish not immediately under his charge, and shall there preach or exhort the people, shall be denied and secluded the benefit of any law of [135] this Colony made for the support and encouragement of the gospel ministry, except such ordained minister or licenced person shall be expressly invited and desired so to enter into such other parish and there to preach and exhort the people, either by the settled minister and the major part of the church of said parish, or, in case there be no settled minister, then by the church or society within such parish.

2. *And it is further enacted by the authority aforesaid,* That if any association of ministers shall undertake to examine or license any candidate for the gospel ministry, or assume to themselves the decision

of any controversy, or as an association to counsel and advise in any affair that by the platform or agreement abovementioned, made at Saybrook aforesaid, is properly within the province and jurisdiction of any other association, then and in such case, every member that shall be present in such association so licencing, deciding or counselling, shall be, each and every of them, denied and secluded the benefit of any law in this Colony made for the support and encouragement of the gospel ministry.

3. *And it is further enacted by the authority aforesaid,* That if any minister or ministers, contrary to the true intent not under his immediate care and charge, the minister of the parish where he shall so offend, or the civil authority, or any two of the committee of such parish, shall give information thereof in writing, under their hands, to the clerk of the parish or society where such offending minister doth belong, which clerk shall receive such information, and lodge and keep the same on file in his office; and no assistant or justice of the peace in this Colony shall sign any warrant for the collecting any minister's rate, without first receiving a certificate from the clerk of the society or parish where such rate is to be collected, that no such information as is abovementioned hath been received by him or lodged in his office.

4. *And it is further enacted by the authority aforesaid,* That if any person whatsoever, that is not a settled and ordained minister, shall go into any parish and (without the express desire and invitation of the settled minister of such parish (if any there be) and the major part of the church, or if there be no such settled minister, without the express desire of the church or congregation within such parish,) publickly preach and exhort the people, shall for every such offence, upon complaint made thereof to any assistant or justice of the peace, be bound to his peaceable and good behaviour until the next county court in that county where the offence shall be committed, by said assistant or justice of the peace, in the penal sum of one hundred pounds lawful money, that he or they will not again offend in the like kind; and the said county court may, if they see meet, further bind the person or persons offending as aforesaid to their peaceable and good behaviour during the pleasure of said court.

5. *And it is further enacted by the authority aforesaid,* That if any foreigner, or stranger that is not an inhabitant within this Colony, including as well such persons that have no ecclesiastical character or licence to preach as such as have received ordination or licence to preach by any association or presbytery, shall presume to preach,

teach or publickly to exhort, in any town or society within this Colony, without the desire and licence of the settled minister and the major part of the church of such town or society, or at the call and desire of the church and inhabitants of such town or society, provided that it so happen that there is no settled minister there, that every such preacher, teacher or exhorter, shall be sent (as a vagrant person) by warrant from any one assistant or justice of the peace, from constable to constable, out of the bounds of this Colony.

Study Questions

1. On what grounds do the ministers of the New Haven association oppose the revival? How does the revival threaten "the established constitution of this government"?

2. What is the apparent relationship between the ministerial associations and the colonial legislature? What is the process by which opinion becomes law?

3. What was the intention of the Anti-Itineracy Act? How would it affect the New Haven Separatists? Why is itineracy such a major threat?

FIVE

Controlling the Campus, November 1741–November 1742

While "Moses and Aaron," in the phrase used by Governor Law to speak of ecclesiastical and civil authority, forged their response to the Great Awakening, tensions at Yale College continued to mount. At almost the same time that the General Consociation was meeting at Guilford, Clap demonstrated his willingness to take firm action against student dissidents on his own campus: at the end of November 1741, he expelled one of the most promising scholars in the college, David Brainerd, whose memoirs have been excerpted earlier in this volume. The fullest account of Brainerd's expulsion [#23] was written soon after his early death by Jonathan Edwards, in whose house the young missionary to the Indians—he became interested in them the year after he left Yale—came to die and to one of whose daughters he had been engaged.

Clap's next dramatic action—closing the campus—is noted briefly in a Boston newspaper [#24]. A more personal account of campus activities in the first months of 1742 is contained in the diary of a Yale freshman, John Cleaveland (1722–1799) [#25], who returned to his family in the town of Canterbury when Clap sent the students home. (For a later episode involving both Cleaveland and Canterbury, see Section VIII, #45–#50.)

The Connecticut General Assembly had been kept informed of Clap's difficulties; the Governor himself had even referred to them in his May 1742 address (see #20). A committee of the Assembly was formed and soon submitted its report on the troubles at Yale [#26]. The reaction to these troubles by a man who did not personally witness them but who was generally sympathetic to the revival is contained in a letter to George Whitefield in England written by the respected and elderly Boston minister Benjamin Colman (1673–

1747) [#27]. Thomas Clap's own account of developments in the College and in the New Haven church—where the separation was by this time a month old—appears in his June 1742 letter [#28] to Solomon Williams (1700–1776), minister of the first church in the town of Lebanon, Connecticut. Like Benjamin Colman, Williams was a distinguished man who was sympathetic toward the Awakening but critical of its more extreme manifestations.

The pastor of the second church in Lebanon, Eleazar Wheelock (1711–1779), a 1733 graduate of Yale, was one of the most actively committed partisans of the revival in New England. His diary entries for mid-June 1742 [#29] record his experiences on an evangelical itineration which took him through New Haven. Wheelock's letter to his wife [#30], written shortly afterward, describes some of the same events. An indefatigable itinerant himself and a staunch defender of the principle of itineracy, Wheelock nevertheless continued to maintain his ties to the established churches. He never criticized other ministers in public, and he voiced strong opposition to some of the later developments spawned by the Awakening, including indiscriminate church separations and public preaching by lay "exhorters." After the end of the revivals, Wheelock became interested first in teaching and then, like David Brainerd, in aiding the Indian population; the Indian school he started at Lebanon in 1754 was moved to Hanover, New Hampshire, sixteen years later, where it became known as Dartmouth College.

A second letter that Clap wrote to Solomon Williams of Lebanon's first church [#31] continues to present the Rector's view of developments in New Haven during the summer of 1742. In November, after the College had reopened, Eleazar Wheelock received a letter from his fifteen-year-old stepson, John Maltby, who was living in New Haven. Maltby's letter [#32] reveals something of the atmosphere on and around the campus that autumn.

23

Jonathan Edwards:
Account of David Brainerd's Expulsion

November 1741

It could not be otherwise than that One whose Heart had been so prepared and drawn to God, as Mr. Brainerd's had been, should be mightily enlarged, animated and engaged, at the Sight of such an Alteration made in the College, the Town and Land, and so great an Appearance of Men's reforming their Lives, and turning from their Profaneness and Immorality, to Seriousness and Concern for their Salvation, and of Religion's reviving and flourishing almost every where. But as an intemperate imprudent Zeal, and a Degree of Enthusiasm soon crept in, and mingled it self with that Revival of Religion; and so great and general an Awakening being quite a new Thing in the Land, at least as to all the living Inhabitants of it; neither People nor Ministers had learn'd thoroughly to distinguish between solid Religion and its delusive Counterfeits; even many Ministers of the Gospel, of long standing and the best Reputation, were for a Time overpowered with the glaring Appearances of the latter: And therefore surely it was not to be wondered at, that young Brainerd, but a Sophimore at College, should be so; who was not only young in Years, but very young in Religion and Experience, and had had but little Opportunity for the Study of Divinity, and still less for Observation of the Circumstances and Events of such an extraordinary State of Things: A Man must divest himself of all Reason, to make strange of it. In these disadvantagious Circumstances, Brainerd had the Un-

---

Jonathan Edwards (ed.), Life of Brainerd, pp. 19–21.

---

happiness to have a Tincture of that intemperate indiscreet Zeal, which was at that Time too, prevalent; and was led, from his high Opinion of others that he looked upon better than himself, into such Errors as were really contrary to the habitual Temper of his Mind. One Instance of his Misconduct at that Time, gave great Offence to the Rulers of the College, even to that Degree that they expell'd him the Society; which it is necessary should here be particularly related, with it's Circumstances.

In the Time of the Awakening at College, there were several religious Students that associated themselves one with another for mutual Conversation and Assistance in spiritual Things, who were won; freely to open themselves one to another, as special and intimate Friends: Brainerd was one of this Company. And it once happened, that he and two or three more of these his intimate Friends were in the Hall together, after Mr. Whittelsey, one of the Tutors, had been to Prayer there with the Scholars; no other Person now remaining in the Hall, but Brainerd and these his Companions. Mr. Whittelsey having been unusually pathetical in his Prayer, one of Brainerd's Friends on this Occasion asked him what he thought of Mr. Whittelsey; He made Answer, *He has no more Grace than this Chair.* One of the Freshmen happening at that Time to be near the Hall (tho' not in the Room) over-heard those Words of his; tho' he heard no Name mention'd, and knew not who the Person was, which was thus censured: He informed a certain Woman that belonged to the Town, withal telling her his own Suspicion, viz. that he believ'd Brainerd said this of some one or other of the Rulers of the College. Whereupon she went & informed the Rector, who sent for this Freshman and examined him; and he told the Rector the Words that he heard Brainerd utter, and informed him who were in the Room with him at that Time. Upon which the Rector sent for them: They were very backward to inform against their Friend, of that which they look'd upon as private Conversation, and especially as none but they had heard or knew of whom he had uttered those Words; yet the Rector compell'd them to declare what he said, and of whom he said it.—Brainerd look'd on himself greatly abused in the Management of this Affair; and thought, that what he said in private, was injuriously extorted from his Friends, and that then it was injuriously required of him (as it was wont to be of such as had been guilty of some open notorious Crime) to make a publick Confession, and to humble himself before the whole College in the Hall, for what he had said only in private Conversation.—He not complying with this Demand, and having gone once to the separate Meeting at New-

Haven, when forbidden by the Rector, and also having been accused by one Person of saying concerning the Rector, that he wondered he did not expect to drop down dead for fining the Scholars who followed Mr. Tennent to Milford, tho' there was no Proof of it (and Mr. Brainerd ever profess'd that he did not remember his saying any Thing to that Purpose) for these Things he was expell'd the College.

Now, how far the Circumstances and Exigences of that Day might justify such great Severity in the Governors of the College, I will not undertake to determine; it being my Aim, not to bring Reproach on the Authority of the College, but only to do Justice to the Memory of a Person who I think to be eminently one of those whose Memory is blessed.—The Reader will see, in the Sequel of the Story of Mr. Brainerd's Life, what his own Thoughts afterwards were of his Behaviour in these Things, and in how Christian a Manner he conducted himself, with Respect to this Affair; tho' he ever, as long as he lived, supposed himself much abused, in the Management of it, and in what he suffer'd in it.

His Expulsion was in the Winter Anno 1741, 2, while he was in his third Year in College.

24

Boston *Evening Post*:
Account of the Troubles at Yale

April 26, 1742

From Connecticut [comes a report] that in divers Parts of that Colony, they are in great Confusion on religious Accounts; and that

Boston *Evening Post*, April 26, 1742; quoted in Franklin B. Dexter, *Documentary History of Yale,* pp. 355–356.

at Yale College in New-Haven the Divisions are so great, that the Students have all left it, and are gone Home. They are in Hopes that the General Assembly which is soon to meet, will find out some Expedient for composing their Differences.

25

John Cleaveland: Diary of a Yale Freshman

1742

[Jan.] 15. This day is friday and I declamed the first time that ever I declamed [illegible] all the time and was something affrited, and Betts was very much affrited, but before I was up out of my bed in the morning I had many thoughts about my backsliding from god my first husband, and all this [time] I have bin very heedless about spiritual things. This night after prayers in the hall Jones prayed in Halls roome very affectionately. After I came home I and Williams Sange a Hymn and [after] that there came up five more and we sang a hymn and so we separated and went away and Williams and I had a considerable discourse concerning religion, and after he went away we prayed and I was the mouth to speak but was exceeding blind in spiritual things. This day I have heard also a horrable story conscerning Brainerd: how that people suspect that he set up a letter or paper upon a mans door and said we are stoute men and the first time that we meet with [you] whether by night or by day we will pull out your tongue out of your throat and break every bone that you have in your body and clear the town of Mr. Wrascall.

From a photostat of the original manuscript in the Yale University library.

16. This day being Saturday, Dickinson is gone to a meeting to hear Sir Woodbridge preach.—This day Mr. Clap expounded upon Christ as a mediator between god and man, and as both god and man, this night after our meeting I heard Strong primus [that is, the older of two students named Strong] say that Mr. Stoddard of Woodbury is come out very bright in the work of the Lord, and as before he was wont to say it was the work of the [Devil], so now he says the Divill is in those that oppose the work of the Lord. Mr. Clapp prayed this night better than ever I have heard him since I have been at New-haven.

17. This day being the Sabbath I went to hear Mr. Noyes preach in the forenoon on Ecclesiastes 9.5, and in the afternoon on 1st of Peter 1.7. This day has been a very cold day in so much that many Scholars went from meeting before the meeting was over; this night we have had a meeting. We read, sang and prayed twice, after and before meeting. I received some money of my companions, about six shillings, and after the meeting was over I spent my time very shamefully and loosely considering the right and it s[eems] as if I were [re]turned like the Dog to his vomit or the sow that was washed to her wallowing in the mire again.

18. This day being Monday I have been very cold in religion and as it were a running downhill and from the Lord Jesus Christ, O that the Lord would smite my dead soul with his spirit and cause me to hear his voice, that the bones which he hath broken may rejoice.

The day has been wet, [a] lowering day, some snow and some rain. This day I have heard the Seniors dispute upon the words, *istud homini indubitabile esset quod non cognoscitur*. This day Lord primus was called before the Seniors for carrying himself unbecomingly and this night I spent with the Lymans and Ely and we had some Discourse concerning moving out of the College if we could see our way clear and if we could have some ministers on our side. I drank tea this night with Ely, and after I came home I discoursed with Mr. Mix concerning getting out of commons, and this night Dickinson went and talked with Mr. Clap about going into the college in the place of Britt.

19. This day I have I think more errands than any Day I know of and it has been the worst day for going on errands that ever I went on. I went to Rossiter and Darling and he sent me to widow Allens and when I had got almost to college Fisk primus and he sent me to Tod's to get him a horse, and after I came back he sent me to Captain Munsons, and at night after prayer Dor sent me to Sykes to get a pair of shoes for him.

This day Dickinson went in to college to Live. I think [illegible] burden from and gro colder and colder in things of Religion. This day I went first to Sir Weatherton to be instructed in ciphering. The Seniors disputed in the Hall upon *non* [illegible] *lactione, indiferantis.*

20. This day is Wednesday. Mr. Clap preached in the Hall on 2nd of Peter 1.10, Wherefore give all diligence to make your calling and election sure. and [his] doctrine Was this:

It is our great and indispensable duty to use our utmost diligence to make [sure] our calling and election; and I think he preached the best that ever I heard; he seemed to preach experience.

This night I was absent from the meeting in the college, and studied very industriously but [was] very cold in religion.

21. This day being Thursday, Mr. Case was persecuted by the people of Milford. He was put in prison and the people had a Court about [it.] the people the belongs to the water-side and they put one man in the prison, and I with some more of my class asked Mr. Whittelsey whether we might go to the Court.

This day I have walked very far from god my creator and very senseless of my danger.

The meeting in the college was omitted for the sake of the Court and many other things.

This night Williams and Field supped with me and after supper we sat and sang some of Doctor Watts Hymns.

This night Betts prayed with me and after that Betts and Draper were a bed. Draper seemed to be very discontented with Betts.

22. This day has been kept as a day of prayer by some of the Scholars in the College, especially by the seniors. This night Mr. Humphreys preached in the hall and in the time of exercise I seemed to be some concerned but afterward I returned Like the Dog to his vomit to my dullness and deadness; time passeth away and my time draweth nigh and I grow duller and more stupid.

23. This day being Saturday. Mr. Clap expounded in the hall upon the free will of man. This night we had a meeting in Hawleys room and we sang first and then prayed twice. This day I have heard some precious news concerning the Lord Jesus Christ, riding upon the word of truth at Weathersfield and a form of the work spreading at Norwalk. O that I might hear such news every day and not only hear of it but see.

24. This day being the Sabbath. In the forenoon Mr. Noyes preached on 1 of Peter 4.18. In the afternoon Mr. Whittelsey preach[ed] on Luke 13.24. This night Mr. Clap prayed above an hour

as I judge and I was as stupid as stupidity itself all the while he prayed. After prayer we had a meeting and began to pray according as the Class is placed. This day I heard of Mr. Graham and Mr. Bellamy and Mr. Mills coming to New Haven to preach.

25. This day is Monday and has been kept by me very loosely. O that I had a heart [that] would not turn aside from the right or from the left. This day I and Draper did out like two silly fellows without any sense of future and Divine things. We scuffled together like two dunces and I worried myself very much and did no more good then if I had been a flinging fire brands arrows and Death. This night I spent with Beebe, Field and Lord, after that I came home. I had some discourse with Draper concerning his vileness in the meanwhile[.] I was all over covered with guilt and sin. I heard that Mr. Robbins preached a fast at the Water Side and we have some prospect of his preaching tomorrow.

26. This day been attended with much disturbance in this town.

This night Sir Woodbridge preached in the hall upon Hebrews the 3rd, 12—the third time that ever he preached. This night we had a battle concerning religion, about Brainerd and many others of the same class or of the same sort. Landlord Mix claimed to talk as if the work which is in the Land was of the Divil and I thought that my Landlord was disturbed, and I was very plain with him, plainer then ever I was with him.

27. This day being Wednesday has been a gameing day among us. There has been preaching at Mr. Cooks about twenty rods from the college almost all day. Mr. Clap would not let us go to hear him preach. Mr. Mills preached two or three sermons. Some of the Scholars went to hear him preach: Some of the seniors and some of the juniors. I was almost resolved to go Let what would fall out, but I had not the courage to do it. At night after prayers Lyman, Williams and I [went] to visit Russell and Sturgeon and we spent the night with them.

28. This day being the Thursday. In the room after prayers in the Hall I received a letter from my brother Elisha Cleaveland and it was full of gall and honey, full of bitter and sweet. I heard that the Lord by Death had taken away my brother Moses. O that the Lord would sanctify the death of my brother to the Salvation of my soul.

After that mead, this bitter news, I heard the Lord had smiled upon my father's family with the mercys of David; I heard that this blessed work of the Lord had gone through my father's family: O that it may be a Saving Work upon each of their hearts.

This night Mr. Whittelsey preached in the Hall and I thought he was a very good orator but for a preacher I did take no liking to him. After the meeting was over I went into Fowlers Room and sat with him and Tracy and spent the night until twelve a clock in discoursing on religion and we prayed once.

29. This day I have been in a bewildered condition and have not hardly known what to do. I went and discoursed some with Strong, and after that I [re]moved into college and sat and drank tea with some of my class mates, and this night reasoned with Betts & Draper. But I seem at last too stupid and dead in religion and vital piety. This day the Separate party were set off by the Court and have Liberty to have Meeting by themselves, and they appointed their meeting to be at Mr. Lieut. Mix.

30. This day being Saturday. I have spent it after a sordid state without a sense of my own Deplorable estate, and have Stopped in things of a religious nature. This day I was put in Commons. This night I have been exceeding dull the like I have not known since I came to College.

31. This day being the Sabbath. Mr. Noyes preached in the forenoon on Matthew the 25th 46th, and these shall goe away in to Everlasting punishment: I thought some other text might [have] done the turn as well as that. And in the afternoon Mr. Whittelsey preached concerning the Spiritual Death that possesseth the hearts of all men, And after meeting and the prayers [in the] Hall Clarke and [I] went to hear Mr. [?] preach [at] Lieutenant Mix's and he preached exceedingly well.

[Feb.] 1. This day being Monday and the first day of the month. I have spent it very oddly and in a Dead and Sluggish manner in the things of a religious nature. O that my soul might be drawn out in Love to the god of heaven and earth. O that I might See and taste that the Lord is pleasant O that I might have raptures of joy let into my Soul that my Soul might be drawn out in a reflection of Love to the god of heaven. This day Mr. Clap gave us a lecture concerning these New Lights as people call them in a Reflecting way. He seemed to talk as if these people were quakers, who go under the name of New Lights. I think he said that [they] had taken oath against the religion of the country, and also he said it would not do for the Colony to bring up or the Colony would not bring up Scholars to swear against the Religion of the Colony, and also he said he believed that our religion was the true religion of Jesus Christ and we should find it so if we would compare it with the word of god.

---

2. This day being Tuesday I have still been a going on more Stupid then ever, & am a ripening for the Eternal flames. O that my soul might be Relieved by the Spirit of god. This night I sang a Hymn or two with Leavitt and Williams. It seems sometimes to me [as] if I never did desire to turn to the Lord again.

3. I had this day some talk with Strong primus about Religion and also this night some with Rosseter, and again I spent this night until nine of a clock, and after I came home I spent the night in writing a Letter to my father in laying open my case to him.

4. This day I Lived in great expectation of hearing Mr. Robbins preach but he failed in coming and Mr. Noyes had a Lecture and preached himself.

5. This day being friday. Mr. Clap fined Hawley five Shillings for speaking the truth in the Hall: and the truth was that he stayed at home because of the coldness of the air and of the preacher. This night I was called before the gentlemen sophomores for scandalously Reproaching of them and was very smartly Reproved by them; but they got nothing by it—neither did I.

6. This day being Saturday, Mr. Clap expounded on Justification: after Dinner the Seniors had a meeting in Hawley's Room and we made four prayers and so concluded. This night after prayers in the Hall Woolsey asked me to go and errand and also said he had leave from Mr. Whittelsey. This [night] Lyman 2dus had a kind of a battle with Phelps.

7. This day being the Sabbath. Mr. Noyes in the forenoon preached on Solomons Songs 5.1, and after Sermon he administered the Sacrament. I was exceeding cold in spirit in time of worship and in the afternoon Mr. Clap preached on the 7th 4. of Matthew. This night we had a meeting and Cook prayed first and Russell concluded, and after meeting [we] Concluded concerning having meeting every night among us.

8. This day I have walked very Loosely before god. I have had but a small sense of my guilt and sin. This day has been a very stormy day. This night we sat up the nightly meeting in our class. This night I went an errand for Rudgers and I went to Bradleys and spent the Evening with Strong in Religious Discourse.

9. This morning a moravian followed the Rector into the hall and after prayer he desired to preach but it was not granted to him, but notwithstanding he spake some, but the scholars would not stay to hear him. And again this night he aforementioned came into our meeting and one of the Seniors asked him to pray and after prayer he

asked for a Bible and when he had obtained [one], he read a verse in the 2nd of Titus and so in his way preached until Mr. Whittelsey sent for the people to come down, and so he broke off and blessed them and as he went from college he shook off the dirt from his feet.

10. This day Mr. [Samuel] Whittelsey of Wallingford preached at New Haven today on 7 of Romans 21. He preached at first very well but to finish he spoilt it all. This night there has been a counsel in the Library about Mr. Pierpont, and Mr. Noyes and Mr. Pierpont disputed.

11. This day the counsel broke up in the Library and Mr. Robbins was turned out of their meeting and the case came out against Mr. Pierpont and his brethren. This afternoon Mr. Robbins preached on John 3.5 but I did not hear him, and this night [I] broke out and went and heard him, and he preached on Genesis 19.17. And he spoke as a man sent from god to warn me of my sin and danger, but O the vileness and stupidity of my own heart, all the calls and invitations of god to me a sinner don't seem to have any impression upon my heart.

12. This day being friday. The Seniors Declaimed in the Hall, and finished by declaiming all but Strong. This day we were taken up into the Large garret to be tormented by the Sophomores and three of my class were fined for unmanners. This day I have walked very cold in Religion. I have lived very far from god. My thoughts have wandered very much from worshipping god. O that I might have a sense of heavenly and divine things.

13. This day being Saturday. Mr. Clap expounded on Church Discipline. This day I have been very dead and dull in the Religion of Christ. This night I had some talk with Winchell about our deadness in Religion, and he seemed to be very Relenting.

14. This day being the Sabbath. Mr. [Samuel] Whittelsey of Milford preached in Mr. Noyes's place, and he preached on James 1.18 of his own will begat he us. This day I felt as if I were returning to my lusts again without Restraint.

15. This day I have been very cold and dull in Religion. This night I wrote two letters, one to Mr. Mills and the other to Zena Lothrup.

16. This day I wrote a letter to my parents and this night I spent with Williams tertius in Mr. Whittelsey's room, but O I do not know what to do for my Self, I Sin so fast down hill.

17. This day I have been very cold and dull in Religion. This night Mr. Clap preached 1 of Peter 2.21, but it had but a poor affect upon me. I know not what to do with my self, I am so stupid in things

of Religion. I am so careless about my own soul, my precious and immortal soul.

18. In the fore part of the day I Remember nothing Remarkable, but this afternoon I had some discourse with Lockwood; and after I came home I received a Letter from Sir Lewis from Canterbury and there I heard of the conversions of my brethren and sisters and also of the wonderful exploites [?] of the Lord.

19. This day the Juniors began to declaim again the second time. At receiving a Letter last night from home I was something concerned after I got to bed about [it], and so I have been all day but after a stupid sort; I spent some talk about the deadness of my heart with Leaming. This night I have tended upon the buttery.

20. This morning having the care of the buttery I was to Ring the bell; but over slept myself, so the Rector called me a Sleepy head for it. This day Mr. Clap expounded on adoption, justification and sanctification, and this afternoon I spent with Brainerd primus and heard some heavenly news from Canterbury concerning my brother and sister, how Remarkable full they are. This night after meeting I spent with Lockwood in discoursing on Religion and our dead souls, how that we are conforming to the world.

21. This day being the Sabbath. Mr. Noyes preached on Hebrews 10.31th and he [was] some[what] better than I have heard him. This afternoon Mr. Whittelsey preached on John 3.16th, and he preached very well, I think the best that ever I heard him. This day I have been something concerned under great doubts about myself. This night I had some discourse about our Stupidity.

22. This day I have been in a more stupid estate then ever: O the perverseness of my heart. This afternoon Ely and I took a circuit round by Bradleys and so to Jones to hear Mr. Humphreys preach, but he was taken sick and could not come. Brainerd primus [that is, David Brainerd] prayed: and after prayers in the hall I went with Lockwood, and Rowland prayed, and after him Brainerd secundus.

23. This day I have had some sweet discourse with Mr. Kinberley about Religion; he seemed to me to be a sweet child of god: this night after prayers in the Hall we had a meeting together [and] Brainerd prayed. After the meeting was ended Brainerd, Ely, Lyman 2nd and I went to Lockwood's room. We sang an hymn, and as we were about to pray Winchell spoke in opposition to it and said he did not allow it, and after many words to convince him of his error, Brainerd, a sweet child of god as I trust, as he took leave of Draper

and Betts he spoke in an exhorting and drawed some tears from his eyes. He seemed to be something affected by his discourse.

24. This day morning I was something out of case in very great bodily pain. This morning I was absent from prayers and recitation; this day the consociation sat at Guilford &c. This afternoon the Seniors had a fast. Some of [the] Juniors and freshmen Joined with them. I was so stupid it seemed to me that I was left of the Lord to myself. This night I received a Letter from my father, sister and Brother. I seemed at first to be as overcome with I know not what. I read my Letters and heard that my fathers house was like a Little Bethel. This night I laid my case some before my classmate Lymans; this night Cogswell and Throop came to college.

25. This day I have been in a confused condition, as if it were without any relenting for Sin. This day I have had many thoughts about my father's family: I thought much concerning their happiness. This afternoon I spent my time with Lockwood and his chamber mates: this night I was at the meeting, and after meeting I stayed and read my Letters to Russell, Williams and some more of my class, and spent my time with them till nine o clock; and now I feel like a flint stone, stupid dead and dull.

26. This day I read of a comets being seen in the south, by many people; I find myself more and more inclined to the world: when I am at my meeting I am dead and I am about my senseless affair. I seem to have no sense of heavenly and divine things.

27. This day I took a walk with Leavitt to Johnsons, and we had a considerable deal of discourse together about our stupidity and also concerning the times, dreams, and the Like. This night I have had much discourse about going to hear Mr. Bellamy preach, more discourse then I think was profitable. But O that I might have a sense of my stupidity and distance from god, amen.

28. This day being the Sabbath. Mr. Bellamy preached at the Separate meeting, and I had a considerable discourse about going, but happened to fall through, and so I heard Mr. Noyes preach from Matthew 25.42, and in the afternoon I went to hear Mr. Bellamy preach from Matthew 11.22. I was something concerned about myself, there were some in convictions; this night I think I have shook off my convictions.

[Mar.] 1. This day hath passed over with much commotion. I went in the morning to the separate [meeting] to hear Mr. Bellamy, and he preached from the words of Paul, that I glory in nothing save in the cross of Christ. He preached excellent well and I was under some convictions, but it soon wore off. In the afternoon I went again to hear him and he preached from the words of Christ (viz) Strive to enter in at the strait gate, for many shall seek but few shall enter. Many of the children of god were enlivened and stirred up by the Spirit of god. After prayers in the Hall the Seniors had a meeting and Throop was filled very full by the spirit of god. We were called down by some of the Seniors, and it was the sweetest meeting we have had since we came to college. Mr. Bellamy and Mr. Pierpont came to visit us in college. We signed a Letter to send to Mr. Tennant.

2. This day I made accounts with Mix and paid him 9-12-0. This night I went to Mr. Pierponts and there were a number of the children of god as I trust. Brainerd primus repeated a sermon.

3. This day Mr. Stiles preached but I did not Like him. I spent this afternoon with Russell. Leavitt and I took a walk to see some distressed souls, and I was Like a stone all the while. It seems to me sometimes that I am undone forever. But I can't realize eternal things.

4. This day I have walked very closed in sin: I haven't got rid of this Self yet, and perhaps never shall. This night a chorus was attended by some of the scholars in the Reverend Rectors house. This night I wrote two letters—to my father one; to my sister one.

5. This day hath been very stormy; this day I have been asleep in my sins unconcerned about my future state. This night the sophomores and freshmen had a chorus: o the Desolation of Zion. I wrote some letters to my Brothers and Sisters today.

6. This day Draper proposed to me about living together, and to keep Batchellor's hall. This day I have still kept on my course in sin and Levity. O that I might be delivered from this fountain of sin and corruption.

7. This day being the Sabbath. Mr. Noyes preached on 1 Cor. 11.24. He administered the Sacrament, and in the afternoon he preached on Titus 3.5—not by works of righteousness; and he made a miserable hand of it. This night I was absent from our stated meeting. Spencer, Brainerd and Brown carried on meeting. I retired to my closet and read some of Mr. Joseph Allens works: and was something affected.

8. This day I have been more dull than ever. I grow more stupid every day: this day I helped make up the commons bills. This day Draper got a place for him[self] and I to live at.

9. This day I went to visit Brainerd and his Brethren and we were very handsomely treated by them. Williams 3 and Leavitt were

my Brethren. O I remain very Stupid and set notwithstanding my many privileges.

10. This day being the quarter day. I have been very much perplexed and stupified: this night I have seemed like a flint stone, dead in things of religion. Lockwood and I had considerable discourse about our hearts: we prayed together: we sang an hymn and very nearly [?] we spent the night together.

11. This day being thursday. Sir Woodbridge came home and so I left the college and came to Mr. Bradleys. I have had no sense of heavenly and divine things. My soul hath been involved in the world in Lust and corruptions of my heart: O that I might have a sense of heavenly and divine things: I seem to be sealed up like a stone.

12. This day I was fined one penny for being tardy. This day the venerable Rector came off his journey. This night the sophomores had a chorus in Copp's room. This night after meeting as [I] was coming home I felt something affected within myself: but it had [no] abiding in me: but I am become more stupid daily: O for an interest in the Lord Jesus.

13. This day seems to be more like spring than any day hath been since this month came in.

14. This day being the Sabbath. After prayers William 2 went home with the Reverend Rector to get leave to go to meeting, but he would not suffer him; but said if [he] was conscience bound he might go home for a little time, while the times grow better. This day Mr. Woodbridge preached on 2 Cor. 13.5. In the afternoon he preached on the 20th verse of 3rd of Revelations: but I was like a stone all the while.

15. This day I have had some discourse with a certain young woman about religion. This day I have been exceeding cold in religion: this day hath been exceeding cold as cold as any hath been this winter as I think.

16. This morning hath been very cold; and I also. My soul seems to be out of reach of all the calls of god. This night I heard that Mr. Clap was about getting a minister to preach in the hall. I heard this day that Mr. Cheney [of] Waterbury has drowned himself not long ago. This night I have been still as dead as before, and stupid like a stone: O the incredible ingratitude that dwells in my breast.

17. This day Sir Woodbridge preached a Lecture in the meeting house on Matthew the 3.3, prepare ye the way of the Lord, make his paths strait: he made a very good discourse. I felt a little stirred up at his preaching, but it was presently over: and [it was] but five minutes

before I was dead as a stone again in Religion. O the incredible obdurateness of my heart.

18. This morning I had a very beautiful meeting:—I dreampt that I was brought to behold my parents, Brothers and Sisters rejoicing in the Lord: and some of my relations rejoicing with them. I thought that my eyes bursted almost with a sight of them. This day I have been very rude considering my circumstances. My case I fear is very bad. This night I heard that Mr. Clap had forgave Throops going to meeting at the Separate [society].

19. This day Mr. Burr preached on 3 John 11 verse: I have no greater joy then to see my children walk in the truth. I thought I felt some of the spirit of god working upon me: but it was presently went away. Lloyd seemed to be something touched with the preaching.

20. This afternoon Mr. Burr preached again on Matt. 11.28— come unto me all ye that labour and are heavy laden & I will give you Rest. He spoke exceeding well from that text: but I was like a stone under his preaching. This night Mr. Parsons preached in the Hall: & he preached from the first of Nahum—the Lord is good, a stronghold in the day of trouble, and he knoweth them that trust in him. But none of this seemed to take hold on me: and why because of my sins and iniquities: O that my iniquities were subdued and that I had an interest in the Lord Jesus Christ, who died to redeem the sinfull children of men——amen and amen.

21. This day being the Sabbath. Mr. Burr in the forenoon preached from 1 of Peter 4.18—if the righteous are scarcely saved, where will the wicked and ungodly appear. He set forth the terrors of it very lively indeed, in truth; but I felt all the while like one sealed up—without any concern [illegible] anymore than common when Live ministers. I have returned to my lusts like the dog to his vomit. This afternoon Mr. Bellamy preached in the meeting house and he preached from the 13th chapter 7 & 8 verses. O he set it forth in the most lively manner that he could: the preaching semed to have some hold on me a little while, but it soon went off. This night Mr. Burr preached in the Hall from those words [?] in Matt. 6.33 but seek ye first the kingdom of god. He applied it to the Scholars in particular. I was something affected a while but my convictions went off, and [I became] stupid. Ely and I went and prayed together in a lot.

22. This day in the afternoon Mr. Bellamy preached on [blank space in the manuscript]. I was like a stone, without any warmth. This night Mr. Wilbert preached in the hall on Phil. 3.8. Lord primus seemed to be something convicted by the sermon. This night Mr. Par-

sons preached at the Separate meeting. Mr. Lockwood came into town tonight.

23. This day at noon I took a walk with Lord primus and Russell and we had a considerable deal of discourse about religion and our corrupt hearts. This afternoon Mr. Robbins preached at the Separate meeting. This night Mr. Burr preached in the Hall from Ecclesiastes 11.9.

24. This day I wrote a letter to my parents. This day Lord 2 went from college. This night Mr. Burr preached a sermon from John 3.7—Marvel not that I say that you must be born again. After I had got into my room I felt very much concerned about myself: but it soon went off.

25. This day being [word crossed out]. I walked about like a vagabond. This afternoon Mr. Burr preached in the meeting on Philli. 3.3. He preached exceeding well, but I was like a stone under his preaching.

26. This day we have had no preaching from those ministers of god that have preached so frequently of late. This night at the prayers Lee heard a noise in one of my ears, which put me a thinking pretty much a little while.

27. This morning about break of day I seemed something distressed about my wretched state by nature and practice. This afternoon Mr. Burr preached [illegible] in the meeting house, from Luke 16.31—if they hear not Moses and the Prophets, neither will they be persuaded if one should rise from the dead.

28. This day being the Sabbath. Mr. Burr preached in the forenoon from these words—(viz) the kingdom of heaven dont consist in meats and drinks. This afternoon he preached from Galations 4.19th —my little children of whom I travail in birth again, until Christ be formed in you. Since last friday I have heard thirteen sermons from the ministers as I trust. [?]

29. This day I do not remember much what hath been acted. This night Ely set sail homeward. This night we [had] no meeting in our class.

30. This noon I had some discourse with Strong 1 about my vile condition.

31. This day being the last day of the month. We finished the evangelists. This night I with some more got a berth, for a voyage home. I am in things of religion very dull, and lifeless.

[Apr.] 1. This day was a very broken day with me. I sent my things aboard this night in order for a voyage home: but being stormy we did not set out or sail. This [night] I took my leave of my School fellows.

2. This day we set sail from Newhaven for New London: but the wind being against us we drove about all night, but as we came along the vessel rubbed upon a rock, which affrited us very much. After that I was almost overcome with sickness by being upon the sea, and I endured a very bad night, and we came upon the horserace which tossed us very much.

3. This day I arrived at New London at one o clock in the afternoon, and we took a boat and set sale for Norwich: and we arrived there at about five o clock: and after that Draper and I traveled till nine o clock and came to Deacon Lothrops.

4. This day being the Sabbath I came to Canterbury meeting and Mills preached from Psalms 8.2. At noon I was something distressed when I came to see my mother, brothers and sister, in great Joy. I think I never saw such a meeting.

I seem to wear off my convictions and it will be a wonder of mercies if I am ever brought from sin.

5. This day I have been something concerned about my poor immortal soul, but have had poor slighting conviction. This night I went to Captain Browns to a meeting: and we had a very full meeting.

6. This day I took a ride with my father to my brother Josiahs. This night there was a meeting and some were filled. I went also to Mr. Averys to see them.

7. This day being a fast. Mr. Avery preached from the 19th of Luke 41—he came near the city, and looked on it, and wept over it.

8. This day I were off all my convictions, as it were, by lose discourse. This night brother Josiah related to me his experiences.

9. This day I were something convicted of sin, but nothing hearty. This night we had a meeting at grandmother Paines. The christians were full. I was struck into convictions but I wore them off very suddenly.

10. This day I have been something concerned about my precious soul, but I still am trampling upon the blessed saviour and redeemer.

11. This day hath been a very rainy day, it being the Sabbath day. Mr. Mills preached from Matt. 6.10—thy kingdom come, thy will be done: on Earth as it is in heaven. I seemed to be like a stone all day.

12. This day I went down into town. This night Mr. Mills preached a sermon from Luke 18.1—pray always and not faint. We

had some of us a very live meeting. I was in some distress but I wore it off. This night I tarried at Uncle Solomon Paines.

13. This morning I had a considerable discourse with uncle Solomon Paine about religion. He related to me his experiences. This afternoon Mr. Mills preached from 1 Cor. 1.30—of him are you in Christ Jesus, who of god are made wisdom, righteousness, sanctification and redemption. After him Mr. Baker preached from the words concerning the five virgins. His words seemed to have a very great affect upon the audience. I was in considerable distress for myself, but many more were more distressed for me than I was: there were a very great stir indeed.

14. This morning Mr. Baker preached a sermon at uncle Johnsons. Some seemed to be alive and some dead. After sermon a company of us went to Newent to hear Mr. Meachum and Sir Judd. There were something of a stir there and there [were] some very bold opposers.

15. This day I went with Mr. Meachum and uncle Elisha Paine to the west farms and there Mr. Meachum [preached] very well—and there was a considerable stir among the Christians.

16. This day I have almost lost my convictions. This [day] uncle and I set out for home. This day I had some acquaintence with Sir Lewis.

17. This day I stayed at home some part of the day. I took a walk with Ant Constance up to grandmother Paines, but I have been very careless about my future estate this day. O that I had faith in Christ. Amen and amen.

18. This day being the Sabbath. Mr. Mills preached from 1 of John 3.1—behold what manner of love the father hath bestowed upon us that we should be called the sons of god. I was something concerned. This day Ebenezer was taken into the church.

19. This day I went to visit Sir Lewis. He and I went to the Lower end meeting: and he was very full of the divine spirit and all were filled that ever were filled.

20. This forenoon I spent with Lucy Cleaveland. This day Jabez Fitch's wife came out full of the divine spirit. O that the Lord would still go on with his work.

21. This day I kept school for Sir Lewis: I have been in a very stupid condition all the day, without a sense of divine things. This night we had a meeting at Uncle Elisha Pain's. There were some full of the spirit as I trust but none in distress as I apprehended, but in a stupid condition as to things of a spiritual nature—amen and amen.

22. This morning I have been in a strange condition, but what shall I do for myself. My case is very sad and sorrowful indeed, for I am blind and naked, and don't apprehend it. This day father related to me his Experiences, how that he was brought out of darkness into marvelous Light. This day hath been a heavy day with me. I have been groping in the dark without one ray of Light.

23. This day I have spent idly and very dronishly and [without] any feeling sense of gods power, and of Christ's beauty. This afternoon Mr. Mills preached from Mark 16.8—and the Lord commended the unjust steward because he had done wisely: for the children of this world are in their generation wiser than the children of light. He preached considerable well from those words, but I did not seem to get much good from it by my negligence. This night after I came home William Bradford and I took a walk among the hills and mountains to pray, and as we returned Bradford seemed to have something of the spirit with him; but I was like a sealed stone. This night I heard of a bird's crowing before a mans door at Say-brook, and I heard of a beast's having a monster at Lyme.

24. This morning I have been in a dreadful senseless condition full of all manner of wickedness, and full of all droneishness, and sloth. Seems to me sometimes if my case was irrecoverable, and desperate, indeed for a glance as it were. This afternoon Samuel Adams died.

25. This day being the Sabbath, Mr. Mills preached from Luke 16.8 in the forenoon, and in the afternoon he preached from Hebrews 2.3—how shall we escape if we neglect so great a salvation. This day I have been exceeding full of vile thoughts and wanderings. I heard that Sir Judd was to preach at Plainfield today. The people were very dead today at meeting and there were no exhortation.

26. This day I spent in the forenoon in the Mill-house sometimes in prayer, and sometimes in reading god's holy word. This afternoon Mr. Mills preached a funeral sermon upon the death of Mr. Samuel Adams from the 131 Psalm 2 verse—Surely I have behaved and quieted myself as a child that is weaned of his mother: my soul is as a weaned child. The children of god were very live at the funeral, a spirit of exhortation was very much poured down upon them. Two persons were struck into convictions: I trembled for a little space of time, but I felt like a sealed stone, and do yet remain so.

27. This day I met Mehetable Brown upon the way (as I went to meeting) exceeding full of the spirit of god. This night the people had a very brave meeting. Many of them were full &c.

28. This day I spent with a friend L—y C————nd (id est) (the bigger part of the day) in religious discourse: this afternoon Sir Lewis and I went to visit Mr. Mills: and we abode there all the night; I went for the doctor [?] for Mr. Mills.

29. This forenoon I spent at uncle Johnson's and in traveling. Sometime I spent with Samuel Fellet's wife in discoursing upon religion. Some discourse I [had] with Enos Hide upon the way: and some with Stephen Backus. This afternoon I spent (some part of it) in hearing an opposer talk &c.

30. This day in the forenoon I have been a wandering about almost like Cain. This afternoon Mr. Wadsworth preached from Romans 8 chap. 9 verse (viz) but ye are not in the flesh, but in the spirit, if so be that the spirit of god dwell in you. There was something of a Revival among the Christians: after meeting, a company of us went to uncle Henry Cleaveland's and seemed to have a considerable meeting; I seemed to be a cast away: I could not join with them in praising the Lord. This night I was wonderfully called upon by god to repent and accept of Christ: but I would not. Pomroy exhorted me, Ebenizer Parson's wife and Sir Lewis: but I seemed to refuse all. There was a great Revival among them there: we prayed three times there: but [I] felt as stupid as stone. O when shall I return from my wickedness unto the living and true god? This night Sir Lewis stayed at father's and he was pretty full of the spirit of god, as I trusted.

This month is ended, etcetera. Finis.

[May] 1. This day I spent in mocking under a cloak of prayer. This afternoon I went with Sir Lewis and Olive Johnson and Lucy Cleaveland to Mr. Avery's: but I seem[ed] to be [in] a lethargy and a sleepy condition: O the foolishness of delaying.

2. This forenoon Mr. Avery preached from Hebrews, 2.16—for verily he took not on him the nature of angels, but the seed of Abraham. This day I partook of the sacrament, but in a dreadful cold condition. Widow Spalding came out full of joy: and there were some of a jangle between Mr. Avery and the brethren. This afternoon he preached from Galations 5.24—and they that are Christ's, have crucified the flesh with the affections [and] lusts.

3. This day I went to Trooping and stayed there a few minutes; and then went with Sir Sprout and Sir Lewis to uncle Johnson's: and there Sir Sprout exhorted me exceeding well: but how did I receive it, o but poorly. I did seem at first something pressed at my heart, and as I came home I felt very much concerned: o what shall I do that I may be saved, what shall I do that I may obtain Eternal Salvation?

4. This day I stayed at home, in a loitering frame, stupid and senseless and unbelieving.

5. This day I went to Preston, and there Mr. Mosely preached from John 7.33—then said Jesus unto them, yet a little while am I with you and then I go unto him that sent me. I seemed all the while like a stupid stone. There was a considerable stir among the people, some in distress, and some rejoicing in their Redeemer.

6. This day Mr. Mosely preached from Luke 22.48—but Jesus said unto him, Judas, betrayest thou the Son of Man with a kiss? He preached exceeding well: and he was very earnest that souls should flee to the Lord Jesus Christ for Salvation: but I still refused his glorious calls and invitations. There were a considerable Revival among the Christians, and something of a stir among sinners: but I was like a stupid stone having a heart as hard as an adimant.

7. This day I did work about an hour out of doors. This afternoon Mr. Moseley preached from Hebrews 3.7–8—Wherefore as the holy ghost saith today if ye will hear his voice, harden not your hearts, as in the provocations, in the day of temptation in the wilderness. He preached exceeding well from those words: but I was all the while like a hardened wretch: sealed up. After he had finished Mr. Mills preached from Malachi 2.7—for the priests lips should keep knowledge, and they should seek the law at their mouth, for he is the messenger of the Lord of hosts.

8. This day spent about trifles, for I don't remember much what I spent that with, but I had many thoughts about myself: I had some talk with John Adams: about religion.

9. This day being the Sabbath. Mr. Mills preached from Psalms 2.12—Kiss the son lest he be wroth while he is in the way. This afternoon he preached from Pro. 3.6—in all thy ways acknowledge him: and he shall direct thy paths: he seemed to preach considerable well, [but] I have felt like a stupid stone. This day old Chuffy was struck into convictions, and uncle Solomon exhorted him: but I was stupid as a stone: and what I am at a loss: sometimes it seems to me my case is almost despairable, and sometimes I have no sense where I am going.

10. This day I went to Woodstock: and as I went I received a letter from Nathaniel Draper. This night I had a great contest with Joseph Morse and one Childs concerning the works of god.

11. This day I went to see John Morse and there I wrote a letter to Chandler. I was at Joshua Chandler's and there we sang a hymn.

[Here the manuscript ends.]

26

The General Assembly: Report on Yale

May 1742

The Comtee appoynted to take into consideration that paragraph in his Honours Speech (made to this Assembly) relateing to the unhapie ciercomstances of the Colege, pursuant to the order of this assembly, have made Inqueiery of the Reuerd Rector of sd Coledge, and of others likelie to Inform us respecting the State thereof, and after deliberation, take leaue to Report to your Honour, & to this Honourable Assembly, as followeth.

That Sundry of the Students of sd Colege, haue as the reuerd Rector Informeth us by the Instigation perswation & example of others, fallen into Seueral Errors in principal and disorders in practice, which may be uerry hurtfull to Relegion, and Some of them Inconsistant with the good order, & gouerment of that Societie.

Perticulerly, Some of the Students haue fallen into the practice of Rash Judgeing & censureing others, euen Some of the Gouernours, teachers & Instructors of the Colege, as being unconuerted, unexperienced & unskillfull guids, in matters of Relegion, and haue thereupon contemtuously refused to submit to theire authoritie, and to attend upon & harken to theire Relegious Exercises & Instructions, but rather to attend upon the Instructions & directions of those to whome the care of Instructing ye Students is not commited.

Some under-Graduate Students haue made it theire practise by day & night, & Some times for Seueral days together, to go about in

Franklin B. Dexter, *Documentary History of Yale*, pp. 356–358. From the original in the Connecticut Archives, Connecticut State Library, Hartford.

the Town of Newhauen, as well as in other Towns, and before greate Numbers of people, to teach & Exhort, much after the same maner, that ministers of the Gospel do, in theire publick preaching.

That much pains hath been taken, to prejudice the minds of the Students, against our Eclesiastical constitution and to perswade them to dissent & withdraw from the way of Worship & ministry Established by the Laws of this Gouerment, and to attend on priuate & Seperate meetings and that Sundry of the Students haue so don, in contempt of the Laws & authoretie of the Coledge.

that these things haue occationed great expence of precious time, by disputs among the Scholers, and Neglect of theire Studies & exercises at Colege, and haue been a hinderance to the florishing of Relegion & uital pietie in that Societie, and if Tolerated, may defeate the good ends & designs of it's Institution.

Your Comtee thereupon are humbly of opinion, that it is of greate Importance, both to our Ciuil & Eclesiastical State that the true principals of Relegion & good order be maintained in that Seminary of Learning.

and that it be Recommended to the Reuerd Rector, Trustees & others concerned in the Gouerment & Instruction of the Colege, to be uerry carfull to Instruct the Students in the true principals of Relegion, according to our confession of faith & Eclesiastic constitution; and to keep them from all Such errors as they may be in danger of Imbibeing from Strangers & foraigners, and to use all such proper measures, as are in theire power, to preuent theire being under the Influence & Instruction of Such as would prejudice theire minds against the way of worship & Ministry Established by the Laws of this Gouerment, and that order & authorety be duly maintained in that Societie; and that those should not Injoy the preueledges of it, who contumatiously refuse to Submit to the Laws, orders & Rules thereof, which haue been made, or shall be made, according to the powers & Instructions giuen in theire Charter, but we thinke it highly reasonable, that all proper meanes be first used with Such Scholers, that they may be reclaimed & redused to order, before they be dismissed the Colege as Incorageable.

Your Comtee are also Informed, that at a late meeting of the Trustees, they concluded, that in order to the remoueing the diffeculties of the Colege, it was proper that Some experienced Graue Devins repayer to Newhauen, and there to Instruct the Scholers by theire Sermons, that may be by them prepared for that end; and forasmuch as such devines must be taken from other pulpits, and the Trustees not haveing money in theire Treasury, suffetient to hire a person, to suply such pulpit or pulpits; we therefore recommend it to this assembly to Grant to the Trustees a suffetient Sum, to enable them to hire a meet person to suply such pulpit or pulpits.

All which is Submited by your humble Seruts.

James Wadsworth
Jos. Whiting
Jer. Miller
E. Williams
Samll. Hill
Jonth. Hait
Jno. Griswold
Ebenr. Gray

In the Upper House. The aforegoing Report read accepted & approved.

Test George Wyllys Secrety.

Concurred with in ye Lower house

Test Jno. Fowler Clerk

27

Benjamin Colman to George Whitefield

Boston, June 3, 1742

Rev. and dear Sir,

Our good Brother, Mr. Prince tells me that in a Pacquet, he has read from you this Day, You complain of my Neglect in not writing to you. The whole Reason of which was (if you will allow it to pass for any Reason at all) that I imagined you was on your Voyage to Georgia near the Times, when I received your kind Letters, the last of which was on board the Vessel on your Way to Scotland. The Rev. Mr. Willison of Dundee, has lately refreshed me with a most brotherly Letter, respecting your first Visit in N. Britain, and congratulating me on the good Spirit, he thinks I have testified in my Sermon on the Doves, towards you, and I find he bears the same humble fervent Mind you-ward, which he would he find and love in me. He tells me that since your Visit to their Kingdom, Religion begins to look with another Face in some of their principal Cities; but he wants to see the Colleges and Students impress'd as many of ours were. I Hint to let you know, that ours impressed at Cambridge and Boston, have gone on in their Studies, and come forth into Service since, in a happy Manner of Spirit: One of whom is now first with Mr. Webb. But at New-haven Things have not proceeded with the like Prudence, Calmness and Modesty; and there has been too much Division and Animosity among the

---

Massachusetts Historical Society, *Proceedings,* LIII (1919–20), pp. 214–215.

Ministers and Churches in Connecticut. The fervent, pious Mr. Devenport, and Mr. Crosswell, have been too much under the Impressions of a heated Imagination, and no doubt often preached under actual Fevers, judging and censuring the spiritual State of Ministers and People; who could not go into the Way and Length, of singing thro' the Streets to and from the House of God, and favouring Exhorters of no Gifts, or prudence for publick Speaking. Some very young Students also, I hear have taken upon them, to go about exhorting, and one of them has lately visited from Northampton down to us, and gone from hence to Portsmouth in Newhamp-shire. He preach'd for Mr. Prince several Times; but Dr. Sewal and Mr. Copper told me, he needed more to be at his Studies. I look upon him to be greatly Spirited to serve Souls but wanting Furniture. We have advised our own Students not to rush forth so unprepared, but to be waiting upon God for Gifts, Grace, and holy Zeal. Mr. Willison bewails much the envious and uncharitable Divisions and Separation in Scotland for smaller Matters, as if they could not allow Good to be done by those who are not of their own Persuasion, and Party in all Respects; and it is with a surprizing Pain, on account of the Messrs Erskines and associate Presbytry, their Weakness, when I read, that even they should be ready almost to disown you; because you would not confine yourself to them; but ministred equally (and I hear with Equal Acceptance and Success) with the established Pastors, and in their Assemblies: I heartily joy (my dear Brother) that you acted with this catholic Spirit among them, and will not be ingrossed by any Party. . . .

[Signed,]

Benjamin Colman

28

Thomas Clap to Solomon Williams

New Haven, June 8, 1742

For the Revd Mr. Solomon Williams of Lebanon

Revd and Dear Sir

I was very sorry I could have no more Conversation with you at Hartford upon the present perplexed State of Affairs. The Trustees seemed generally to be fixed and determined that order and government should be Supported in College, and to obviate some objections proposed it as an expedient that sundry of the Trustees should come and preach here each a Sabbath, and if that did not fill up the time till Mr. Burr should come they proposed that you and Mr. Russell should be desired to come and preach. The Committee of the Assembly, as I heard drew up a Report that it should be recommended to the Governours of the College to take special care to uphold Order and Government in that Society, and to use their utmost endeavors to prevent the Scholars from running into errors, Disorders &c and those who would not be Subject should not enjoy the Priviliges of that Society &c. But I understood that some of the Comtee were not willing to come into it [that is, approve the report] unless a Clause was added to Recommend it to the Trustees to nominate some Judicious Divines to come and preach there for the present, and that money be granted out of the Public Treasury to pay a Preacher that should

---

From the original in the Glatz Collection, The Historical Society of Pennsylvania.

---

preach in their Room. But I was informed by sundry members of both Houses that the Assembly were not generally pleased with that Clause; and so, tho' the Report was accepted in the Lump, yet no Bill in form was drawn for granting the money. And so that scheme seems to drop. At present I suppose Mr. Noyes will [ex]change with some of the Trustees and perhaps some others near at hand, and I hope Mr. Burr may be here in about a month. It is probable that you may come here to bring your Sons and if it would Suit you to be here upon the Sabbath I should be glad. The Scholars of late seem to [be] much more cool, submissive and orderly than they were before the Vacancy [vacation], and some that I have discoursed with freely acknowledge their fault and promise Reformation. And I should have an agreeable Prospect that all things would go on well, if others would let them alone. And indeed I never tho[ugh]t that the fault was originally much in the Scholars, but principally in others who think That Religion is but promoted by Commotions, separations, over-turnings and the like, and who have done their utmost endeavor to bring the Scholars over to their Party. Messrs Devotion, Breck & Woodbridge told me that they read the late N[orth] Hampton result to Mr. Pierpont, and he declared that it had [been] drawn up in the Cabinet Councel office; it could not have been more calculated to defame the Interest of Religion. Mr. Edwards is Scarce allowed to be a good man. Your Sermon about the 2 Childrens Visions is exceedingly Condemned. It is reported here that Mr. Wheelock is to come next Sabbath and administer the Sacrament to the Separate Party and preach to them a month. I should be very glad to know how you advised him in the affair. In expectation of waiting upon you here in a short time I remain

Your Assured Friend
and Humble Servant,

Thomas Clap

P.s. Be pleased to give my service to Majr Fowler, and read to him this Letter if you please because it is in part an answer to his.

29

Eleazar Wheelock: Diary

June 1742

June 9, 1742. Came to New Haven. Understood, that the authority had been consulting how to take me, and that Col. Whiting had given out great words, and had said, that I should not preach but once in town.

June 10. Went to morning prayers at college. Afterwards was invited to breakfast with the rector (Mr. Clap). I went over: he seemed to be very much set against the separate meeting, charged them with great disorder; insisted upon it, that we ought to proceed against those we think not converted, according to the rule, Matt. xviii. 'First go and tell him his fault, then take two or three more,' &c. I told him, I could not believe, that that rule was ever intended to be improved so, for a man's being uncoverted was no trespass against me. Again, it is no scandal; and if it is, then all mankind are born scandalous. I asked him to tell me the steps of procedure with such. He said,—'Go and tell him his fault, then take two or three more: then go to your association.' I supposed, that they would be generally in the same case and not suitable judges: he said, I must deal with them as before. I asked him what I should do, when hitherto I have condemned and they justified. He said, that it would be very proper to print upon it. I asked him what I should do for the people of the country, who were going by thousands to hell. He said, I

William Allen, "Memoir of Rev. Eleazar Wheelock, D.D., Founder and First President of Dartmouth College," *American Quarterly Register,* X (1837), 17.

should deal with them after the same manner. He seemed to have a remarkable faculty to darken every thing. Preached at 6 o'clock, Ps. xxxiv. 8, with freedom. Understood, that Col. Whiting had been over to the governor to consult him about me, and that the authority met in the evening upon it.

June 12. Sabbath day. Preached three sermons, John v. 40, with two uses according to Matt. xv. 21, and Matt. xxii. 12; the third from Rom. ix. 22, with great power. A young woman from North Haven said, she would go to the New Light meeting and see how they acted. She did not question but she should hear some of them cry out. This she spoke with scorn, deriding them. She came, and was the first, that cried out in great distress. There were also many others in great distress. The children of God refreshed. The people in general so prejudiced, that they won't come to hear me.

June 13. Stayed at home to receive such as wanted to consult me. Was full all day. Was visited by many dear Christians; heard dreadful accounts about Mr. N.'s conduct with them, when under their concern.

June 14. Preached Ps. xci. 11. The children of God much refreshed.

30

Eleazar Wheelock to His Wife

New Haven, June 28, 1742

My Dr & Lovg Wife
Yours by Br D'port [Davenport] came. Gratefull indeed, to hear of my dear absent Family & flock, whom may God still preserve &

From the original in the Dartmouth College Manuscripts, Dartmouth College.

Bless. Ye week before least I preached 10 sermons. I told you in my Last of ye Power of God at Derby. Last week I preached 10 times again. My Journey was to Guilford, where we saw a Great Shaking among Dry Bones, & hell break lose and in a Rage at it. We also saw a Great Shaking at Branford & something at East Haven. They tell me in the two former places it was greater than even had been seen before in them. Dr Br Munson ye Barer was with me, to whom I Refer you for a more full & perticular account of matters. We had much of God with him there. I am this Day going to preach round 'tother way as far as Stratford. Things in this town are much more calm than they were; I mean as to ye Spirit & temper of people. Mr. Clap with ye Rest of ye Chh Comtee are gone to see if they can get Mr. Burr. I have not seen Mr. Noyes since I came to town. I have been proposing terms of reconciliation: viz., yt. the matters of grievance relating to Mr Noyes shod be heard by a Councill of Ministers yt Live Remote: viz., Messrs. Dickinson, Pemberton, ye Boston ministers Sol. Williams, Mr. Lord &c. I don't think yt there is any prospect yt Mr. Noyes will Submit to it, & unless those grounds of their first Separation can be Removed, I dont think there is any hope of union. Mr. Clap sticks as fast to Mr. Noyes as his Shinn and loves him as his eyes and counts him a Sound Orthodox Man—& indeed I dont at all wonder at it, for I believe they think much alike. Mr. Clap Refuses to Let me preach in ye College or to let ye Scholars come to hear me. O yt God wod give him another heart.

It is not yet certain whether I shall stay one or two Sabbaths more. I wod have you get Dr. Williams to preach ye Last if you can, & then if I shod come home he will be there to assist me. I am exceedingly worn out with Constant Labour and much Watching. I have ye young woman now by me, of whom I informed you in my last, under Deep Concern. Dr Br Pierpont & Sister give Love to you & ye family, & he his Love to Br Josiah Lyman. I have you, my Dearest, & ye Dear family, daily in Remembrance. Before God, my heart is with you. Give my love to Br Wright, to Dr Betty, John, Sarah, Theodora, Ruth, and take as much as you can Reasonably Desire yourself from

> Your Constant faithfull Loving Husband and
> Companion in tribulation & in ye kingdom &
> Patience of Jesus Christ,
>
> Eleazr Wheelock

Br Deodate (whom I trust [illegible]) is a firme opposer I hear.

Friends here are generally well. Give my hearty Love to all my Dear People as you have opportunity.

31

Thomas Clap to Solomon Williams

New Haven, July 16, 1742

For the Revd. Mr. Solomon Williams of Lebanon

Revd and Dear Sir

I received Yours of the 9th Instant and am very Sorry that since we have always so well agreed in our Sentiments about Religion that now our different Situation or Information should make us think Differently about some Circumstantials in it. When I took my pen in hand I Intended to have wrote largely and to have set sundry Facts in a Clear light. (Especially such [as] relate to some part of my Conduct), which I am Satisfied you have taken up very wrong Coceptions about, or otherwise you would not have wrote as you did. But finding that much writing is always tedious to me and a great Consumer of precious time, I am necessitated to Defer them all till I have an opportunity of Personal Conversation with you. And am very sorry I happened to miss of it in two Instances wherein I so much depended upon it. I must only mention one thing:————

I was the first that mentioned the Proposal of some of the

From the original in the Glatz Collection, The Historical Society of Pennsylvania.

Trustees and others coming to preach at New-Haven, and with some difficulty brought the major part of the Trustees into it. But finding many difficulties arose in putting it in execution, I was in hopes when I finally wrote to you that Mr. Burr's coming would have accomodated all: which Indeed was the expectation of the Trustees at their Meeting. But since Mr. Burr is not likely to come at all, I am desirous to prosecute the Proposal of the Trustees in the bast manner we can, and accordingly I expect that the Trustees will Preach till the 8th of Augst, Mr. Russell on the 15th and I desire that you would be pleased to come and Preach in the meeting house here on the 22nd. I know not how it should come to pass that the members of the Assembly should give such a different account about their Proceedings about giving money for a Candidate &c. I have several times sent to the Secretary for a Copy but as yet have Recd none, so I know no more about that matter than I did before. But if from the Information you have recd you can depend upon the Assembly to pay a Candidate that shall preach for you I shall be glad. But perhaps you can get your Pulpit easily supplied without any Regard to the Assembly.

I am quite Tired and Sick of all public Controversyes. They are destructive to all the natural and spiritual Comforts of Life. I wish I could live a more retired life wherein I could be more of a master of my own time and tho[ugh]ts and enjoy more Communion with God. So hoping to see you in a little time, I remain with due Regard to Madam

Your most Humble Servant,

Thomas Clap

P.S. According to my Promise in my former Letter I have sent you a Copy of Mr. Tennant's Letter to Mr. Dickinson. You may be assured that it is genuine because I have compared it with the original now left with me. Mr. Tennant when he was at New-Haven very much ran into all those extravagancies which he mentions in his Letter except that of Singing in the Streets. And which was the Leading Cause of all our Difficulties and Confusion, and now the good Gentleman sees his error and is willing to Acknowledge it [in] the most open manner that can be desired. And to beg those to be at peace that he has set at Variance. Oh that others would follow his example before they have kindled such a Fire and cannot be quenched. It grieves me that Men of Religion and Sense should so much Favour and Cherish such extravagancies under pretense of Promoting Vital

Piety! When it is evident from Reason and sad experience that they are most pernicious and Destructive to it.

32

John Maltby to Eleazar and Mrs. Wheelock

New Haven, November 18, 1742

Hond: Father and Mother:

I should have wrote before but have had no opertunity. O My father and Mother my Soul Dried up in this wilderness of Sin and Coruption. O my leaness my leaness it testifies against me, O that the Lord would Shine into my soul and Set it on fier with his Love: if he should so do, he would be to me as the Shadow of a Great Rock in a weary Land, then should I Set under his Shadow with great Delight and his fruit would be sweet to my taste O that it were so, the world the flesh and the Divil wont have it so by any means. But the Lord will have it so if he Pleases tho all hell were ingages in the war. But O that I had a true sorrow for sin, and so Brought to submit Intirely to the Lords will Let it be what it will.

This is a land of Drouth and famine, where no water is; in short here's a famine for the word, here's nothing to feed upon but Jesus Christ. If one lives here and live in the Exercises of the Graces of the spirit, they must live intirely upon the Lord and what shall I do? I am a great way from the Lord, O that I could get neare to him and tell him all my wants as my father. If you think it worth your while, tell our Christians from me a poor unworthy worm that they

---

From the original in the Dartmouth College Manuscripts, Dartmouth College.

---

know nothing what Priviliges they have; they know nothing what it is to go without Preaching 2 or 3 months, and when they had Preaching to be scorn'd and vilified for it, both those that Preach and those that heare. Their is very litel Religious Discourse among Christians; Christians are Dreadfull Dead here and Conform in a great measure to the world. The opposers Rise and the Children of God sink down. There seems to be no might nor Strength in a great many of them; the opposers seem to Reign and have the upper hand of the blessed Children of God. O that our Christians could sutably Prise their advantages, while this lital flock of Christ has no Pastor to lead and guide them but are as it were Scatered about to and fro and Revening wolfs are thick, seeking to Distroy them. They have [not] a Pastor that can under God lead them and guide them in the way that is Good and Right. O that our Christians were made in some measure to Prise their advantages, but they will not till they are made to. O my soul has Longed for to [be] with them and have Christian Conversation with them, but maybe it will not be so. When I shall see them if the Lord ever Permits it to be? O that God would make me intirely resined to his will in Every thing.

I am now living at Mr. Pierpont's, for what Reason you may easily conclude, tho the boys all attributed it altogether to Carnal Reasons my Removing. I told them it was truely for the good of my own and their soul, that I did move. At last they said I was mad. I told them I was not mad but could Pity them and Pray for them as heartily as ever I could in my life, and so gave them a word of Exortation and prayed with them, but I did not take my Leve of the family that night; but the next night [as] I took my Leve of them, I desired the Leftenant, if he had anything against me or knew of anything I had been wrong in, to indevor to make me see, but he said he had nothing against me but was intierly Easy with [what] I had done and thought it was for the best; and so taking my Leve of the family, Desiring their Prayers for me I departed and came [to] Mr. P. on the Day before thanksgiving and have no small thanks to give to the Lord the Giver of all mercies.

Mr. Buel is not yet come home and things Remaine in Respect to that just as they were when you was here. I have bought me a [illegible] hankerchife and 5 oringes, which oringes I send to you with this Leter, concluding they will be acceptabel to you. The hankerchiefe cost 18 and 6 pence, the oringes be 5. I am now in good Health, blessed be God for it; blessed be God, he helps me in my Learning; I am now in Caslatio [?]. Sir, if you have got one I should be glad you would Send it to me if I stay here as soon as you can. This, Hond. Father and Mother with my Duty to you and love to Sisters and Love in special to good Mr. Wright and all Christian friends. Desiring earnest Prayers to the one [illegible] for me a poor unworthy worm. And now, Hond. Parents, hoping that you will forgive and correct what is wrong in you poor unworthy son, Desring your Prayers continually for me, all the throne grace for me [your] most unworthy Son and Servant, I now Subscribe myself your

John Maltby

P.S. I saw Mr. Brainerd and Buel the last night. Mr. Brainerd told me tha you was all well, blessed be God for it. I have not yet Received any Leter, but Mr. Sprout was here the last Sabboth, who told me Mr. Reid wod be here ye next Saboth, who had a Leter for me and some other things.

Study Questions

---

1. Compare the picture of Yale you get from the "Report" of the General Assembly Committee with that from John Cleaveland's diary. Why did Clap send the students home?

2. What was the situation that John Cleaveland encountered when he returned to his home in Canterbury? How does this compare with the situation in which a radical student today might find himself when he returned to his home town?

3. What is Clap's strategy in the summer of 1742, as revealed in his two letters to Solomon Williams and in the Wheelock documents?

4. Why does Clap remain so respectful of Jonathan Edwards in the face of Edwards' support of the revival? What is Clap's relation hip with moderate New Light ministers in general?

SIX

Controlling the Colony, June 1742–June 1744

The General Association of Connecticut ministers, assembled at New London for their annual meeting in June 1742, passed a series of resolutions dealing with the continuing effects of the Great Awakening on the churches [#33]. Later that same summer, New London became the scene of an altogether different sort of assemblage: the "Shepard's Tent" was established under the leadership of the radical New Light minister Timothy Allen (1715–1806). A 1736 graduate of Yale, Allen had been pastor of the church in West Haven until his expulsion by the New Haven County Consociation in May 1742. (He was expelled principally because he had preached that reading the Bible without the presence of God's spirit "will no more convert a sinner than reading an old almanac." Opponents of the revival spread the word that Allen had compared the Bible to an almanac.) Two months after his expulsion, Allen traveled to New London, probably because that town, like New Haven, contained a group of people who had turned against their minister—himself a New Light—and begun to hold private religious meetings of their own. Allen became the leader of these separatists, but at almost the same time he set up the Shepard's Tent—an academy intended to train young men for the evangelical ministry. It was hoped that the Tent would lure potential or actual students away from Yale. In any case it threatened to institutionalize precisely the kind of evangelical activity that both the civil and ecclesiastical authorities had been trying to put down. In direct response to Allen's school, the Connecticut General Assembly, during its October 1742 session, passed "An Act

Relating to, and for the Better Regulating Schools of Learning."
[#34].

The failure of this act to put an immediate end to the Shepard's Tent can be seen from Timothy Allen's letter of February 1743 to Eleazar Wheelock [#35]. The Tent collapsed early that March, however, as an indirect result of an unrelated incident which probably did more to discredit the New Light party than any other single episode of these years: the New London book-burning. The book-burning was the responsibility of James Davenport, the itinerant from Lond Island whose earlier activities had precipitated the crisis in the New Haven church almost a year and one-half earlier, and who had subsequently been arrested and removed from the colony on two evangelical trips in 1742. Early in March 1743, Davenport sailed on still another visit to Connecticut; but this time he restricted his activities to the single town of New London, where he had encountered a most encouraging response the previous year. (By the end of 1742, in fact, the town had replaced New Haven as the center of religious upheaval in the colony.) On this occasion, Davenport convinced his followers in New London to build a great bonfire near the town wharf and to throw upon it all the symbols of their old, unsanctified lives—symbols which included, on Davenport's recommendation, many of the religious books which held honored places in the library of an orthodox eighteenth-century Congregationalist, but which Davenport now condemned as legalistic and not sufficiently spiritual. The book-burning—other items consigned to the fire apparently included fine clothing and similar luxuries—provided opponents of the revival with some extremely effective ammunition. A worried delegation of New Light ministers, including Jonathan Edwards, soon arrived in New London to repair what fences they could. (Edwards himself, for example, preached a sermon in the regular church, "bearing witness against the prevailing disorders, caused by enthusiasm.") At any rate, little was heard about the Shepard's Tent after this incident, and its director Timothy Allen soon departed for Rhode Island. In 1744, partly at the urging of Eleazar Wheelock and other New Light ministers, James Davenport publicly apologized for his actions of the previous three years [#36].

In the meantime, the New London affair and other more symbolically incendiary acts performed by both itinerant ministers and the lay exhorters whom they inspired caused the General Assembly of the colony to enact two further pieces of legislation: the first and more significant of the two, passed at the May 1743 session, revoked the 1708 Toleration Act under which dissenters had been guaranteed freedom of worship [#37]; the other, approved the next October, put stronger administrative teeth into the year-and-one-half old anti-itineracy act [#38]. A letter written early in 1745 to the governor of Connecticut by the Boston minister Benjamin Colman, a moderate and respected New Light [#39], suggests the reputation that colony was coming to acquire in the rest of New England.

33

Resolutions of the General Association on the Revival

June 15, 1742

This general association being of opinion, that the God of all grace has been mercifully pleased to remember and visit his people, by stirring up great numbers among us to a concern for their souls, and to be asking the way to Zion, with their faces thitherward, which we desire to take notice of with great thankfulness to the Father of mercies: Being also of the opinion, that the great enemy of souls, who is ever ready with his devices to check, damp and destroy the work of God, is very busy for the purpose: we think it our duty to advise and intreat the ministers and churches of the colony, and recommend it to the several particular associations, to stand well upon their guard, in such a day as this, that no detriment arise to the interest of our great Lord and master Jesus Christ.

Particularly, that no errors in doctrine, whether from among ourselves, or foreigners, nor disorders in practice, do get in among us, or tares be sown in the Lord's field.

Benjamin Trumbull, *A Complete History of Connecticut*, pp. 172–173.

That seasonable and due testimony be borne against such errors and irregularities, as do already prevail among some persons; as particularly the depending upon and following impulses and impressions made on the mind, as though they were immediate revelations of some truth or duty, that is not revealed in the word of God: Laying too much weight on bodily agitations, raptures, extacies, visions, &c.: Ministers disorderly intruding into other ministers parishes: Laymen taking it upon them, in an unwarrantable manner, publicly to teach and exhort: Rash censuring and judging of others: That the elders be careful to take heed to themselves and doctrine, that they may save themselves, and those that hear them: That they approve themselves in all things as the ministers of God, by honor and dishonor, by good report and evil report: That none be lifted up by applause to a vain conceit, nor any be cast down by any contempt thrown upon them, to the neglect of their work; and that they study unity, love and peace among themselves.

And further, that they endeavour to heal the unhappy divisions that are already made in some of the churches, and that the like may for the future be prevented:—That a just deference be paid to the laws of the magistrate lately made to suppress disorders: That no countenance be given to such as trouble our churches, who are, according to the constitution of our churches, under censure, suspension, or deposition, for errors in doctrine or life.

34

The General Assembly
Condemns the Shepard's Tent

October 1742

An Act relating to, and for the better regulating Schools of Learning.

Whereas by sundry acts and laws of this Assembly, they have founded, erected, endowed and provided for the maintenance of a college at New Haven, and inferiour schools of learning in every town or parish, for the education and instruction of the youth of this Colony, which have (by the blessing of God) been very serviceable to promote useful learning and christian knowledge, and, more especially, to train up a learned and orthodox ministry for the supply of our churches: And inasmuch as the well ordering of such publick schools is of great importance to the publick weal, this Assembly, by one act entituled An Act for the encouragement and better improvement of town schools, did order and provide, that the civil authority and selectmen in every town should be visitors, to inspect the state of such schools, and to enquire into the qualifications of the masters of them and the proficiency of the children, to give such directions as they shall think needful to render such schools most serviceable to increase that knowledge, civility and religion, which is designed in the erecting of them; and in case those visitors shall apprehend that any such schools are so ordered as not to be likely to attain those good ends proposed, they shall lay the state thereof before this As-

Charles S. Hoadly (ed.), *Public Records of Connecticut,* Vol. VIII, pp. 500–502.

sembly, who shall give such orders thereupon as they shall think proper; as by the said act may more fully appear: And whereas the erecting of any other schools, which are not under the establishment and inspection aforesaid, may tend to train up youth in ill principles and practices, and introduce such disorders as may be of fatal consequence to the publick peace and weal of this Colony: Which to prevent,

Be it enacted by the Governor, Council and Representatives, in General Court assembled, and by the authority of the same, That no particular persons whatsoever shall presume of them [164] selves to erect, establish, set up, keep or maintain, any college, seminary of learning, or any publick school whatsoever, for the instruction of young persons, other than such as are erected and established or allowed by the laws of this Colony, without special lycence or liberty first had and obtained of this Assembly.

And be it enacted by the authority aforesaid, That if any person shall presume to act as a master, tutor, teacher or instructor, in any unlawful school or seminary of learning erected as aforesaid, he shall suffer the penalty of five pounds lawful money per month for every month he shall continue to act as aforesaid. And every grand-jury, within any county where such school or seminary of learning is erected, shall make presentment of all breaches of this act to the next assistant, justice of the peace, or county court.

And be it further enacted by the authority aforesaid, That the civil authority and selectmen in each town, or the major part of them, shall inspect and visit all such unlawful schools or seminaries of learning, erected as aforesaid, and shall proceed with all such scholars, students or residents in such school, and all such as harbour, board or entertain them, according to the laws of this Colony respecting transient persons or inmates residing in any town without the approbation of the selectmen.

And be it further enacted by the authority aforesaid, That if any student or resident in such school shall pretend that he is bound as by indenture an apprentice to learn any manual art or trade, and the said civil authority or selectmen shall suspect that such indenture was given only as a colour to reside in said town contrary to law, that then it shall be in the power of the said civil authority to examine all the parties to such indenture under oath, in all such questions which they shall think proper, relating to the true intention of such indenture and their practice thereon; and if it shall appear to the said authority or selectmen, or the major part of them, that such indenture was given upon a fraudulent design, as aforesaid, that then such authority shall proceed as if no such indenture had been made.

And be it further enacted by the authority aforesaid, That no person that has not been educated or graduated in Yale College, or Harvard College in Cambridge, or some other allowed foreign protestant college or university, shall take the benefit of the laws of this government respecting the settlement and support of ministers.

Always provided, Nothing in this act be construed to forbid or prevent any society allowed by law in this Colony to keep a school, by a major vote in such society to order more parish schools than one to be kept therein, and appoint the school or schools to be kept in more places than one in such society.

This Act to continue in force for the space of four years from the rising of this Assembly, and no longer.

35

Timothy Allen to Eleazar Wheelock

New London, February 27, 1743

The Revd. Eleazer Wheelock
Pastor of ye North Church in Lebanon
Revd. & dr Br.

The blessed Lord Seems to be coming, to get to Himself a Kingdom again, ye dr Xns [Christians] were never under such distinguishing teachings here as now; & for some time past, they have ye most self abasing Discoveries of their own Hearts, & ye unspeakable Vile-

From the original in the Dartmouth College Manuscripts, Dartmouth College.

ness of their Natures; ye most amazing Apprehensions of ye infathomable Step of Exalting & redeeming Love in X Jesus;—& ye most powerfull Pleadings for Immortal Souls, that (I think) I ever saw. They have (especially such as dwell near ye Lord), unceasing Expectation of glorious Things att ye Door. It has pleased ye Lord, to make it a most Sweet Time with me, for near 3 Weeks past, so yt many Times I have been even Swallowd up in God; I had been for a g[rea]t while legally tugging after Mortification, & real Transformation into ye lively Image of Jesus X; & tho' I knew Nothing co'd do it but ye fresh & clear Manifestation of divine glory; yet I still sought it, as it were, by ye Works of ye Law, as I constantly, certainly do, unless I am beholding ye Glory of God Shining in ye Face of Jesus X; & then I inherit Liberty, a glorious Liberty, & feel that I do; & indeed this is a Sweet Way of keeping ye Law, vis. thro' believing in him who was certainly ye End of ye Law (as a Covenant or way of Life) to Faith, or rather to ye Subject of it, be it who it will. The Lord's way is in ye g[rea]t Deep, & my Soul does constantly magnify ye Lord, especially for his absolute Sovereignty. The Glory of God—& ye Wisdom of God,—& ye most infathomable & unsearchable Riches of Grace, & freest Love—which do shine in ye new Covenant Way of Life, I can only tell you my Soul is astonishing att; it seems to turn my Eye off to write much, or to damp me, for words scarce touch ye thing; my dr Br, when you are really in God, you have it all. Tis amazing grace yt ever I knew ye Lord is gracious, by Tasting; & tho' by this Means I have often known it; yet I think, so long together, never so much as now; I never saw—Me—Such a Heap of Stuff; a mere Mass of all abominations; I think, ye very Roots of ye Fountains of ye g[rea]t Deep, never appear'd in their own natures, & colours so clearly; truly in God's Light, we see Light! & this has let me in to ye most wonderfull, wonderfull views of Richest, Richest, freest Grace; of God; oh ye Grace! oh ye Grace! my soul sees oceans, boundless oceans of Grace; & to see yt it rises—& every motive to its display towards one Soul, so absolutely & solely, from Ye Eternal Mind; lays open a Field of everlasting Wonders which for many days I have beheld, with sweet astonishment generally; oh yt ye last & Strongest Hold of Satan (my own Nature) were utterly subdued & demolished; for indeed, dr Br, nothing [illegible] is from ye glory, but that; & my [illegible] for nothing so much as to be every [illegible] transforming into the Image thereof, [illegible] there in it comes & appears before God.

It has been a Sweet Season also in ye School much of ye Time this Fortnight. Ye power of Grace, & Love of God, are wonderfully display'd here among ye dr Youth. Last night, Fuller & several more were quite overcome with ye Powerfull Love of God, & even now while I am writing I hear ye most passionate pleadings of several of them much overcome. Several instances of Liberality towards ye Tent [i.e. the Shepard's Tent] lately, among which is a Choice Bell, having this Motto—Glory to God Alone; which indeed seems as if [it] was a Part of yt Prophecy, Zach. 14:20. Number [of students] in ye School is 14, & 2 more presented but not yet accepted, so yt Building as soon & as fast as it can be done, seems to be of Necessity. We have tho't of Building Small, & so more as tis wanted; many materials [such] as Timber, Carpendry, Hinges, Window Frames, Stones, are given sufficient, I suppose, for present want, & by 2 or 3 men from Boston, promis'd last week to send to it directly about 2500 of Boards. Workmen, i.e. Labourers are still wanting, & if you do find any wishing to bestow their Labour, please to tell them. I believe you will account it a Service done to this Branch of ye Interest of our dr Saviour.

I sho'd be glad [if] dr Mr. Pomeroy co'd see this, to whom I wo'd have written now but ha'nt time by this opportunity; but hope I shall soon; whose Prayers, & yours, I desire for ye Shepards Tent, & me yr unworthy Br. P.S. g[rea]t Sufferings have been exceeding Sweet to me, which I noways expect to escape, but X in you is a blessed Portion. Farewell. Ye Lord jesus be with yr Spirit. Amen.

Timo. Allen

36

John Davenport's Recantation

July 18, 1744

Messrs. Kneeland & Green: Please to give the following paper of my Retractation a place in the Gazette, and you will oblige

Your humble servant,

James Davenport

Although I don't question at all but there is great reason to bless God for a glorious and wonderful work of his power and grace in the edification of his children, and the conviction and conversion of numbers in New England, in the neighbouring government, and several other parts, within a few years past, and believe that the Lord hath favoured me, though most unworthy, with several others of his servants, in granting special assistance and success, the glory of all which be given to Jehovah, to whom alone it belongs; yet, after frequent meditation and desire that I might be enabled to apprehend things justly, and I hope I may say mature consideration, I am now fully convinced and persuaded that several appendages to this glorious work are no essential parts thereof, but of a different and contrary nature and tendency; which appendages I have been, in the time of the work, very industrious in, and instrumental of promoting, by a misguided zeal; being further much influenced in the affair by the false

Boston *Gazette,* July, 1744; quoted in William B. Sprague, *Annals of the American Pulpit* (8 vols., New York, 1856), Vol. III, pp. 86–88.

spirit which, unobserved by me, did (as I have been brought to see since) prompt me to unjust apprehensions and misconduct in several articles, which have been great blemishes to the work of God, very grievous to some of God's children, no less ensnaring and corrupting to others of them, a sad means of many persons questioning the work of God, concluding and appearing against it; and of the hardening of multitudes in their sins, and an awful occasion of the enemies blaspheming the right ways of the Lord, and withal very offensive to that God, before whom I would lie in the dust, prostrate in deep humility and repentance on this account, imploring pardon for the Mediator's sake, and thankfully accepting the tokens thereof.

The articles which I especially refer to, and would, in the most public manner, retract, and warn others against, are these which follow, viz:—

The method I used, for a considerable time, with respect to some, yea many, ministers in several parts, in openly exposing such as I feared or thought unconverted, in public prayer or otherwise, herein making my private judgment (in which also I much suspect I was mistaken in several instances)—I say, making my private judgment the ground of public action or conduct, offending, as I apprehend, (although in the time of it ignorantly,) against the ninth commandment, and such other passages of Scripture as are similar, yea, I may say, offending against the laws both of justice and charity, which laws were further broken.

2d. By my advising and urging to such separations from those ministers, whom I treated as above, as I believe may justly be called rash, unwarrantable, and of sad and awful tendency and consequence. And here I would ask the forgiveness of those ministers, whom I have injured in both these articles.

3d. I confess I have been much led astray by following impulses or impressions, as a rule of conduct, whether they came with or without a text of Scripture, and my neglecting also duly to observe the analogy of Scripture. I am persuaded this was a great means of corrupting my experiences, and carrying me off from the word of God, and a great handle which the false spirit has made use of with respect to a number, and me especially.

4th. I believe, further, that I have done much hurt to religion, by encouraging private persons to a ministerial and authoritative kind or method of exhorting, which is particularly observable in many such, being much puffed up, and falling into the snare of the devil, while many others are thus directly prejudiced against the work.

5th. I have reason to be deeply humbled that I have not been duly careful to endeavour to remove or prevent prejudice, (where I now believe I might then have done it consistently with duty,) which appeared remarkable in the method I practised of singing with others in the streets, in societies frequently.

I would also penitently confess and bewail my great stiffness in retaining these aforesaid errors a great while, and unwillingness to examine into them with any jealousy of their being errors, notwithstanding the friendly counsels and cautions of real friends, especially in the ministry.

Here may properly be added a paragraph or two taken out of a letter from me to Mr. Barber at Georgia, a true copy of which I gave consent should be published lately at Philadelphia. I would add to what Brother T. hath written on the awful affair of books and clothes at New London, which afford ground of deep and lasting humiliation, I was, to my shame be it spoken—the ringleader in that horrid action. I was, my dear Brother, under the powerful influence of the false spirit, almost one whole day together, and part of several days; the Lord showed me afterwards that the spirit I was then acted by, was in its operations void of true inward peace, laying the greatest stress on externals, neglecting the heart, full of impatience, pride, and arrogance; although, I thought, in the time of it, that 'twas the Spirit of God in an high degree. Awful indeed! My body, especially my leg, much disordered at the same time,* which Satan and my evil heart might make some handle of. And now may the Holy, Wise and Good God be pleased to guard and secure me against such errors for the future, and stop the progress of those, whether ministers or people, who have been corrupted by my word or example, in any of the above mentioned particulars; and if it be his holy will, bless this public recantation to this purpose. And oh! may He grant withal that such as, by reason of the aforesaid errors and misconduct, have entertained unhappy prejudices against Christianity in general, or the late glorious work of God in particular, may, by this account, learn to distinguish the appendage from the substance or essence,—that which is vile and odious from that which is precious, glorious and Divine, and thus be entirely and happily freed from all those prejudices referred to; and this in infinite mercy through Jesus Christ. And to

---

* I had the long fever on me, and the cankry humour raging at once. [Davenport's footnote]

---

these requests, may all God's children, whether ministers or others, say Amen.

J. Davenport.

37

The General Assembly Repeals the Toleration Act

May 1743

This Assembly observing the growing difficulties in this Colony through the misunderstanding of the law entituled An Act for the ease of such as soberly dissent from the way of worship and ministry established by the laws of this government, made in favour of such as do soberly dissent from the way of worship and ministry established in this Colony: And notwithstanding this Assembly have resolved, that those commonly called Presbyterians or Congregationalists should not take benefit by said law: yet some of the parishes established by the laws of this Colony, through the said misunderstanding, have been greatly damnified, and by indirect means divided and parted, without any sufficient reason for the same; for that those which have gone from such parishes were of the same opinion with such as could not take benefit by said law: Which mischief to prevent,

Be it enacted by the Governor, Council and Representatives, in General Court assembled, and by the authority of the same, That the said law, entituled An Act for the ease of such as do soberly dissent, &c., shall be repealed and made void, and the same is hereby repealed and made void.

Charles J. Hoadly (ed.), *Public Records of Connecticut,* Vol. VIII, pp. 521–522.

And be it further enacted, That, for the future, that if any of his Majesty's good subjects, being protestants, inhabitants of this Colony, that shall soberly dissent from the way of worship and ministry established by the laws of this Colony, that such [180] persons may apply themselves to this Assembly for relief, where they shall be heard. And such persons as have any distinguishing character, by which they may be known from the presbyterians or congregationalists, and from the consociated churches established by the laws of this Colony, may expect the indulgence of this Assembly, having first before this Assembly taken the oaths and subscribed the declaration provided in the Act of Parliament in cases of the like nature.

38

The General Assembly
Strengthens the Anti-Itineracy Act

October 1743

An Act in Addition to one Law of this Colony entituled An Act for regulating Abuses and correcting Disorders in Ecclesiastical Affairs.

Whereas in the last paragraph of said act it is provided and enacted, 'that if any foreigner or stranger, that is not an inhabitant in this Colony, including as well such persons that have no ecclesiastical character or lycence to preach as such as have received ordination or lycence to preach by any association or presbytery, shall presume to preach, teach or publickly to exhort, in any town or society within this Colony, without the desire and lycence of the settled minister and

Charles J. Hoadly (ed.), *Public Records of Connecticut,* Vol. VIII, pp. 569–570.

the major part of the church of such town or society, or at the call and desire of the church and inhabitants of such town or society, provided that it so happen that there is no settled minister there, that every such preacher, teacher or exhorter, shall be sent (as a vagrant person) by warrant from any one assistant or justice of the peace, from constable to constable out of the bounds of this Colony:' And it being found by experience that, for want of further provision, the good ends proposed are defeated; and some persons that, pursuant to the aforesaid law, have been taken and carried out of the bounds of this Colony, have immediately returned again, and by preaching and exhorting as aforesaid have greatly disquieted and disturbed the people: Which for the future to prevent,

Be it enacted by the Governor, Council and Representatives, in General Court assembled, and by the authority of the same, That when it shall so happen that any person that is a foreigner or stranger, and not an inhabitant in this Colony, shall at any time after he has been, by order of authority as aforesaid, transported out of the bounds of this Colony, return into the same again, and shall in any town or society in this Colony preach, teach or exhort, contrary to the true intent and meaning of the aforesaid law, it shall be the duty of any one assistant or justice of the peace, that shall be informed thereof, to cause such person to be apprehended and brought before him, and if he shall be found guilty, to give judgment that such person shall become bound in the penal sum of one hundred pounds lawful money, to his peaceable and good behaviour until the next county court in the county where the offence shall be committed, and that such person will not offend again in like manner; and also, that such offender shall pay down the cost of his transportation. And the county court may, if they see cause, further bind such offender to his peaceable and good behaviour during the pleasure of said court.

39

Benjamin Colman to Governor Law

Boston, January 21, 1745

[May it Please your Honour]

My last Letters from London, from Dr Avery & Dr Watts, oblige me to do myself ye Honour to write to you, on ye unhappy affair of Mr. Winthrops Debt to ye late Revd & learned Dr Hunt of London, with whom I sometimes held Correspondence by Letters while he lived, & am ye more bound now to serve ye Sorrowful Widow & her Children wherein I am able.

I am equally bound, it is true, & truly inclined, not to disserve ye worthy & desolate Mrs Winthrop & her children, who are in my Eye & Heart more than bereaved; and from my Heart I wish 'em all ye just Regards from your Honour & ye Government that can possibly be rendered 'em.

But how hard is ye Case in this crooked World, when between Persons & Families equally hond & beloved by us, we cannot be just to One without bearing hard upon ye other.

Having two Copies of ye Case sent me, I forward one of them to your Honour, tho' I am satisfied you have it already from Dr Avery.

He writes me, that he hopes your Honour will take kindly from Him, & from ye Committee of ye Dissenters, what he has wrote you in their Name respecting ye Law about Itinerant Preachers: he indeed

Connecticut Historical Society, *Collections,* XI (1907) [The Law Papers], pp. 250–251.

trembled (he sayes) for your Charter. I hear there were some lately in Prison near Lebanon, glorying in their Sufferings, & preaching daily to those yt will come to hear 'em, moving their Compassions. I hope God will graciously direct ye Government in this matter, & preserve you both in State & Church, in Civil and Religious Order, Rights & Priveledges.

I beg ye Favour of your Honour to salute from me the Honble Lt Governour Wolcot, & let him know that ye Pacquet I received from him about (or something more than) a Year agoe got safe to ye Hand of your worthy Agent Mr Palmer, one of my Friends to whom I directed it being dead before it arrived; & he has wrote me that he that have ye Advantage therefrom to know how to act & answer, in Case any thing be moved by Mr Mason, before he receive his particular Directions or Order from your Government.

Sir, that your Life may be prolonged for ye Service of your Colony in State & Church, & also Mr Wolcots; & having served your Generation by ye Will of God, your Sleep may be sweet in Jesus, is ye Prayer of Him who under ye Infirmities of Age asks your Prayers for him, & is

Your Honours
most Obedt Humble Servt

Benjamin Colman

Study Questions

---

1. On the basis of the various laws and resolutions included in the section, how successful do you judge the Connecticut authorities to have been in dampening the revival? Does the direction of their energies change between 1742 and 1744?

2. Do you think that the ministerial associations, the General Assembly, and other Old Light groups and individuals comprehend what is really going on in their society? What do you think is their understanding of these events?

3. To what extent do the "excesses" of the revival stem from the presence of unsettled or disturbed individuals? How convincing is Davenport's own analysis (in his "recantation") of his earlier activities?

SEVEN

Two Commencements, September 1743–September 1744

Among those who came to New Haven for the 1743 commencement was an ex-student whom Thomas Clap could not have been happy to see: this was David Brainerd, who had been licensed as a regular minister by the Fairfield County East Association several months after his expulsion from Yale. (The Fairfield County East Association was the one county organization in Connecticut that was firmly New Light in membership and policy—as early as 1740 it had tried to recruit George Whitefield—and during 1741 and 1742 it issued ministerial licenses to a whole series of young candidates who would probably have been turned away anywhere else in the colony.) Brainerd's diary account of his visit [#40] records his attempted rapprochement with the college administration.

Another individual whose relationship with Clap had been less than warm was Eleazar Wheelock, the New Light minister from Lebanon (see #29–30). He too had a request to make of the Yale rector—in reference to his stepson John Maltby, who was about to enter the College as a freshman [#41]. Clap replied to Wheelock's letter some two months later, in November 1743 [#42].

At commencement the following September (1744), one of the speeches—the first Yale commencement address to be printed since Edwards' "Distinguishing Marks"—was delivered by a tutor at the College named Chauncy Whittelsey (1717–1787), the very man whom David Brainerd had insulted three years before in the offhand remark that led to his expulsion. Whittelsey's address, "The True Notion of a Faithful Improvement of our Talents" [#43], was hardly designed to appeal to the New Light sensibility. (A short time later, as it turned out, Whittelsey left both the College and the ministry in order to go into business. After gaining a sufficient fortune through the faithful improvement of his *own* talents, Whittelsey at length returned to the ministry and ended his days, appropriately enough, as Joseph Noyes's successor in the pulpit of the New Haven church.)

By the early fall of 1744, the impact of the Great Awakening on Yale College seems to have subsided measurably. The only public hint of continuing concern for the stability of the campus appears in the vote of the college trustees prescribing a maximum age limit for entering freshmen [#44]. And even this vote might have been construed to refer to problems of an earlier day: for both David Brainerd and Samuel Buell (another former student—B.A. 1741—whose irregular ordination by the Fairfield County East Association had provoked something of a scandal) were over the new age limit when they first entered the College.

40

David Brainerd Visits New Haven

September 1743

Tuesday, Sept. 13. Rode to New-Haven. Was sometimes dejected; not in the sweetest Frame. Lodged at ——. Had some profitable Christian Conversation, &c.—I find, tho' my inward Trials are great, and a Life of Solitude gives 'em greater Advantage to settle and penetrate to the very inmost Recesses of the Soul; yet 'tis better to be alone, than incumber'd with Noise and Tumult. I find it very difficult maintaining any Sense of divine Things, while removing from

Jonathan Edwards (ed.), *Life of Brainerd,* pp. 80–83.

Place to Place, diverted with new Objects, and fill'd with Care and Business. A settled steady Business is best adapted to a Life of strict Religion.

Wednesday, Sept. 14. This Day I ought to have taken my Degree;[1] but God sees fit to deny it me. And tho' I was greatly afraid of being overwhelmed with Perplexity and Confusion, when I should see my Class-Mates take theirs; yet, in the very Season of it, God enabled me with Calmness and Resignation to say, The Will of the Lord be done. Indeed, thro' divine Goodness, I have scarcely felt my Mind so calm, sedate, and comfortable for some Time. I have long fear'd his Season, and expected my Humility, Meekness, Patience and Resignation would be much tried [2]: But found much more Pleasure and divine Comfort, than I expected.—Felt spiritually Serious, tender and Affectionate in private prayer with a dear Christian Friend to Day.

Thursday, Sept. 15. Had some Satisfaction in hearing the Ministers discourse &c. 'Tis always a Comfort to me, to hear religious and spiritual Discourse. O that Ministers and People were more spiritual and devoted to God.—Towards Night, with the Advice of Christian Friends, I offered the following Reflections in Writing, to the Rector and Trustees of the College (which are for Substance the same that I had freely offered to the Rector before, and intreated him to accept) and this I did that if possible I might cut off all Occasion of Stumbling and Offence, from those that seek Occasion. What I offered, is as follows.

Whereas I have said before several Persons, concerning Mr. Whittelsey, one of the Tutors of Yale College, that I did not believe he had any more Grace, than the Chair I then lean'd upon; I humbly confess, that herein I have sin'd against God, and acted contrary to the Rules of his Word, and have injured Mr. Whittelsey. I had no Right to make thus free with his Character; and had no just Reason to say as I did concerning him. My fault herein was the more Aggravated, in that I said this concerning One that was so much my

---

[1] This being *Commencement* Day. [Jonathan Edwards' note]

[2] His Trial was the greater, in that, had it not been for the Displeasure of the Governours of the College, he would not only on that Day have shared with his Class-Mates in the publick Honours which they then received, but would on that Occasion have appeared at the Head of that Class; which, if he had been with them, would have been the most numerous of any that ever had been graduated at that College.—[Jonathan Edwards' note]

Superiour, and one that I was obliged to treat with special Respect and Honour, by Reason of the Relation I stood in to him in the College. Such a Manner of Behaviour, I confess, did not become a Christian; it was taking too much upon me, and did not favour of that humble Respect, that I ought to have expres'd towards Mr. Whittelsey. I have long since been convinced of the Falseness of those *Apprehensions,* by which I then justified such a Conduct. I have often reflected on the Act with Grief; I hope, on Account of the Sin of it. And am willing to lie low, and be abased before God and Man for it. And humbly ask the Forgiveness of the Governors of the College, and of the whole Society; but of Mr. Whittelsey in particular. And whereas I have been accused by one Person of saying concerning the Rev. Rector of Yale-College that *I wondered he did not expect to drop down dead for fining the Scholars that followed Mr. Tennent to Milford;* I seriously profess, that I don't remember my saying any Thing to that Purpose. But if I did, which I am not certain I did not, I utterly *condemn* it, and *detest* all such Kind of Behaviour; and especially in an Undergraduate towards the Rector. And I now appear, to judge and condemn my self for going once to the separate Meeting in New-Haven, a little before I was expell'd, tho' the Rector had refused to give me Leave. For this I humbly ask the Rector's Forgiveness. And whether the Governours of the College shall ever see Cause to remove the Academical Censure I lie under, or no, or to admit me to the Priviledges I desire; yet I am willing to appear, if they think fit, openly to own, and to humble my self for those Things I have herein confess'd.

God has made me willing to do any Thing, that I can do, consistent with Truth, for the Sake of Peace, and that I might not be a Stumbling-block and Offence to others. For this Reason I can cheerfully forego, and give up what I verily believe, after the most mature and impartial Search, is my Right, in some Instances. God has given me that Disposition, that if this were the Case, that a Man has done me an *hundred Injuries,* and I (tho' ever so much provoked to it) have done Him one, I feel disposed, and heartily willing humbly to confess my Fault to him, and on my Knees to ask Forgiveness of him; tho' at the same Time he should justify himself in all the Injuries as he has done me, and should only make Use of my humble Confession to blacken my Character the more, and represent me as the only Person guilty, &c. Yea, tho' he should as it were insult me, and say, He knew all this before, and that I was making work for Repentance, &c. Tho' what I said concerning Mr. Whittelsey was only spoken in private, to a Friend or two; and being partly overheard, was related to the Rector, and by him extorted from my Friends; yet, seeing it was divulged and made publick, I was willing to confess my Fault therein publickly.—But I trust, God will plead my Cause.[3]

---

[3] I was witness to the very Christian Spirit Mr. Brainerd shew'd at that Time, being then at New-Haven, and being One that he saw fit to consult on that Occasion. (This was the first Time that ever I had Opportunity of personal Acquaintance with him.) There truly appear'd in him a great Degree of Calmness and Humility; without the least Appearance of Rising of Spirit for any ill Treatment he supposed he had suffered, or the least Backwardness to abase himself before Them who he thought had wrong'd him. What he did was without any Objection or Appearance of Reluctance, even in private to his Friends, that he freely open'd himself to. Earnest Application was made on his Behalf to the Authority of the College, that he might have his Degree then given him; and particularly by the Rev. Mr. Burr, of Newark, one of the Correspondents of the Hon. Society in Scotland; He being sent from New-Jersey to New-Haven, by the rest of the Commissioners, for that End; and many Arguments were used; but without Success. Indeed the Governours of the College were so far satisfied with the Reflections Mr. Brainerd had made on himself, that they appeared willing to admit him again into College; but not to give him his Degree, 'till he should have remain'd there, at least a Twelve-Month, which being contrary to what the Correspondents, to whom he was now engaged, had declared to be their Mind, he did not consent to it. He desired his Degree, as he thought it would tend to his being more extensively useful; but still when he was deny'd it, he manifested no Disappointment or Resentment. [Jonathan Edwards' note]

41

Eleazar Wheelock to Thomas Clap

September 1743

Revd. Sr:

I have herewith sent my Son whom I Committ to your Care under God. I believe you will find him (& ye young man, viz. Clark, who Comes with him) Studious, Sober, peacible, and orderly. It is with no small concern yt I send him, Chiefly on Religious Accounts, being credibly informed of ye prevalency of Arminian Principles in College, which, I know, exceeding well suit with ye pride & Corruptions of ye Carnal Mind. And also I cant but think your principles & practise in some respects Contrary to the Natural Rights and Liberties of all man-kind, and especially to what has been boasted as one of ye Glories of our Colleges, yt they breath a Catholick air. You know, Sr, yt my principles are Catholick & yt I hate Every thing in Religion yt has the Least Shew or appearance of Tyranny or opression, & therefore will pardon me in writing as I do. I have a Great Desire yt these young men shod have ye Liberty of hearing Such Ministers of Christ as they Desire to hear when they have Convenient Opportunities for it, but when I Consider how fruitless the request has been when made by others who have more interest in yourself than I have, my hopes are Cutt off at once.

After I saw you I had some Encouragement of their Boarding att Mr. Cooke's. If yt shod fail, you may remember I spoke to you

From the original in the Dartmouth College Manuscripts, Dartmouth College.

for ye South Garrett. I Earnestly Desire they may Live together. & if they shod Live in College, may I begg one favour of you, viz., yt my Son may be Waiter in ye Hall. It may be of advantage to me, & I think yt my poverty demands it if that be ye Rule (as I suppose it is) yt you go by in that matter. My outward Circumstances are very Strait and Difficult by reason of a very Numerous and Chargable family, and also, you know, I am Deprived of my Living, at Least of ye Benefit of a Law to Secure it to me (with how much Justice & Righteousness ye world will See another Day) Whereby I have Suffered much allready & am Like to Suffer More as Religion Declines) *NB* among us. My son has been very infirm & can bear but little hardship. I don't know but he will need to Ride sometimes; if his State of health shod Require it, I begg ye favour of you yt he may have ye Liberty: Rev. Sr, I heartily wish your prosperity & ye presence of God with you in your important Concerns. & tho we have the unhapiness to think Differently in Some things, yet I am, Rev. Sr,

Your assured Friend & very Humble Servt

Eleazr Wheelock

P.S. I have seen a Copy of Mr. Eliot's Lettr to you & yours to him; and as to one Clause in this, viz., Respecting my advising you not to go to College, it is an Absolute ———. I never said so nor thought so, but [rather] the contrary, and always manifested to you yt I thought it your duty to go, & I have appeald to ye whole assocn who have judgd yt Mr. Eliot was wrong in yt matter.

Yrs, E.W.

P.P.S. I presume, Revd. Sr., it will be gratefull to you to hear of ye Religious Affairs of this part of ye Country, & for yt purpose I shall improve this vacant minute. Things in general in these parts are much more Calm & Settled. Those who have been ye Subjects of ye Late Work generally grow in prudence, and I hope in acquaintance with their own hearts. Ye body of ye people in these Eastern towns where the work has prevaild seem satisfied more than they were yt it is indeed a glorious work of Divine Grace. A Spirit of Conviction seems to be allmost wholly gone. Some seem to be Settled Down in Security, yet ye Reformation remaining is very great. & that *Dreadfull* Religion which consists so much in fire, Bitterness, & Censoriousness, I think is Dying, and People seem generally convinc'd yt it is not true Religion. Tho' we have never had it among us, it has been in some other

---

places. When I look back upon my own conduct in ye Late Season, I can see many Steps which it seems I cod mend had I ye opportunity again; and I Desire ever to be humbled for whatever I have done to prejudice others against ye truth. I am weary of Controversies and Disputes. I long (I think) for ye peace of Jerusalem.

42

Thomas Clap to Eleazar Wheelock

New Haven, November 17, 1743

For the Revd. Mr. Eleazar Wheelock of Lebanon
Revd. Sir,
    I received your Letter with your Son. He and Clark chose to live in the Chamber you had bespoke for them. I should have been willing to have gratified you in making your son Waiter, but I had promised it before. I have not heard anything of his being weakly since he came. I gave him Liberty once to ride to see his uncle. He and the rest of the Scholars carry themselves very well for ought I know. Thro the generosity of the Assembly we are able to maintain a third Tutor so that the Freshmen have a Tutor to themselves, which will be a great advantage. The College seems at present to be upon most accounts under very good Circumstances. None of the Scholars that I know of any way Interest themselves in the Differences at New Haven, and I hear no Disputes about any thing. Mr. *Cooke*'s, Mr. *Graham*'s and Mr. *Mills*'s son, etc., came to our communion. *Tuttle, Allen* and *Tallmadge* have given public Satisfaction for breaking off from Mr. *Noyes* and his Church and have by them been Received and Restored. I hope your Information about the spreading of

From the original in the Boston Public Library.

Arminian Principles in College is in a great measure, if not wholly, Groundless. You gave me a hint, which you desired should be kept private, that Mr. Tutor Whittelsey had asserted some Arminian Principles to Mr. White of Windham, and since the Commencement I understand that there has been a great noise and Clamour about it in the Country. Whereupon I examined Mr. Birdsell [?] and Sr. Ingersoll, who were present at the Dispute, and both say they heard no such thing as is Reported. I also examined Mr. Whittelsey and he says that the principles which he always holds and professes are: that it is not Just so suppose that God should require of any man to do what wasn't in his power in his Primitive State; but that it is Just to Require it now in his fallen State, because the man has Sinned away his Power, yet he cannot Sin away his duty. If Mr. White had supposed that Mr. Whittelsey had held any Corrupt Principles, he should have informed me of it at his House or at my House at the Commencement, where we had 2 or three hours Discourse about various things but heard nothing of that; and I having at that time heard nothing of it but that private hint from you, I did not think to say anything to him. Now to make a noise and Clamour about the Country that the Instructors of the College are Corrupt in their Principles, and to say nothing of the Rector or Trustees does not seem to me to be fair and Christian treatment of the College or the officers of it. But it seems to be part of that persecution which we are to expect, to suffer for the Cause of Christ. Indeed, as I told you in your Parish, I had always been concerned lest Arminianism should prevail in the Country; and was now more concerned than ever, for these 2 reasons: 1, because so many had run into a Tincture of the other Extreme of Antinomianism; 2, because those who had done so had charged almost all the rest with Arminianism—even those who had the most Established Character for Calvinists. Witness: Mr. *Croswell, Allen, Symmes,* etc., against Mr. *Dickinson* & the Boston ministers. This has brought Arminianism into a sort of Credit, having the better Company on that Side. And if a man be really an Arminian, he lies under no greater Imputation than the most Steady Calvinist. I believe the best way to suppress Arminianism is to be Slow in Charging, but sure in proving of it against any particular persons.

I am, Sir,

Your humble Servant,

Thomas Clap

I hope you will excuse my haste.

43

Chauncy Whittelsey:
A Faithful Improvement of our Talents

September 9, 1744

To The Young Gentlemen
Graduated Batchelors of Arts
at Yale-College, Sept. 12th, 1744

The following Lines were penn'd with a peculiar Eye to your Instruction and Benefit; and what-ever Reception they may meet with from Mankind (whose Candour I crave) *I securely trust them with You, being perswaded that You will peruse them with delight, as they were composed by your hearty Friend, under the Influence of an upright desire to know and speak the Truth. I recommend them to you as an honest Token of my real concern for your Usefulness and final Happiness: And as they are now made publick at your Request and Charge, they are therefore justly inscribed and presented to you,*
By your Affectionate and Faithful
Friend and Tutor,
Chauncey Whittelsey.

Chauncy Whittelsey, *A Sermon Preach'd at New-Haven on the Sabbath Preceeding the Public Commencement, Sept. 9th, Anno Dom. 1744. Wherein Is Considered the True Notion of a Faithful Improvement of Our Talents, and the Wisdom of Being Early and Constant Therein* (New London, 1744).

To The Class Graduated Anno Domini, 1744

Occasioned by the Sermon preached upon the Sabbath before their Commencement, by their Excellent Tutor the Ingenious Mr. Chauncey Whittelsey.

If you would be what this Discourse design'd,
Some great Example always keep in Mind;
The Force of Reason may command Assent,
But living Vertue gives a President;
How all it's sacred Rules in Practice shine,
And speaks the Pattern and themselves divine:
That gains the Understanding to approve;
This courts the Will with all the Charms of Love,
The *Author* then before you always place,
And when you read his Precepts, view his Face
In them you're only told how to be great,
In him you plainly see that happy state:
Strain ev'ry Nerve, on ev'ry Feature gaze;
The more you imitate, the more you praise:
If near the bright Example you arrive,
Your Names with his shall mouldring Time survive;
From Age to Age with great Applause be past
As long as *English, Greek* or *Latin* last.
Thus Virgil ey'd the *Grecian* Bard divine,
And aim'd at *Homer*'s strength in ev'ry Line:
He very near the noble Copy came,
And rais'd his own, on his great Master's Fame.

         J. Hubbard Esqr.

The Nature and Wisdom
of a Faithful Improvement of Our Talents

Matthew XXV. 29.
For unto every One that hath shall be given, and he shall have
abundance.

These are the words of Jesus Christ our great Teacher, Lord and
Saviour; the Discourse He is here upon is the parable of the Talents,
by which is represented to us in a lively manner the Obligation we
lye under, as Moral Agents, honestly and faithfully to improve the
Powers and Advantages we severally enjoy: And as this will be my
chief aim in the ensuing Discourse, it will not be an improper Digres-
sion from my main Subject, to give a general & plain Exposition of
the whole Parable; in doing which I will give the Story in brief and
in my own Language, with the Spirit, the Application of it, desiring
each one for himself to regard the text as I go along.

The Parable begins at the 14th Verse of this Chapter, and is
introduced to illustrate and enforce the Exhortation offer'd in the
verse preceeding V. 13th, *Watch ye therefore, for ye know not the*
Day nor the Hour in which the Son of man cometh. As tho' he had
said, Since you are wholly uncertain when the Bridegroom, the great
Head of the Church and Judge of the World will come and call you
to an account, therefore stand ye prepared *continually,* be *always*
vigilant and industrious in the Service assign'd you in the World.
Then follows the Parable, *For the Kingdom of Heaven is as a Man*
travelling, &c. Or (as in the Original, Osper gar Anthrōpos Apodē-
mōn,) *It is as a Man travelling, &c.* As tho' he had said, The Matter
I am upon, the Reasonableness and Importance of this Exhortation,
may be aptly represented by this Similitude. *A Man being* about to
travel into some distant Country, call'd together his Servants, and
distributed his estate among them, to be taken care of and improv'd
by them in his absence: but he divides his Goods among them, *not*
equally, but for wise Reasons he committed to one a much greater
portion of his Estate than to another; to one he gave five Talents, to
another two, to another one. Having thus wisely setled his business
at home, he set out on his Journey. Thus God deals with Mankind.

The Heathen World in general, he left to the Guidance of their own rational Powers, and the small assistance of some obscure Traditions; The Jewish Nation he favour'd more highly; to them at sundry times and in divers manners he spake and made known his Will by the Prophets: But in these last days he hath spoken unto us still *more fully* and *clearly* by his Son. So likewise among particular Men in the same Age and under the same Dispensation, some are favour'd with richer Advantages to know and more and stronger Motives to practice, the Will of God, than others.

The Similitude goes on, V. 16th, Those Servants with whom the Master had intrusted his Estate behav'd very differently in their Lord's absence: Some, by their honest Industry, made those Improvements which were reasonably to be expected; whil'st others carelessly neglected, or ungratefully misimprov'd their Lord's Money; He that had receiv'd five Talents gain'd other five, but he that had receiv'd one went and hid it in the Earth.—Thus Mankind act toward God, the great Landlord of the World: Some, like rational Beings set themselves diligently to Study the Will of their Maker, and faithfully to improve the Powers they are endow'd with, and the advantages of every kind that they enjoy, for gaining useful Knowledge, cultivating vertuous Habits, and doing good in their day: while others spend their time in Idleness, or consume their Strength in Vanity and Wickedness.

To proceed, V. 19th, After a while the Lord of those Servants returns home, and calls them all to an account for their Conduct and the Improvement they had severally made of that Portion of his Estate which he had betrusted them with; accordingly they all appear before him, and now their Reception with their Lord is as different as their Conduct was in the Improvement of his Money: They that had wisely and industriously applied themselves to their Lord's Service, were accepted, commended and rewarded: But they that had been foolishly negligent; and had unjustly misimprov'd their Time and Talents, were frowned upon, condemned and punished.— And thus God the great Lord and Judge of the World, will deal with Men: They, who have thankfully received and wisely improv'd the Gifts of Heaven, for the advancing the noble Designs of divine Goodness, who have honestly sought after and conscientiously practised the righteous Will of God, they will be accepted with approbation & applause, and honourably rewarded; each one in a Just Proportion to his particular Improvements: On the other hand the Wicked and the Slothful will be cloathed with shame, publickly condemned and deservedly punished.—This is the Substance of the Parable, with the true Meaning the Application thereof. . . .

That our Talents (at least many of them) will be increas'd by a faithful Improvement of what we have, is indisputably evident *from Experience and Observation.* That the Influence of Custom is exceeding great, every one will be irresistably convinc'd, who critically observes himself or his fellow Men. An Action, which at first was not to be perform'd, but with much difficulty and Labour, by Custom, or a frequent Repetition, becomes easie and delightsom, that is, the Power we have to do the same Action or Actions of the same Kind, our natural Powers, by a repeated successful exercise, are increas'd, or exercised with more ease and success, and that many times in a great and unaccountable manner, when the Attempts, the Efforts in the exercise of them are frequent and vigorous; or, as applied to the present Case, thus, *the rational Study and industrious Practice of Vertue, will render it easie and delightsom,* and a Man will thereby be enabled to proceed, to make Progress therein, to still greater and greater Degrees of Perfection.—Agreeable hereto has been the Observation of the Wisest Men, and best Writers upon humane Nature in all Ages; accordingly this is one of the Precepts which Pythagoras is said to have deliver'd to his Disciples, *Optimum vitae Genus eligito et Consuetudo faciet jucundissimum,* choose that Course of Life, which is most excellent, and Custom will render it the most delightful. Yea, Mankind have so generally made this Observation, that it has obtain'd as a common Proverb, that *Use is a second Nature,* which is not more vulgar than true; the Meaning of which I take to be this, that an Action by being frequently practis'd, becomes as familiar and easie, as if we were prompted therto by some natural Biass or Inclination of Mind.

And as our natural Powers do thus grow stronger by proper exercise, so our Advantages of gaining Knowlege and practising Vertue, are naturally inlarg'd by a faithful Improvement. This is evident thus; what ever Knowlege we obtain by an honest and faithful Improvement of the Advantages, we now enjoy, may it self be made Use of, as a proper Means to gain still further Knowlege; and as our Knowlege is increas'd, so our Obligations, our Motives to the Practice of that, which is right, are also increas'd; And the Considerations, the Motives, by which we are excited to the Practice of our Duty are won't to have continually more Weight and Influence upon the Mind, by being seriously meditated and diligently practis'd upon. This I will attempt to make more obvious by an Instance;—The

Revelation of the Gospel is a great Advantage we enjoy: Now, by honestly studying the more plain and intelligible Parts of this Revelation, we gain that Knowlege, which may be it self a great Advantage to us, whereby to understand the more obscure and difficult Parts and Passages of it; and the better we understand the Gospel, the more shall we become acquainted with the Inducements, that are therein set before us, to the Practice of Religion; and the more we ponder upon those Inducements, upon the Blessings held forth in the Promises of the Gospel, the more valuable are they won't to appear; and the more necessary to make us truly happy, and so they will have the greater Influence on our Minds. Thus it is evident *from Experience and Observation* that our Talents will be (*such is the Nature of the Humane Soul*) increas'd by a faithful Improvement. . . .

Hence we see the great Wisdom of being early and in earnest in improving the Talents that we are severally betrusted with. He that begins soon, who sets out upon this Business in the Morning of his Days, in the Bloom of Life, and applies himself hereto with Vigour and unwearied Industry, he will flourish like *the Palm Tree* and grow like the *Cedar in Lebanon.* And are not the Thoughts of advancing the *Dignity* and *Perfection* of our Natures, of rising into a more exalted Sphere among Intelligences; are not the Hopes of becoming more nearly allied to the Superiour Spirits of the Angelical World, are not these sufficient to fire our Breasts with a holy *Ambition,* to animate our Zeal, to strengthen our *Resolutions,* that we will make this the *incessant* Pursuit of our Lives?

But they who are in their youthful Days, are more especially regarded in this Inference; the Exhortation therefrom speaketh as unto Children, to those who are in the *Spring of Life:* to them therefore I will offer a few thoughts, chiefly such as are suggested by the preceeding Discourse; the which as they may be profitable to all, so I recommend them particularly to the Consideration of those *Youth of this Assembly,* who enjoy peculiar Advantages for gaining useful Knowlege, and whose Good I am bound, by the Station in which Providence hath plac'd me, especially to consult. Wherefore that you may be fully, even *practically* convinc'd that it is a point of the *highest Wisdom* for you to be early and *in earnest* in improving the Talents you are betrusted with, Consider,

1. Hereby you will keep out *vicious Habits,* which will otherwise take Possession and quickly get *deep rooted* in the Soul. The Mind of Man is like a Garden; the which, unless it be prudently taken Care of, and steadily manur'd will be soon overrun with Weeds, with

Briars and Thorns; which when once they have got the Possession, can hardly be rooted out again, the which notwithstanding must be effected before the Ground will yield any profitable Increase. So the Minds of Men, unless they are prudently and diligently taken care of, unless they *early* and *in earnest apply* themselves to the Improvement of their Talents, to the right use of their Powers, they will quickly become *habituated* to do evil. Those that are indolent and vicious will naturally and by the strange Influence of Custom wax *worse and worse:* to them, the gaining of true Knowlege and the Practice of Vertue and the Exercise of real Piety, will become *more and more* difficult; this will be the natural and *sure* Consequence of their Negligence and Wickedness. By neglecting Study & Labour, honest Enquiries after their Duty & manly Efforts in doing it, Men become *more and more* averse thereto. Errors, being entertain'd for truths without a through Examination, Prejudices being long indulg'd become *deep-rooted* and have such a *Sovereign Command* in the Soul, that it is almost impossible to get freed from them, or to escape their destructive Influence. Rational Resolutions having been repeatedly drawn up, and as repeatedly violated, at length become weak and insignificant; and the Man, like the door on its Hinges, is easily mov'd backwards and forwards; tho' he frequently makes some Efforts toward a Reformation, yet, *Unhappy!* they are so languid and faint that they prove *wholly ineffectual.* Again, The Passions, by unreasonable Compliances gain Strength *mightily,* and become Lordly and uncontroulable, demanding and obtaining of the Man a quick Obedience to their *Sovereign* Dictates. And for *such a one* to learn to do well is like the *Ethiopian's changing his Skin and the Leopard his Spots. Unhappy Man,* who, when ever his Eyes shall be open'd by Serious Consideration, will weep over himself and with an aking heart cry out and say, Oh! *that I had known in my Day the things of my Peace!* For to free the Mind from Prejudices, that have been *long* receiv'd, to mortify vicious Inclinations, which have grown *strong* by Custom, and to subdue *old* Habits, that are become *stubborn* and *deep rooted* in the Soul, this is like *cutting off a right hand, and plucking out a right Eye;* 'tis like tearing the Flesh from the Bones, and is not to be effected, but by *great* pains and Sorrow, by repeated *severe* Resolutions, and with the *utmost* Difficulty. Is is not then *desirable,* is it not a point of *great Wisdom* for *you* to avoid this unhappy Condition by being *early and in good earnest* in improving the Talents, which you are severally betrusted with? Consider,

2. Hereby you will *engage the divine Favour and Blessing* with you in all your Ways, and have *just* Reason quietly to confide in the Providence of God for a *sufficient Supply* of the Good things of this Life. This is clearly evident and may be justly concluded from the moral Perfections of God, his Regard to Vertue, his Approbation and Care of them, *that walk uprightly before him,* who make it their daily Business to *serve God and their Generation faithfully.* There are also in the Word of God many Passages express to this Purpose; even too many to be enumerated here; *I have been Young,* says the Psalmist, *and now am old, yet have I not seen the Righteous forsaken, or his Seed begging Bread,* Psal. XXXVII. 25. Agreeably our Saviour says to his Disciples, Mat. VI, 31, &c. *Therefore take no thought,* that is, be not anxiously concerned, saying, *what shall we eat or what shall we drink, or wherewith shall we be cloathed,—For your Heavenly Father knoweth that you have need of these things. But seek ye first the Kingdom of God, and his Righteousness and all these things shall be added unto you,* that is, as far as God in his Wisdom shall see to be best. And verily this is an *inestimable* Blessing: what every wise considerate Soul would esteem the *riches,* the *best* Portion, that *could* fall to his Lot in the World. What more valuable Inheritance could any one wish *for himself,* or his *dearest Friend;* yea what better could a *tender Father* crave for his *only Son,* than this, that he be always under the *fatherly Care and Protection of Almighty God;* that he have his Portion dealt out to him by *infinite Wisdom and Goodness* engag'd for his good, so that he have just reason to think that even when he is afflicted, God *All-wise* does hereby but chasten him, as *a Father a Son in whom he delighteth,* for *his* Profit, that he may be made Partaker of his Holiness; this is indeed the most happy state of Existence, that Earth can boast, than which as to this Life no Mortal can frame a higher Wish. Surely then, I may recommend it to you as a point of the *greatest Wisdom,* that you apply your selves *early and in earnest* to the Improvement of the Talents committed to your Care. Especially if you consider also,

3. By this means *you will be useful* in the World. This is evident from the Nature of a faithful Improvement of our Talents, as before explain'd. And what can be a more *agreeable Self-reflection* than this, to be conscious that we have been *designedly* the means of Happiness to our fellow Men? that we have *labouriously endeavour'd,* as we had Power and Opportunity, to alleviate their Sorrows and promote their Welfare? What Pleasure more *Heavenly and Godlike?*

What can afford a more solid and manly self-Approbation than, to be conscious, that we have in our Sphere of Action been imitating the *Fountain of Happiness,* who is *Good unto all, and whose tender Mercies are over all his Works,* and of whose Goodness we our selves have largely receiv'd. *Doubtless* this is such *Solid* Delight as renders it a Point of *true Wisdom* for you who are yet in the Morning of your Days to pursue it *diligently,* and accordingly to apply your selves *quickly* and *with Intenseness* to the faithful Improvement of the Talents, you are betrusted with. *I might add here,* that *this, your being thus useful in the World,* will be the most effectual Way to cause your Names to survive with Honour when you are dead; For it has been an ancient Observation, that how *injudiciously and partially* so ever the World treats Mens Characters, while they live, yet when their Bodies are mouldred to Dust, their Names are generally us'd with a *more just* and *equal* Regard to their *Deserts.* Such was the wise Observation of King Solomon, Prov. X 7. *The Memory of the Just is blessed; but the Name of the Wicked shall rot.* And this, tho' it be not the most weighty Consideration, yet is it *not below* the *lawful* desire of a *Wise Man,* or a *Saint.*

4. By the Improvement of your Talents you will stand *continually prepared for Death,* and while you live, will become *daily more and more ripe for Glory.* How ever your Names may be unjustly treated by Men, yet God, *the Father of your Spirits,* will assuredly deal with you *in Mercy* and *Faithfulness.* They who are diligently imployed in their Lord's Business; who are like a faithful Servant prudently waiting for his Master's Coming, they when ever they shall be seised by the King of Terrors, may calmly give up the Ghost, trusting safely in the Grace and Truth of God, who will not *take his loving Kindness from them, nor suffer his Faithfulness to fail.*

And as all, who are *thus faithful to the Death, shall receive a Crown of Life,* so each one will finally be advanced in Glory in Proportion as he had made Progress in Grace and excell'd in good Works: *He that gains ten Pounds, will be made Ruler over ten Cities.* They, who having been *early and in earnest* in improving their Talents, have brought forth much Fruit and been *singularly* Vertuous, they shall *shine as the Stars for ever and ever.* Since then these things are so, *what manner of Persons ought you to be?* Is it not a point of true Wisdom and of great Importance for you to apply your selves *immediately* and *diligently* to the Improvement of the Talents committed to your Care?

It now only remains that I conclude with a brief Address to those at whose desire and for whose Sake especially this Discourse was composed.

My Beloved Pupils, You have been (as I trust you are sensible) the Objects of my *daily Concern* for years past, while I have been endeavouring *in the Integrity of my Heart and with the Skilfulness of my Hands,* to season your Minds with useful Knowledge and to win your Hearts to the Love and Practice of Vertue: And now your Welfare here and hereafter; your Usefulness on Earth and Happiness in Heaven, I acknowlege, do justly claim a share in my fervent Wishes; Accordingly, it is among the Sincere and most ardent Desires of my Soul, that you may be Blessings in your Day, and Blessed for ever; The which will surely be your *happy Portion,* if you are but faithful in improving, what God, the Great Housholder, your Creator, and *Heavenly Father* has committed to your trust. Let me then direct you, yea let me *beseech* you to esteem and treat *this* as the great Work, the main, the proper Business of your Lives, to make *this* your constant Employ.

Let it be the honest Aim of your Minds, the Centre of all your Schemes, the Drift of all your Actions, to promote *the noble Designs of infinite Goodness,* to advance the Interests of solid Religion and the Good of Men.—And in pursuing these worthy Designs, take for your Guide that Rule, which your *All-wise* and *faithful Law-giver* has favour'd you with, the *Holy Scriptures; The Law of the Lord is perfect, converting the Soul; the Testimony of the Lord is pure, making wise the Simple; the Statutes of the Lord are right, rejoycing the Heart; the Commandment of the Lord is pure, enlightning the Eyes; the Fear of the Lord is clean, enduring for ever; the Judgments of the Lord are true and righteous altogether.—Take care* to act always upon Principles that are *intelligible and just;* examine carefully and *impartially* the Principles which you imbibe; their *Meaning* and *Evidence;* see that, *like Men,* you understand in what Sense and *why* you believe them; It can never be pleasing to God, it can't be becoming a rational Being, it can't be serviceable to true Religion, that we should believe we know not *what* or *why.*—In the Improvement of all your peculiar Privileges, be *prudent* as well as *industrious:* Such is the faithful Servant; he is one that is not only active, but also Considerate and Thoughtful how he may accomplish his Master's Business to the best advantage; so *here:* In this Business you will stand in need of Skill and Fore-Thought; here is Room for the profitable exercise of much *Prudence* and *Sagacity* wisely to pitch upon those Ways of living, to contrive those Methods of acting, to project and judiciously to Scan and perfect in the Mind those particular *Schemes,* which will be most serviceable to the great Ends of your Being.—And as you must be thus Prudent and Wise to do Good; so let me exhort and perswade you to be *very industrious;* this Matter both requires and deserves the greatest Diligence; *Incline your Ears unto Wisdom and apply your Heart to Understanding; yea, cry after Knowlege and lift up your Voice for Understanding; seek her as Silver, and search for her as for hid Treasure; for Happy is the Man that findeth Wisdom, and the Man that getteth Understanding; the Merchandise thereof is better than the Merchandise of Silver, and the Gain thereof than fine Gold; she is more precious than Rubies, and all the things you can desire are not to be compar'd unto her.*—And as you are but entering upon the active Part of Life, your Experience being yet but small, and your Passions lively and strong, you will find that you lie much expos'd to the *Violence of Temptations,* which will many times assault you on a sudden, at a time and in a manner you expected them not; be exhorted therefore to seek daily *Assistance from God,* and to accustom your selves to *frequent, serious* Meditation on the *great Motives* of the Gospel, that by this means you may cultivate that *strength* of Resolution and *steadfastness* of Mind, by which you may be habitually prepar'd for, and may successfully withstand your Enemies.—These thoughts, together with what was offer'd more generally in the preceeding Discourse, I, *in sincere Friendship* and concern for your Welfare, recommend to your *serious Consideration.* For if these things be in you, *they will cause that you be not barren or unfruitful;* Hereby you will become *Plants of Renown,* such as both God and Men will *delight to honour;* Hereby you will be *Blessings* to the Places, where you shall live, a *Credit* to your respective Families, a *Comfort,* a *Joy* to your Parents; and by this means you will *greatly rejoice my Heart,* even mine. Finally as You are about to take your leave of me and each other, however we shall be separated in Life or at Death, let this, whil'st we live be our steady Purpose and Conscientious endeavour: *to serve God and our Generation faithfully in our respective Places,* then shall we meet together again beyond the Grave, and rejoice together in each others Friendship and in Glory everlasting, *which God of his infinite Mercy grant through Jesus Christ our Lord,* Amen.

44

Proceedings of the Yale Trustees

September 12, 1744

Att a meeting of Trustees of Yale College in New haven Sep 12th 1744

Then Present

	Tho Clap Rectr
	Jared Eliot
	Samll Cooke
The Revd Messrs	Samll Whittlsey
	Josph Noyes
	Anthony Stoddard
	Benj. Lord
	Danll Wadsworth

The Question being put Whether Mr. Buell, being ordained in the manner he was shall Barr him of his masters degree, Resolved in the Negative Provided that this act Shall never be brought as a Precedent.

Whereas the originall design of this College as declared in the Charter was for the Training up youth in the arts and Sciences it is agreed and voted that after the End of this vacancy no person Shall be admitted a freshman into this College who is more than twenty one years old, unless by Special allowance of the Trustees or their Committee.

Franklin B. Dexter (ed.) *Documentary History of Yale University* . . . *1701–1745* (New Haven: 1916), pp. 365–366; from the original minutes in the Yale Archives.

That the Rector with the advice of any two or three of the Trustees apply himself to the Genll Assembly in Octr next to Revive the motion for Erecting another College house; or to Repair the Rectors house also to Purchase additionall Lands to the College yard.

A Draught of a new Charter for Yale College being Red at this Board, voted that the Sd draught be delivered to Coll. Fitch for his Perusal and best thoughts upon it; for which we order him five pounds old Tenor and that the draught by the advice of two or three Trustees by the Rector be presented to the Genll Assembly in Oct next, desiring that they would be Pleased to Pass it into an Act.

Jared Eliot Scribe

Study Questions

---

1. How does Eleazar Wheelock, a passionate Calvinist, come to plead for "the natural rights and liberties of all mankind"?

2. On the basis of the documents printed in this and earlier sections, describe the relationship between Thomas Clap and Eleazar Wheelock.

3. Compare Whittlesey's 1744 sermon to the Yale student body with Pemberton's 1741 sermon to the same group.

EIGHT

The Cleaveland Expulsions, November 1744–April 1745

When the twenty-year-old freshman John Cleaveland returned to his native town of Canterbury after Rector Clap closed the Yale campus in May 1742 (see #26), the situation he found at home was almost as inflammable as the one he had just left in college. The church in Canterbury, like that in New Haven, was being swept by revival and dissension. The previous year its minister had resigned under difficult circumstances, and a replacement had not yet been found. In the meantime, a succession of itinerant evangelists, Eleazar Wheelock among them, had preached irregularly to the congregation until the anti-itineracy legislation of 1742 rendered such activities illegal. At about the same time, several members of the congregation took it upon themselves to preach (or "exhort," as the current usage had it) in and out of the Canterbury meeting-house—a practice unacceptable if not altogether unknown in the churches of New England. Most prominent among these lay exhorters were two of John Cleaveland's uncles, Solomon and Elisha Paine.

The congregation could not agree on the selection of a new minister, because it was hopelessly split on the issues raised by the revival. A majority of the actual church members (that is, full communicants) backed the Awakening, but it was opposed by a majority of the entire town (or the "parish," as Cleaveland referred to those members of the congregation who attended the church without taking communion or being legally entitled to vote in affairs). The situation was complicated even further by the fact that the church had never ratified the Saybrook Platform, which would have permitted the Windham County Association—dominated by Old Lights—to settle the dispute. Indeed, early in 1743 the church voted to continue operating under the much older Cambridge Platform, which granted each congregation almost complete independence from any higher ecclesiastical authority. Therefore, when the town appealed to the county Consociation late in 1743 for help in selecting a minister, most of the church members refused to recognize the jurisdiction of this organization. For their part, the church members voted to call a ministerial council of their own, composed of sympathetic New Lights. Both sides finally agreed to try out an ostensibly neutral candidate named James Cogswell, a young man who had been graduated from Yale in 1742. When it became apparent, however, that the new candidate was basically out of sympathy with the revival, the New Light party refused to agree to his ordination. Cogswell remained in Canterbury and continued to occupy the pulpit, however, and early in 1744 his opponents—a majority of the church members together with a smaller part of the "parish"—withdrew from his preaching and began to hold regular worship services in private homes under the leadership of the two Paine brothers. The church building itself was physically closed to them, and at least one member of the group was actually arrested and jailed during the summer of 1744 on the charge of unlawfully exhorting and breaking the peace during the sabbath. (When Elisha Paine himself had left Canterbury the previous year to preach in a nearby town, he too had been imprisoned for three months under the anti-itineracy law.) Meanwhile, the supporters of Cogswell proceeded with plans for his ordination. It was a difficult situation; there were many people and convincing arguments on both sides; each party had some justification for claiming that it was the authentic church in Canterbury and that its opponents were the "separatists." By the end of summer (1744) scores of the town's residents found themselves threatened with fines and jail terms, and the civil authorities guarded the meetinghouse against unauthorized (New Light) use.

This was the situation that John Cleaveland encountered when he returned to Canterbury in September 1744, for the two-month vacation following college commencements in the eighteenth century. While in Canterbury, Cleaveland (along with his younger brother Ebenezer, who had just entered Yale as a freshman) followed his own wishes and his parents' example by attending the New Light meetings conducted by his uncles, Solomon and Elisha Paine. When word leaked back to Thomas Clap that the Cleaveland brothers had been seen at a "separate" gathering, the Rector decided to make an example of the two students.

Public reaction to the expulsion of John and Ebenezer Cleaveland is suggested by an anonymous letter on the subject in a New York newspaper [#45] and by the fact that Clap felt compelled to reply in kind [#46]. Shortly afterward, the Rector published an extended defense of his action, "The Judgment of the Rector and Tutors of Yale College, Concerning Two of the Students, Who Were Expelled" [#47]. At about the same time, John Cleaveland prepared his own "Just Narrative of the Proceedings" [#48], which for some reason was never printed. A letter to Cleaveland from Eleazar Wheelock in March 1745 [#49] gave the young man moral support and practical advice. The Cleaveland brothers' memorial to the Connecticut General Assembly, along with that body's response [#50], closes the present volume. While the tract is not included here, the students at Yale expressed *their* reaction to the expulsions by printing, at their own expense, a new edition of John Locke's *Essay on Toleration.*

45

A Letter to the New York *Post-Boy*

March 17, 1745

A Letter from a Gentleman in Connecticut, to his Friend at New York.

Sir;

The Friendship you have always honoured me with, encourages

New York *Post-Boy,* March 17, 1745; quoted in Franklin B. Dexter, *Documentary History of Yale,* pp. 370–371.

me to trouble you with this Letter, upon an Affair, I think very extraordinary in its Kind, as well as Consequences: It is a Fact that, I believe, will not be controverted by any Person in the College; it is as follows; Two of the Students went, the last Vacation, to see their Parents; at the Time of their being at home, they were by them persuaded, desired or ordered, to go and hear a neighbouring Minister preach, who is distinguished in the Colony by the Name of a New-Light; they accordingly went, it may be with their own Inclinations, without any Persuasion, Desire or Order of any Person; for I can't say which it was, but go they did: When the Vacation expired, they returned to College: The Governors of the University were informed, they had been to hear a New-Light Preacher; it is of little Consequence how the Information came, or who was the Informer; but the Fact was, they had been to hear such a One; for which, and for no other Cause, they were both expelled the College. How this is agreeable to Reason, Justice, or the Principles of natural Equity, I can't see. . . .

You must excuse me, if I am a little warm upon this late Stretch of College Power; it is the utmost Cruelty and Injustice, take the Thing in what Light you please: Had the civil Magistrates undertaken the Affair, and punished them for a Breach of the Law of the Colony (lately made to prevent the New-Lights from disturbing the Government) that might have been just, but for a College to inflict so cruel a Punishment for a Crime not committed within their Jurisdiction, and for which they had not the least Glimpse of Authority, is not a little surprising. . . .

I am,

Your most obedient humble Servant,

HEZEKIAH W———R.

46

Thomas Clap to the New York *Post-Boy*

New Haven, April 18, 1745

Mr. Parker,

I have seen in your Post-Boy of the 18th of March last, an anonimous Letter publish'd, giving an Account of the Expulsion of two Scholars; which was therein asserted to be for no other Reason, than going to hear a neighbouring Minister preach who is distinguished in this Province by the Name of a New Light; and this fact, he says, will not be disputed by any Person in the College. It is surprizing to me, that any Person should assert such a notorious Falshood, or expect it should find Belief: For it is known to the World, that a great Number of the Ministers in this Colony have the Name of New Lights, and sundry of them have Sons at College; and that the Scholars have always had free Liberty to go and hear any of them, and there never was any Thought of a Prohibition: Tho' this indeed is true, that they were prohibited from following Lay-Exhorters, and Separations, whoever preach'd at them. I don't think it is worth while for me to give a particular Account of this Affair . . . . . . But this is the best Account that can be given of it in a few Words, that they were expelled for being Followers of the Paines, two Lay-Exhorters, whose corrupt Principles and pernicious Practices are set forth in the Declaration of the Ministers of the County of Windham . . .

I am &c.

THOMAS CLAP.

New York *Post-Boy*, April 29, 1745; quoted in Franklin B. Dexter, *Documentary History of Yale*, p. 372.

47

Thomas Clap et al.:
Judgment of the Rector and Tutors

1745

It is well known that Messieurs Elisha and Solomon Paine of Canterbury, Lay Exhorters, have advanced sundry Corrupt Principles and Dangerous Errors; by means whereof they have led many People in the Country and especially in the County of Windham, into Schisms and Separations; which had such a threatning Aspect upon these Churches, as gave occasion to the Ministers of that County, unanimously to publish a Letter or Declaration to their People, setting forth the pernicious Nature and Danger of those Errors, and warning them against running after the Teachers of them. And since the Ministers of that County are the most proper Judges in this Case, we shall choose to Represent it in their words.

> You well know there are divers Persons in several of our Societies, who have of late Separated themselves from the Congregations to the which they did belong, and have vented diverse Erroneous and dangerous Principles, calculated to Overthrow the Institution of the Gospel Ministry, to render Vain the Ordinances of Christ's Appointment, to the Perverting of the Holy Scriptures, and making some of the great and most important Doctrines of them appear in a ridiculous

Thomas Clap et al., *The Judgment of the Rector and Tutors of Yale College, Concerning Two of the Students Who Were Expelled; Together with the Reasons of It* (New London, 1745); quoted in Richard Hofstadter and Wilson Smith (eds.), *American Higher Education: A Documentary History* (2 vols., Chicago, 1961), Vol. 1, pp. 74–83.

Light;—And have followed several Persons who have set up for publick Teachers and Exhorters (as far as we can find) on the same
Principles, and draw away the People after them, to the Neglect and
Contempt of the Instituted Worship of God. Some of the most Considerable of these Errors are those that follow.

1. That it is the Will of God to have a pure Church on Earth in this
sense, That all the Converted should be Separated from the Unconverted.

2. That the Saints certainly Know one another, and Know who are
Christ's true Ministers, by their own inward Feeling, or a Communion
between them in the inward Actings of their own Soul.

3. That no other Call is necessary to a Person's undertaking to preach
the Gospel, but his being a true Christian, and having an inward
Motion of the Spirit, or perswasion in his own Mind that it is the
Will of God he should preach and perform ministerial Acts: The
Consequence of which is, That there is no standing instituted Ministry
in the Christian Church which may be known by the visible Laws of
Christ's Kingdom.

4. That God disowns the Ministry and Churches in this Land, and
the Ordinances as Administered in them.

5. That at such Meetings of Lay-preaching, they have more of the
Presence of God than in his Ordinances and under the Ministration
of the present Ministry and Administration of the Ordinances in these
Churches. And hereupon many have Chosen to follow after such as
have set up themselves to be Preachers, Exhorters and Expounders
of the Doctrines of the Scriptures; several of which there have sprung
up of late in this County, the most famous of which is Mr. Elisha
Paine, of whose Mistakes and Errors in these points we have diverse
Intimations.

Then they proceed to recite sundry Evidences, by which it appears that the said Paine has declared,

That it was made manifest to him, that Christ was about to have a
pure church; and that he had not done his duty in time past in promoting Separations and Divisions among the people, and that for the
time to come he should endeavor to promote and encourage Separations, pag. 9. And asserted, That the Saints, by virtue of Grace in
themselves, know the certainty of Grace in another: And charged Mr.
Everet with Blasphemy for denying of it, pag. 11. And that the Union
of a Christian to God or Christ, was the same in kind with the Union
between the Humane Nature of Christ and the Divine; the only
difference was, the Spirit was given to Christ without measure, but

to Believers in measure: And when it was replied, That the Union between the Humane and Divine Nature of Christ, was a Union of the Second Person; but the spirit which dwelt in Believers was the Third Person. Mr. Paine replied, *That they were no otherwise Three Persons, than as they were Three distinct Officers.*

This he insisted upon with many other things of the like nature: Whereupon the said Ministers say;

We thought ourselves bound, for the Honour of Christ & the Welfare of your Souls, to give an account of these things, that so you may see to what danger persons are Exposed in running after such Teachers, and how false are their pretences to the especial Impulses of the Holy Ghost, in calling them to preach,—That God has in his Providence Testified against their Practice; diverse of those who have undertaken this work have fallen into scandalous Sins and Miscarriages, and others into foul and dreadful Errors, miserable Weakness and strange perverting the Word of God.

Then the said Ministers proceed clearly to Confute those Errors from the Word of God and the Nature of the Things, shewing them to be Subversive of the very being of the Christian Church in any visible Form of it. And we cannot but signifie our Approbation of their just and seasonable Testimony against them.

In the next place, it appears to us, That *John Cleaveland* and *Ebenezer Cleaveland,* Students of this College, had imbibed and practiced sundry of those Principles and Errors, by their withdrawing from the publick Worship of God in the Congregation in *Canterbury* and attending upon the Meeting of those *Paines,* and by justifying these Errors before us. Particularly,

1. It appears to us that they had imbibed the Third Error there mentioned, (viz.) *That no other Call is necessary to a person's under-taking to preach the Gospel, but his being a true Christian and having an inward Motion of the Spirit; or a perswasion in his own Mind that it is the Will of God that he should Preach.* Tho' they sometimes added this Proviso, *That such persons had a sufficient Ability to preach or teach to Edification:* And they particularly justified the preaching of the Paines; And *John Cleaveland* said, that *Solomon Paine* could preach better than he could, if he should study Divinity this Seven Years.

---

2. That they had imbibed the Fifth Error there mentioned (viz.) *That at such Meetings of Lay-preaching and Exhorting, they have more of the Presence of God than under the present Ministry: And that the extraordinary influences of the Spirit accompanied the preaching of these* Paines; and said, that thereby they were filled with such a strong and lively Impression of divine Things, as made them *come home Singing along the Streets.*

3. They asserted, *That every true Christian was as much United to God as Christ was;* and brought those words of Christ to prove it. *That they all may be one, even as we are one,* Joh 17.21, &c. But they being Examined about Mr. Paine's denying the Doctrine of the Trinity, said, *They did not know, or had not heard that he did deny it.*

We being apprehensive of the fatal Tendency of these and such like Errors, which the said *Cleavelands* had imbibed, and were likely more and more to imbibe, if they were permitted to attend upon the preaching of the *Paines;* and the danger that they might Infect and Corrupt the College (which would be very definitive to Religion) after discoursing with them several Times, proceeded to give the following Judgment;

Yale College, November 19th, 1744

The Rector and Tutors

Present,
Upon *Information that* John Cleaveland *and* Ebenezer Cleaveland, *Members of this College, withdrew from the publick Worship of God in the Meeting-house* in Canterbury, *carried on by* Mr. Cogswell, *a Licensed and Approved Candidate for the Ministry, preaching there at the desire of the first Parish or Society in* Canterbury, *with the special direction of the Association of the County of* Windham; *and that they the said* Cleavelands, *with sundry others belonging to* Canterbury *and* Plainfield, *did go to & attend upon a private separate Meeting in a private House, for divine Worship, carried on principally by one* Solomon Paine, *a Lay-Exhorter, on several Sabbaths in* September *or* October *last.*

The said *Cleavelands* being several times sent for, Acknowledged the Facts, as above related, and Justified what they had done, and gave in, the Reasons given in Writing by the said Separatists for their Separation, aforesaid; the most material of which are these, Viz. That the first Society in *Canterbury* keep up only the Form of Godliness and deny the Life, Power and Spirituality of it, and had given Mr.

Cogswell a Call in order for Settlement, whom they the said Separatists had declared to be destitute of those essential Qualifications that ought to be in a Minister of Jesus Christ; and therefore cannot join with the Society in their Choice, but look upon it to be their indispensible Duty to Choose one after God's own heart, one that will be able to comfort the wounded with the same comfort wherewith he himself is comforted of God, and not a blind Guide; for then the Blind will lead the Blind into the ditch of God's eternal Wrath. And many of the said Society speak evil of those things, which they the said Separatists receive and hold to be the Effect of the Holy Ghost: Whereupon they look upon it a loud Call to them to come out from among them, &c. And do appoint the House of *Samuel Wadsworth* to be a place to Meet in by themselves to serve the Lord in spirit and in truth.

And the said *Cleavelands* say, That this being the Act of the major part of the Members in full Communion within the said Society, is a sufficient Warrant for them to join with them.

They also say, That the said *Solomon Paine* had sufficient Knowledge and Ability to Expound the Scripture and to Preach the Gospel, and therefore has a right to do it: And therefore they say, That in withdrawing from the publick Worship and attending upon the Preaching of the said *Solomon Paine,* they have not acted contrary to any divine or humane Law.

Whereupon it is Considered by the Rector and Tutors,

1. That we (depending in this matter upon the unanimous Judgment of the Association in the County of *Windham*) do Judge that the said Mr. *Cogswell* is sufficiently Qualified to be a Preacher of the Gospel; and therefore that the Reflections cast upon him, as aforesaid, are groundless.

2. That if there were any Reasons why the said Separatists should not choose to receive Mr. *Cogswell* as their Minister; or if it should be doubtful whether it is convenient that Mr. *Cogswell* should be Ordained where so great a Number are against him, (which things properly belong to the hearing and judgment of a Council) yet we can't see that this could be any Justification of their setting up a Separation in the mean time.

3. That neither the major part of the Members in full Communion, nor any other persons in any Parish or Society, have any right or warrant, to appoint any House or Place for Worship on the Sabbath, distinct and separate from and in opposition to the Meetinghouse, the publick Place appointed by the General Assembly and the

Parish; but on the contrary, all such Places & separate Meetings are prohibited by the ancient Laws of this Government.

4. The principal Reasons assigned for this Separation manifestly import that spirit of uncharitable Censuring and rash Judging of mens Hearts and spiritual State, which has of late so much prevailed in the Country, and which is plainly prohibited in the Word of God.

5. There's scarce any thing more fully and strictly Enjoin'd in the Gospel than Charity, Peace and Unity among Christians; and scarce any thing more plainly and frequently forbidden than Divisions, Schisms and Separations: And therefore nothing can justifie a Division or Separation, but only some plain and express Direction in the Word of God; which must be understood as a particular Exception from the general Rule. And it appears to us that there is no Direction or Warrant in the Word of God to set up a Separation upon the Reasons there assigned.

6. That if it could be supposed that they had a Warrant to Separate from the Meeting-house, Preacher and Congregation where they belong'd, and attend upon some lawful Minister in another place; yet this could not justifie them in attending upon the Ministry or Preaching of a Lay-Exhorter, who has no Right, License or Authority to Preach; and especially of one who is a common promoter of Separations and Disturber of the Christian Peace, not only in *Canterbury,* but also in *Windham, Mansfield* and other places.

7. That this practice of setting up Lay-Exhorters (which has of late prevailed in the Country) is without any Scripture Warrant, and is Subversive of the standing Order of a Learned Gospel Ministry, and naturally tends to introduce spiritual Pride, Enthusiasm and all manner of Disorders into the Christian Church.

Whereupon it is Considered and Adjudged by the *Rector* and *Tutors,* That the said *John* and *Ebenezer Cleaveland,* in Withdrawing and Separating from the publick Worship of God, and Attending upon the Preaching of a Lay-Exhorter, as aforesaid, have acted contrary to the Rules of the Gospel, the Laws of this Colony and of the College, and that the said *Cleavelands* shall be publickly Admonished for their Faults, aforesaid: And if they shall continue to Justifie themseves and refuse to make an Acknowledgement they shall be Expelled.

Thomas Clap, *Rector*

About a Week after this *John Cleaveland* gave in a Paper, wherein he says, *"I did not know that it was a Transgression, either of the Laws of God or of this Colony, or of this College, for me, as a Member of and in Covenant with a particular Church, as is generally owned to be a Church of Jesus Christ, to meet together with the major part of said Church, for Social Worship, and therefore Beg and Intreat that my Ignorance may be suffered to Apologize for me in that respect."*

Upon which it was Considered:

First, That we have no Evidence, and never so much as heard, that that Company of men who Separated from the Congregation at *Canterbury* and Met at the House of *Samuel Wadsworth,* were owned to be a Church of Christ, by any Churches or Ministers (unless by Mr. *Crosswell*) but have always been Informed that they have been look'd upon by the Ministers and Churches in the County of *Windham,* as a company of persons Disorderly, Separated from their own Congregation, by the Influence of the *Paines,* upon the Principles mentioned in their Letter aforesaid; and that they were not the major part of the proper ancient Church in *Canterbury:* Tho we understand that Circumstance is disputed.

Secondly, The Plea, that persons who met at the House of *Samuel Wadsworth,* were the major part of the Church, appears to be a meer pretence, and not the true and real principle of the Conduct of those persons: For these *Paines* have made and preach'd at Separations in *Windham, Mansfield,* and many other places; and we have been since Informed, That the said *Cleaveland* met with the Separations at *New Haven* and *Milford,* in which places there was no pretence that the Separatists were the major part of the Church. So that it is very plain they acted upon the other principles before mentioned, which justifie the Separation of a Minor part as much as a Major.

Thirdly, He had no colour to plead Ignorance; for he had often heard the Rector declare in the College-Hall, *That these Separations and Lay-Exhorters, were contrary to the Word of God,* (tho' perhaps he might not believe it.) And the Book of the Laws and Customs of the College had some time before been read in the *College-Hall;* in which among other things there was this Clause, *That no Student shall attend upon any Religious Meetings but such as are appointed or approved by publick Authority, or by the Rector.* The Laws of the Government which he had broke, were also read to him—And here we think it proper to take Notice of one very false Representation in the Memorial; it is said, *That they Informed the Rector, &c. and begg'd to see them, but were denied.* We have no remembrance, and do not believe, that they begg'd to see the Laws of the College, and know that they never were refused or denied: For we well remember that we had the Laws by us, and read that Paragraph which they had transgressed; and if we did not read it in their hearing it was because they did not desire it, and we supposed that they could not be ignorant of it; at least that the said *John* could not be ignorant, who had been at College Three Years: And some of the Scholars had Transcribed the Laws.

Fourthly, What ever might be his former Ignorance and Mistake, yet after all means of Light and Conviction, he still persisted in Justifying what he had done, and *would acknowledge no Error in it;* tho' sometimes he seem'd to be brought to such a doubt and stand in his own Mind, as that it seemed probable that he would have made some Acknowledgement, if he had not been prevented by ill Advice.—And since the principal End and Design of Erecting this College (as declared in Charter) was, *To Train up a Succession of Learned and Orthodox Ministers,* by whose Instruction and Example people might be directed in the ways of Religion and good Order; therefore to Educate persons whose principles and practices are directly Subversive of the Visible Church of Christ, would be contrary to the Original Design of Erecting this Society. And we conceive that it would be a Contradiction in the Civil Government, to Support a College to Educate Students to trample upon their own Laws, and brake up the Churches which they Establish and Protect, Especially since the General Assembly in *May* 1742, tho't proper to give the Governours of the College some special Advice & Direction upon that account; which was to this Effect, *That all proper Care should be taken to prevent the Scholars from imbibing those or such like Errors; and that those who would not be Orderly and Submissive, should not be allowed the Privileges of the College.* Neither can we conceive that it makes any odds, whether such pernicious Errors are imbibed and practised, and the Laws of GOD and the Civil Government are broken, in or out of the Vacancy or the Town of *New-Haven,* or with or without the Concurrence of their Parents, since the pernicious Consequences thereof to the *College & Religion* will be just the same.

Thomas Clap, *Rector*

Chauncey Whittelsey
John Whiting   *Tutors*
Thomas Darling

New-Haven, May 1st, 1745

48

John Cleaveland:
"A Just Narrative of the Proceedings"

1745

A Just Narrative of the Proceedings of the Revd. & Hon'd. Rector and Tutors of Yale College in New Haven with John Cleaveland and Ebenezer Cleaveland who were members of Said College. Wherein is particularly related, what these members did that was offensive. Also what was said in Several Conferences by Each Side. To which is subjoined Some Remarks upon the Judgment of the Expulsion Exhibited to the public some time since. Made by one of the said members to the said Rector in Conversation.

In the year of our Lord 1741 the Church of Christ in Canterbury, being destitute of a pastor, met and conferred together. [The Church] read Cambridge Platform of Church Discipline and chose a committee from among themselves, to search into the past constitution and practice of said Church and draw up something and make return at the next Church meeting in order that the Church might renew their covenant and make record; and after about fourteen months time of searching into the Scriptures and Platform of Church Discipline the said committee made return at a full Church meeting, and it was voted then by said Church (nemine contradicente) that Cambridge Platform (agreed to 1648), is most agreeable to the former and designed practice of this Church. It was also voted at the same time that it was regular for that Church to admitt persons (even while destitute of a pastor) that are in full communion with

From the original manuscript in the Essex Institute, Salem, Massachusetts.

other Churches and come with a regular dismission to their church immediately hereupon, and for two or three years together members were received into this Church, who came with letters of dismission and recommendations from churches in the vicinity, whereby this church was considerably enlarged. In the meanwhile the late Revival of Religion spread in the neighboring towns, and Canterbury Church appeared then to be no small sheaves in the same blessed influence. But the major part of the town or first parish appeared against it, by refusing to call such minister on probation for the settlement that had appeared to be zealous promoters and abettors of it. So that a division was soon commenced between the Society and the Church— for the ministers the church was for, the Society or Parish was against, and vice versa. And thus the case was till sometime in the beginning of the year 1744. The parish made choice of a minister to settle with them, (but by the way it must be noticed that the controversy between the Church and Parish was in a measure respecting their right or privilege. The Church insisted it was their right by Cambridge Platform to lead the Parish in the choice of a minister, but the Parish insisted it was their right by Sea Brook [Saybrook] to lead). But before the Parish had made choice as above, the Church by writing (April 5, 1744) gave the Parish to understand that they were utterly against settling the person that was called on probation by them, for that they were of opinion from what knowledge or acquaintance they had of him and his preaching, [that] he had not those essential qualifications that ought to be in a minister of Jesus Christ, and therefore declared that they utterly refused to join with the society in improving him for that purpose. But this was regarded but a little it seems by the Society, for without any reply they proceeded to call him as above. Not long after this, even in August following, the Church made a formal withdraw[al] from the Parish—for several reasons. Viz.

1. The Parish had called a man to settle with them in the Gospel ministry contrary to the mind and vote of the Church, even after the same had been manifested to them.

2. The Parish hath declared themselves to be of a contrary way of thinking from us, as to points of discipline, by words and practice.

3. They deny us the liberty of the meeting-house except we conform to their principles, which [meeting-house] we help'd build to worship God in according to our consciences.

4. Many of the Parish spare not to speak reproachfully and blasphemously or evil of what we receive and hold to be the faith and effects of the holy Ghost.

Whereupon they did look upon themselves to be found in duty to withdraw and appoint some convenient place to worship in and to proceed to call a minister on trial for a short time in order for [making] a settlement. But notwithstanding this, in November following a Church meeting was appointed in order to manifest their sentiments more fully respecting the minister the Parish had made choice to settle with them, and the whole church having met according to appointment and the business of the meeting having been opened by the moderator, one of the Church [members], that had been zealously engaged with the Parish in their proceedings—that were contrary to the true principles of the Church—stood up and said: if all those persons that have been admitted into the Church since we have been destitute of a pastor, may be excluded from acting, then *we* shall be free to act with you. Which was by no means agreed to, being contrary to as stated vote of the Church. Then he proceeded and said, he would have all those that looked upon themselves to be under Say-brook regulation of church-discipline draw to the east-side of the meeting-house whereupon they did to the number of 16, and then proceeded to choose a moderator and a scribe and immediately thereupon adjourned to a private house and there made choice of the man the Parish as above had called, for their pastor &c. While the body of the Church being left in the meeting-house were transacting the business of the meeting according to their warning. Here was Separation [of] a minor part of the Church from the major, only upon a pretended [or] at least mistaken notion of their being upon another plan of discipline even when but a few years before they had unanimously voted that they were under Cambridge Platform agreed upon by a Synod of 1648.

While the chief of these things were transacted between the Church and Parish John Cleaveland (who was a member of said Church and was so even before they [were] destitute of a pastor) resided at Yale-College in New Haven being a member of said College and Ebenezer Cleaveland his younger brother was admitted a member of said Society [Cleaveland presumably intended "College" instead of "Society"] in September 1744 at their commencement; but the vacancy [vacation] at College being immediately after the commencement, the said Cleavelands returned to Canterbury to see their friends, where they tarried several Sabbaths. And they being unacquainted with the controversy went, especially the said John, to the meeting-house to hear the minister the Parish had made choice of to preach with them, till he had searched into the Church votes respecting the controversy subsisting, and had understanding in the controversial transactions. By which he was fully satisfied the Church had been greatly imposed upon, and had just reason to withdraw to some other [place] if they would act consistent with their Congregational principles that they were settled upon. But notwithstanding this there arose another difficulty in his mind to bar him from meeting with the Church [:] there was an ecclesiastical rule [not] in Cambridge Platform but in Sea-Brook regulation of Church discipline almost universally practiced upon in Connecticutt, that no person shall preach till they have been examined, licenced and approbated by some Association of ministers, and the man that ministered to the Church had not passed that ceremony. It being a little [out of] the customary way seemed to [indecipherable]. Although he was fully persuaded that the said person was endowed with considerable gifts for edification, this difficulty wrought so as to put him upon enquiring what saith the Scriptures? and he was soon brought to see that all essential [?] gifts were given to the Church, that they were to try prove [them] and that by calling them to exercise themselves and so to approve or disapprove as they found them gifted to edification. Whereby the difficulty was removed out [of] his way, and accordingly he met with the Church till their return to College.

But before their return to College some person to them unknown informed the Rector and Tutors that they had attended said meeting, whereupon they were soon called before said Rector & Tutors at their return of November 19, 1744: and the following conference was held between the Revd Rector and Tutors and the said Cleavelands:

Rector: I have heard that while you were at home in the vacancy you went from Mr. Cogswell a regular and authorized one that the Society at Canterbury had applied to preach with them, and had a mind to settle in the ministry to hear Mr. Solomon Paine a lay-exhorter at a separate meeting—Is it so, or is it not?

John: It is true that we went to hear Mr. Paine exercise his gifts, where the Church of Christ in Canterbury met for divine worship.

R: Why did you go there?

J: The major part of the Church of which I am a member met there by agreement or vote, and farther we do look upon ourselves in this respect to be moral agents, capable of trying things (in religion) for ourselves. Therefore after we had heard Mr. Cogswell a few

Sabbaths, we thought it no transgression to meet with the Church to know how they carried on, whether more agreeable to the word of God than the other? or not?

R: Didn't you go to see whether Solomon Paine had an immediate call from God to preach or no!

J: No sir; neither do we suppose that it was our business to enquire whether he had an immediate call from God to preach.

Whittlesly. Tut [or]: Relating to what you said, how they carried on worship: don't they carry on as other Churches—that is, sing and pray and discourse upon the Scriptures?

J: Yes.

W: But ministers that agree in the aforesaid manner of handling discourses, may differ as to zeal and delivery.

J: We grant it.

R: What call do you hold necessary for a person in order to preach: must he be called by God or by man?

J: He must be called by both God and man.

R: How must a person be called by the spirit of God?

J: In case we had been called ourselves, we could be better able to answer you than we are now.

R: To return. Seeing the meeting you went to was a Separate meeting you are to be blamed (or to that effect).

J: We do not apprehend that meeting to be a Separate meeting properly because they agreed to meet there by a vote (in order to enjoy their Privileges.)

R: A few more than half makes [no] alteration; since they separated upon the same bottom [that is, grounds] (as others) of judging and censuring ministers.

J: That let the meeting be Separate or not Separate we thought we had full liberty when we were [away] from College, or out of New-Haven to go to what meetings we pleased, and it would be no transgression of College laws in case we should accordingly.

W: How could you possibly think so, when the Rector had been so much against it?

J: We made inquiry whether there was any law in College that forbid the members of College going to Separate meetings, and have been credibly informed that the Revd Mr. Williams of Pomfret, who is one of the Trustees of College, hath said there is no such College law, the making of one had indeed been discoursed of but never concluded upon.

R: The laws of God and the laws of College are one (or to that purpose).

J: I do not hold that meeting to be a Separate that I went to, but in case it was I am entirely ignorant of any law in College forbidding my attending upon it.

W: You know it was contrary to the Rector's mind.

R: Well but how came you to hear the Paines preach. They hold errors, at least the lawyer [Elisha Paine] does: didn't you know it?

J: No Sir, we have perceived none.

R: He holds that an unconverted person ought not to pray, and also—   NB

J: I have heard him preach several times but never apprehended him to hold any such doctrine. I have heard him say that an unconverted [person's] prayers are sin, and all that is done without faith is sin.

W. T: Well that amounts to the same, for whatsoever is done without faith is sin and [an] unconverted person can't pray in Faith, therefore it is a sin for him to pray, it amounts to the same. But he holds that every believer is as much united to Christ as Christ is to God.

E[benezer Cleaveland]: What does our Saviour mean when he prays that they may be one in us, as thou Father art in me and I in thee?

R: What do you mean by it?

W: Neither he, nor Paine know what they mean by it.

To which the said John was about to speak his mind, but was prevented [from getting] an opportunity, for immediately hereupon the Rector told them he should dismiss them for the present but should call them again (being not well) for it is a weighty matter said he.

The same night about nine oclock after they had withdrawn a friend came and informed them that he had been to the Rectors and there heard him read a suspension to this effect viz. That Whereas John Cleaveland and Ebenezer Cleaveland members of Yale College in the late vacancy went from Mr. James Cogswell the regular authorized preacher of the Gospel at Canterbury to hear Solomon Paine a lay exhorter at a Separate meeting and have thereby violated the laws of God this Colony and College, I do therefore suspend them from their rights and privileges in College till satisfaction be made and if none be made then to proceed & expel [them]. T. C. R. Y. C., and saw him deliver the same to Tutor Whittlesy to read the next morning in the Hall. At the hearing of which the said

---

Cleavelands were something surprised not dreaming that they should meet with such an expedite severity without further conferring on the affair. Whereupon the said John went immediately to the said Whittlesy's to try if he could not persuade him to defer reading suspension till something further was done, and when he had got there the following conference passed between them. Viz.

John: Sir, I desire to be excused for interrupting you at this unseasonable time of night, for the affair I come upon I apprehend to be of considerable importance.

W. T: Well, and what then?

J: I am informed, Sir, you have a suspension put into your hands to read in the morning wherein I am to be debarred from the privileges of College until &c.

W. T: Well, and what then?

J: I don't understand why you should be so hasty in suspending us, before you had showed us the law we had transgressed: the demerits of the transgression and the conditions of reconciliation. For I suppose it is possible that satisfaction may be made and the difficulty removed without publishing the same by suspension.

W. T: The first thing that we were to do was to inquire into the fact and as to making it public, it is public in its own nature, and ought to be made public here before it could be made up.

J: We acknowledge the fact (that is as above related.)

W. T: Well then the next thing was to proceed to suspension.

J: I don't understand it so, and farther if I have transgressed I am entirely ignorant of what law.

W. T: Your ignorance can be no plea in your defense. You knew the Rector was against such meetings as you went to.

J: Can't you defer reading the suspension till something farther might be done.

W. T: I can't defer it without the Rector's order. You may go to him and if he will give order to defer it I shall then defer [it]. But it will do no good, nothing can be done to any purpose till you are suspended.

The said John having received such answers withall, concluding the Rector was by this time taking his rest, concluded not to go to the Rector. And so when the morning came their suspension was read off which was as above. When this was done the said Cleavelands finding now that they had nothing to do but to study, did accordingly apply themselves thereto without interruption for near the space of a week and then Rector sent for them [and] the following conference passed viz.

R: Well, you have been deemed guilty of breaking the laws of God &c. (as above) and have [been] suspended therefor; I have now waited some time and do now expect you'll make as large a confession as the charge, or else you must be wholly deprived of College privileges.

J: Sir: we are not convinced that we have done anything worthy of such a charge as is said against us and consequently can't make a confession. For we always thought that when we were out of New-Haven we had full liberty to go to what meeting we pleased without a thought of transgressing any College law. Even supposing it were a Baptist's or Quaker's meeting, but especially where the major part of the Church had agreed to meet together for the worship of God of the same persuasion with ourselves.

R: All College laws excepting a few little ones extend farther than New-Haven bounds, and as for Quakers, they are so wrong and contrary to the Scriptures, that it would be very wrong for [you] to go to [their] meeting at any time whatsoever; and as for the Baptists, there were one sort of them that differed but little from us, with whom a person might lawfully meet, in case he was providentially cast amongst them. But as to the meeting that you want to [it] was a Separate meeting notwithstanding they went off by a major vote of the Church [they did so] upon the bottom that other Separate meetings did elsewhere, which spirit of Separation I look upon to be the worst practical thing that ever was brought into the Church. And the reason of their separating was because they judge Mr. Cogswell to be an unconverted man.

J: The Church do not so [judge] that he is unconverted, but say, they are of opinion from what acquaintance or knowledge they have had of him and his way of preaching, that he hath not those essential qualifications, that ought to be in a minister of Jesus Christ.

R: Ah: they looked on him to be unconverted, was all the qualifications, they supposed him destitute of. They do not dispute his learning &c.

J: Supposing that we should grant that the Church did not think him to be converted; no doubt they look on it their duty and privilege, yea: and we suppose Sir you are of the same mind too, to settle in the ministry of them, such as they look on to be pious Godly experienced men.

R: You have no reason to think otherwise of Mr. Cogswell.

J: After all, Sir, I remain entirely ignorant of any law forbidding any member of College going just where he thinks fit when [away] from College and [so] that you might not think we are alone in this ignorance, many of the senior class and some of the graduates have said they should have done the same that we have without the least suspicion of transgressing any College law.

R: Ah. They knew it would be contrary to my judgment and if you do not go according to my judgment you can't expect to enjoy College privileges, but if it be so as you report of them, I suppose they do not think so honorably of my judgment as they ought. So be it. I'll make them know otherwise by my dealings with you.——This was the sum of this conference with the Rector and he dismissed them for that time telling them that if they did not make a confession as extensive as the charge they must be expelled. Not many days after this they were again sent for again before the Revd Rector and Tutors. And then the following conference passed viz.

R: The last time you were before me I laid open your case to you and told you what you should do to be admitted, and having had some time given you to consider on it what you concluded upon.

John produced a paper and gave them containing what followeth viz.

To the Revd. and Hond. Rector and Tutors of Yale College in New-Haven. Revd. & Hond.

It hath been a very great concern and trouble to me, that my conduct in the late vacancy has been such as not to maintain interest in your favor, and still retain the great privileges, that I have enjoyed for three years past under your learned, wise, and faithful instruction and government. Nothing of an outward nature can equally affect me with that of being henceforward wholly secluded [from] the same.

Hond. Fathers, suffer me to lie at your feet, and intreat your compassionate forgiveness to an offending child wherein I have transgressed.

Venerable Sirs: I entreat you, for your paternal wisdom, goodness, and clemency, to make in my case such kind allowance for the want of that penetration and solid judgment expected in riper heads—as tender parents are naturally disposed in respect of their weak children; but more especially I beg to be admitted in the humblest manner to suggest as a motive of your compassion to the ignorant,—that I did not know that it was a transgression of either the Laws of God, this Colony, or of the College for me as a member of and in covenant with a particular Church as is generally owned to be a church of Jesus Christ, to meet together with a major part of said Church for social worship. And therefore do beg and intreat that my ignorance may be suffered to apologize. For in respect of that fact, which to riper heads may appear to be a real transgression; I can assure you, Venbl. Sirs, that I have endeavored to keep and observe all the known laws and customs of College unblamably. And I hope I shall for the future be enabled so to do, if I may be restored to a standing again in my class. Thus begging your compassion, I subscribe, your humble servant and obedient pupil,

New-Haven, Nov. 26, A.D. 1744　　　　　　John Cleaveland.

But this was by them regarded as nothing because there was nothing said against either the meeting or the person that carried on at the meeting: who had neither a degree nor a licence except from the Church that improved him. Therefore they told said Cleavelands they should proceed to farther measures of discipline.

J: Sirs, I should be glad to know what the Scriptures say as to the call of a person to preach.

R: The Scriptures saith, how can they preach except they be sent; and no man taketh this honour to himself but he that is called of God as was Aaron.

J: Has that text in *Hebrews* a reference to ministers being called in gospel-times? (The reason of his thus asking this question was, he apprehended the rule of the Apostles was to set forth that all the High-Priests before Christ, were types of Christ, & so argue that if the types were called of God hence necessarily the antitype must also, which he thought evident from the verse following the forecited words; so also Christ glorified not himself to be made a high-priest, but he that said unto him thou art my son this day &c.)

R: Yes, to be sure.

J: If the call of Aaron is a rule for us to try others by, whether they are called of God, I suppose it to be necessary to know in what manner Aaron was called of God, but of this I am ignorant.

R: He was called by Moses. But it is not necessary that ministers under the Gospel shall be called in the same method as Aaron was. As Aaron was called of God so must all Gospel-ministers, and there are rules in the Gospel directing how they shall be introduced.

J: Is there any other rule of introducing a minister, but by laying on of hands of the Presbytery?

R: No.

J: Then he that preaches before he is ordained or hath had the laying on of the hands of the Presbytery is a bold intruder into the ministerial function. (Now the Rector had said that such as preached without a license were so.)

R: The Church of England do make this an objection against the Presbyterians, but it is supposed by our divines, that such as have power to ordain, have authority [to] license before ordination.

J: If the matter is brought to the opinion of divines, we suppose we can instance some likewise. We have been credibly informed that in some parts of the province of the Massachusetts the candidates are very seldom examined & licensed before they have a call to settle.

R: I believe you'll rarely find an instance (or to that effect).

J: I can instance some [and likewise and one in Connecticut of liberal education (?)] (But the Rector concluded this subject with saying)

R: All that so do, are bold intruders, who do that which they have no business with and therefore since you went to such a meeting to heard a lay-exhorter which was entirely wrong (in case you don't make a full recantation) we shall proceed to expel (or to that effect).

T[utor]: Have you anything more to offer?

E: I have something to offer. When I was at home I was under the care of my parents, and they told me if I did not meet where they met, I could not expect that they would maintain me at College and the meeting not appearing contrary to the word of God, I thought it my duty to obey my parents in this thing.

R: If you went in obedience to your parents, this extenuates the crime, for it is a good thing to reverence your parents. However we are not to make their judgment a rule of our proceeding, but shall proceed according to what appears right to us notwithstanding.

J: Sir, I find it to be a matter of impossibility to serve two masters and am brought into a perfect dilemma for if we don't make a full recantation we must be expelled [from] College and if we do make such a one it will be so grievous and contrary to the mind of our parents they will not support us at College, so that whether we confess or do not confess, we are under a necessity of leaving College.

R: As you say it is a very difficult thing to serve two masters, when they dictate contrarily, and therefore you must choose which of the two you will obey for the future.

J: Sir, if you will overlook this, we will for the future endeavor to persuade our parents to let us go to such meetings as are *not* contrary to the mind of the authority of College.

R: I don't know but I may, if you will openly acknowledge your fault in the Hall.

J. & E: We don't see it to be our duty to make an acknowledgment. And so were dismissed for this time.

Some time after this John of his own accord went to the Rector and the following conference was held between the Rector and him alone.

R: Well, what—

J: Sir, you have granted to us some time to consider which of the two masters we shall choose to serve in this concern. We have thought of the matter and do think it was our duty in that case to obey our parents, and therefore can't go from the same. And having an opportunity for one of us to go home I am come to know [whether] we may not, one of us at least, have liberty to go home as well before as after we are expelled?

R: What do you mean by going home? I don't understand,

[There follows a gap of probably a single page in the manuscript.]

J: I am persuaded it is mentioned in the paper if not in that particular paper containing the most of the reasons. (Whereupon the Rector looked into the paper & found it fully expressed but said however)

R: However I don't suppose that was any material reason but rather a meer quibble and now if you do think that Separations & upholding or letting lay exhorters was the best way to advance godliness, I've no more to say.

J: Sir, we don't look upon some separations and the letting lay exhorters the best way. We are not fully determined concerning them.

R: Well, if you are in some suspence about them we will favour [you] with some time to get satisfaction.

J: Sir, we shall look upon it [as] a favour and do also earnestly desire liberty to ride out of town to ask advice.

R: Well, I will discourse with the Tutors and if they are willing I will indulge your desire. (After some more free discourse he dismissed them.)

Not long after the Rector sent for John and told him he had discoursed with the Tutors, & they had concluded so far to favour them, more than was customary to persons under their circumstances as to let them have liberty to ride out and ask council.

Hereupon said John rode to Stratfield, to see the Revd. Mr. Cook, a gentleman eminent for piety and learning and also one of the Trustees of College, and layed the whole case before him viz. copies of the Churches votes—of their admonition and indeed of the whole of the substance of the above relation, having minuted the same down, and of what had [been] offered to them and desired his advice and in fine the reverend Gentleman told him, he believed they would be undoubtedly expelled, for he could not see how they could in conscience do more than they had done to remove the Censure, and he returned and told the Rector that he found nothing to alter his Mind. After some Discourse said the Rector, Why: Do you really think the Separations at Windham and other places thereabouts are right. He replied that he did not chose to say anything about them either in the way of justification or condemnation, apprehending they had not reference to his case, for he apprehended that the Church he met with did agree to meet at that place—mainly to enjoy their privileges agreeable to their principals of discipline. To which the Rector replied that was nothing but a quibble; and you justify lay-men's preaching don't you? Said John replied that he didn't [think] *that* had any reference to his case either to justify or condemn seeing he didn't apprehend that Mr. Solomon Paine did pretend to preach when he heard him, but only to carry on as a brother in their ex-tremity and if he had preached in any other place [or] time, it had no reference to his case. To which the Rector in some haste said he couldn't have patience to hear his quibbles and if they were settled he told him he should proceed to expel them speedily.

At night the Rector sent for them both and asked them whether they were settled in their minds; they replied that they were still of the same [opinion] as they were before; then said the Rector I shall proceed to expel you tomorrow morning and would have you come hear it, & accordingly they did, and were commanded to depart the Hall and the limits of College no more to return—likewise were the students forbid receiving them into their chambers and of commersing with them lest they should [be] infected by them.

49

Eleazar Wheelock to John Cleaveland

Lebanon, March 9, 1745

Very Dear Dear Brother

Yours of Feby 26 I received but three Days ago; it is very well-come and plesant to me. And how dos your Dear Soul prosper now? I thank God he has been (I trust) purifying, ripening, and fitting you for himself, by all ye Suffering you have been calld to. The Dear Lord grant yt your glorying may still be, and more and more, in the Cross of Christ: in being nothing in yourself but having all in Christ. And fill you more and more with flaming yet prudent zeal; with burning love, & a sound mind, whereby you may glorify him. I need not exhort you to pray for me, for I am ye Chief of Sinners and Less than the Least of all Saints. Amazing it is yt to such an one it shod be given to preach to poor Sinners the unsearchable Riches of Jesus Christ. They are unsearchable indeed; I see them Daily more and more so. I have lately had a trial of the heaviest Cross yt ever I have been calld to in ye Course of my Ministry: viz., to have my own Children, yt Could a Little while ago have pulled out theire Eyes and given them to me, now Count me their Enemy for telling them ye truth. But ye Lord has made even this Cross sometimes light and easie to me. I never before truly understood Gal[atians] 4: 15.16.17.

As to your going into the Jersies, I exceedingly approve of the proposal, and shall be freely willing myself, and Doubt not but my Bretheren in the ministry here will be willing, to contribute what in

---

From the original in the Essex Institute, Salem, Massachusetts.

---

them Lies to ye Design; unless it be tho't best (as in ye opinion of many in these parts) yt you sho'd put in a memorial to ye Assembly next May and pray to be righted & restored to your privilidges in College. Capt. Lee or Majr. Fowler will gladly serve you in the affair. I am much concerned for your Brother, & upon his account especially I do much Desire it. And it may be of much Service to ye College, to which I doubt not you wish well. I wish you wod think of the matter and propose it to Mr. Robbins and other ministers in those parts whom you have been free with. May ye Lord make you, my Dr Br, a pollished Shaft in his hand. Give my utmost Love to Dr Br Robbins & Sister, and accept it yourself from

Your Real Friends & Br Eleazr Wheelock

50

John and Ebenezer Cleaveland: Memorial to the General Assembly

April 1745

To the Honorable General Assembly of the Colony of Connecticut to be held at Hartford in the County of Hartford ye second Thursday of May next; the Memorial of John Cleaveland of Canterbury in Windham County, and Ebenezer Cleaveland a minor of s'd Canterbury, (who comes by his Father Josiah Cleaveland of s'd Canterbury) humbly sheweth:

That said John and said Ebenezer have for some Time been students at and members of Yale College at New Haven under ye

---

From the original in the Connecticut Archives: Colleges and Schools, 280a–d, (Connecticut State Library, Hartford, Connecticut).

---

care of the Revd. Thomas Clap Rector and Chancey Whittlesey, John Whiting and Thomas Darling Tutors and have in all things behaved Themselves according to the Laws and Constitutions of the s'd College & have given none [illegible] of offence to any at any Time During their Abode at sd College; the sd John was one of the Senior Class, & sd Ebenezer being one of the Freshman Class; and had, according to their several Standings acquired a good Degree of Humane Learning.

But may it please your Honours! so it hath happened that ye major Part of Canterbury Chh, of which the said Josiah and the said John are members in full Communion, have of late as they apprehend found it both necessary and a Duty to withdraw Themselves from the Society of said Canterbury and ye minor Part of the Church, and to hold religious meetings by Themselves; Because of an unhappy Controversy that had got in amongst Them, Partly on account of Their different Ways of Thinking about the late Glorious Work of God that has been in ye Land, and Partly (and indeed Principly) relating to Church Government and Discipline. The minor Part of the Church, and the major Part of the Society, have of late declared Themselves off from our ancient Church Confederation, Discipline and Principles, which all along have been Congregational, according to the Platform agreed to at Cambridge by a Synod in 1649; which Confederation was Solemnly renewed at a full Church Meeting (nemine contradicente) at Canterbury January 27 1742/3 after the Church had been for more than Twelve Months by themselves, and [a] Committee (by them for that End specially appointed) looking into and considering the s'd Platform of Chh Government &c. But the minor Part of said Church, after some Time joyning with the major Part of s'd Society, making the major Part of the whole Society, Choose Mr. James Cogswell for their Minister, whom the major Part of ye Church protested against; and so declared that ye minor Part of the Church, and the major Part of said Society, had not any power to Impose a Minister upon them; for that by their afores'd Platform ye right of Choosing a Minister is solely in the Church; and the person then chosen not being agreeable to the Chh; nor could they admitt of such an Infringement of their Priviledges. The minor Part and the Society insisting they had a right by Say-Brook Platform (since they together made ye major Part of said Society) to Choose a Minister; which Platform they then declared they adhered to—it became necessary for the Chh to withdraw from the Meeting House to worship; being not willing to bring their Contention there,—But rather minded, since they could not agree, peaceably to depart to another House to worship him who is the God of Peace.

All which was Transacted while the said John Cleaveland was at New-Haven.—And the s'd Josiah Cleaveland, who is Father to the memorialist, being one of the major Part of sd Church, and one that attended the meeting of the Chh after the minor Part had joyned with ye Society as aforesd—and the said Ebenezer being a minor and under his said Fathers Government.

Thus, may it please your Honours, Matters stood in sd Chh in September and October last in ye time of ye Vacancy at College, in which Time your Honours Memorialists being at home, the said John, a member in full Communion with sd Church, and the s'd Ebenezer under his s'd Fathers Government, Thought it their Duty to attend ye Meeting of the Chh with their said Father; and not to leave ye Assembling with the Chh; verily believing that they therein acted according to the Rule of God's Word: which commands *that we should not forsake the Assembling of ourselves together*. And as we do firmly believe that the Chh has [the] right to Choose their own Minister, so we were well assured that ye minor Part of the Chh with ye Society had Choose Mr. Cogswell Contrary to the major Part of the Chh, and we did and do firmly Believe that the Church ought not to be thus imposed upon. Whereupon, when we returned to College again, some Person to us unknown informed the Revd. Rector and Tutors that we had attended the said Meeting, upon which we were called before the s'd Rector and Tutors on the 19 of Nov. last; when we were examined relating to our going to s'd Meeting [we] freely owned it; and Then in order to give the Revd. Rector and Tutors satisfaction yt our going to that Meeting was not with any factious or Rebellious Mind or Intent, but purely what we Thought was our Duty, we procured copies of our Chh Proceedings which shew our Cause to be as above related, and laid them before ye said Rector and Tutors; which we looked upon and were then of opinion were sufficient to Justofie our attending the said Meeting. We also informed the Revd. Rector &c. that we were entirely ignorant what the Laws of College were, for that we never had oppertunity to see Them; and if our going to the s'd Meeting was a Breach of the College Laws, we humbly pray'd that our Ignorance might for this Time attone for our Mistake; and pray'd that we might see the Laws of College yt we had Transgressed, but were told by ye Rector that the Laws of the Colony were the Laws of College, and Thereupon read to us two Laws of the Collony yt forbid Separate Meetings. We then observed that the Penalties to them Laws annex'd were not Expulsion from College, but only to pay fines. And besides, by the Laws of this Colony (if we had Transgressed Those Laws) we were to have our Tryall in the county where we had offended: which was owned by the Rector. But we were by him informed that the Colony Laws were by Law of College made the Laws of College; which we begged to see but were deny'd, and our Reasons not being satisfactory to the Revd. Rector and Tutors we were thereupon suspended [from] College Privileges; at length admonished; and on the 3d of January Last, we not confessing that we had Broke the Laws of God, this Colony and College (as it was by the Revd. Rector and Tutors required that we should as Terms of Forgiveness) we were in a Solemn and formal manner Expell'd [from] College by the Revd. Rector and Tutors, and cut off from any further Privileges in s'd College, and commanded to depart out of the Limits of the same & never more to return there. Thus were we proceeded against by the meer Arbitrary Will and Pleasure of the Revd. Rector &c. without any Law of College; for there is none to warrant ye Proceedings against us.

Thus, may it please your Honours! we have endeavored in a few words to set forth our Cause, omitting much yt might be said being unwilling to trouble Your Honours with Things that relate to our Cause that are not absolutely necessary to set our cause in a clear and true Light. For may it please Your Honours! as we understand ye Laws of this Colony, the Congregational Persuasion is as much under the countenance of the Laws of this Colony as the Say-Brook Platformists are, and therefore we Think it hard measure indeed to be cut off from our College Privileges meerly for being of the Congregationall Persuasion, and acting agreeable thereto, while the Say-Brook Platformists, Professors of the Chh of England, Seven Day Anabaptists and Quakers have, and have had, free Liberty to enjoy all the Privileges of College—their Principles and Practices (in the Vacancys at College) agreeable thereto notwithstanding.

We therefore humbly pray that your Honours would be pleased to take our case into your Honours Paternal Consideration, and consider our distressed Circumstances; and upon hearing our sd cause and Circumstances thereunto appertaining: Enact and Order in our Favour that we be again immediately restored to our Standing in College and to all the Privileges and Immunities thereof, as if the

---

aforesaid Judgnt of Expulsion had never been pass'd against us; in confidence of which we as in Duty Bound shall &c.

Josiah Cleaveland in behalf of Ebenezer
John Cleaveland

Canterbury April 21st 1745
To the Sheriff of ye County of New Haven, his Deputy, or Constable of New Haven within said County Greeting
In his majesties name you are hereby Commanded to Cause ye Revd. Thomas Clap, Rector of Yale College att New haven, Chancy Whittlesey, John Whiting and Thomas Darling, Tutors of said College, all of said New Haven, to Know that they may if they see Cause appear before the Generall Assembly to be held at Hartford in the County of Hartford on ye 2 Thirsday of May next, that is, to appear ye first Tuesday after ye said Thirsday, to Shew Cause, if any they have, why ye foregoing Prayer should not be Granted. You are also to leave a true attested Copy of ye foregoing memorial and of this writt with each of ye afore[mentione]d Persons (viz) ye Revd. Mr. Clap, Chancy Whitelsy, John Whiting and Thomas Darling at ye place of their usual abode at least 12 Days before said Tuesday.
Fair Not but make Return hereof with your Doings thereon according to Law. Dated in Saybrook, April 23, 1745

Samuel Lynd, assistant

Newhaven, April 27th, 1745 then this Writ was serv'd on the within Nam'd, Revd. Thomas Clap, Mr. Chancey Whitlesy, John Whiting & Thomas Darling by leaving a true & attested copy of it at the usual places of their Abode. Test [attested] Moses Mansfield, Constable of Newhaven

In the upper House
The Question was put whether the Subject Matter of this Memorial should be taken into Consideration at this Time, in order for enacting or ordering thereon as prayed for. Resolved in the Negative, and thereupon it is Resolved that the Memorial be dismissed.

Test George Wyllys, Secrety

1. Compare the church separation at Canterbury with the earlier New Haven separation. In what ways do the divisions between Old and New Lights appear to have deepened between 1741 and 1744? What is the social significance of "lay exhortation"?

2. What different kinds of arguments do the Cleaveland brothers employ in their defense against Clap's criticism? Which of these arguments would Clap find most difficult to counter?

3. Why does Clap refuse to accept the Cleavelands' public apology?

4. Which side in the Cleaveland controversy, and in the Old Light-New Light divisions generally, seems more "modern" in its positions?

5. Compare the New Light movement during the Great Awakening with modern revivalism as practiced by men like Billy Graham.

6. Where would you have stood if you had been a student in Yale College during the Great Awakening?

Appendix A:
The Yale Community

1. Trustees, 1740–1745

Ten Congregational ministers were constituted Trustees of the new College in 1701 by the Connecticut General Assembly; they were appointed for life and were given the authority to choose their own successors.

Trustee	Home Parish	Dates of Service
Jared Eliot (1685–1763)	Clinton	1730–1763
Ebenezer Williams (1690–1753)	Pomfret	1731–1749
Samuel Woodbridge (1683–1746)	East Hartford	1732–1743
Samuel Cooke (1687–1747)	Stratfield (Bridgeport)	1732–1746
Jonathan Marsh (1685–1747)	New Hartford	1732–1745
Samuel Whittelsey (1686–1752)	Milford	1732–1752
Joseph Noyes (1688–1761)	New Haven	1735–1761
Anthony Stoddard (1678–1760)	Woodbury	1738–1760
Thomas Clap (1703–1767)	Yale College	1740–1745 (ex officio)
Benjamin Lord (1693–1784)	Norwich	1740–1772
Daniel Wadsworth (1704–1747)	Hartford	1743–1747

2. Undergraduates, Classes 1741–1748

Each class is listed in order of descending *social* rank, as determined by the Rector during its freshman year. This method of social rather than academic ranking continued until the 1760s.

Class of 1741
William Livingston [New York]
Stephen Williams [Mass.]
Daniel Southmayd (Waterbury)
Richard Mansfield (New Haven)
Thomas Youngs New York
Samuel Hopkins (Waterbury)
Samuel Buell (Coventry)
John Herpin (Milford)
Simon Huntington (Norwich)
James Sproat [Mass.]
Jonathan Judd (Waterbury)
Noah Welles (Colchester)
David Webster (Glastonbury)
Joseph Lamson (Stratford)
John Grant [?]
Thomas Lewis (Waterbury)
Rueben Judd (Farmington)
David Youngs [New York]
John Moore (Windsor ?)
Jabez Huntington (Norwich)

Class of 1742
Joseph Eliot (Killingworth)
William Peartree Smith [New York]
Hendrick Hans Hansen [New York]
Joseph Hawley [Mass.]
Josiah Wolcott (Wethersfield)
Samuel Fitch (Lebanon)
Elizur Hale (Glastonbury)
Asher Rosseter (Guilford)
Jared Ingersoll (Milford)

Class of 1742 (cont.)
Nehemiah Barker [Mass.]
Edward Dorr (Lyme)
Nathan Strong [Mass.]
Isaacus Jones [Mass.]
Jonathan Lyman (Durham)
Jonathan Lee (Coventry)
James Cogswell (Saybrook)
Timothy Griffith
   [Pennsylvania]

Class of 1743
Nathan Whiting (Windham)
Elnathan Chauncey (Durham)
Soloman Williams (Lebanon)
Eliphalet Williams (Lebanon)
Samuel Fisk (Haddam)
David Burr (Fairfield)
Daniel Farrand [New Jersey]
Caleb Smith [New York]
Eleazar Fitch (Lebanon)
Joshua Lathrop (Norwich)
Stephen Johnson [New Jersey]
Myndert Lansing [New York]
Gershom Clark (Lebanon)
William Throop [Rhode Island]
Samuel Huntington (Lebanon)
Joseph Fowler (Lebanon)
Job Prudden (Milford)
Joshua Belden (Wethersfield)
Ichabod Camp (Durham)
Israel Bunnel (New Haven)
David Sherman Rowland
   (Fairfield)
Aaron Richards [New Jersey]
Nathan Dewolf (Lyme)
Thomas Arthur [New Jersey]

Class of 1744
Hezekiah Huntington (Norwich)
Benjamin Woolsey [New York]
William Samuel Johnson
   (Stratford)
Ebenezer Rosseter (Stonington)
Timothy Dwight [Vermont]

Class of 1744 (cont.)

Leverett Hubbard (Hartford)
John Hubbard (New Haven)
Anthony Rutgers [New York]
Caleb Smith [New York]
Samuel Tracy (Norwich)
Alexander Phelps (Hebron)
David Wilcoxson (Stratford)
Agur Tomlinson (Stratford)
Elijah Mason (Hartford)
Jonathan Copp (New London)

Class of 1745

William Russell (Middletown)
Warham Williams [Mass.]
John Haynes Lord (Hartford)
William Sturgeon (Norwalk)
Nathaniel Lloyd [New York]
William Smith [New York]
Thomas Bradbury Chandler
   [Mass.]
Samuel Lockwood (Norwalk)
James Beebe (Danbury)
Jonathan Colton [Mass.]
Siman Ely (Lyme)
Freegrace Leavitt [Mass.]
Samuel Field [Mass.]
Daniel Lyman [Mass.]
Elihu Lyman [Mass.]
David Strong (Lebanon)
Daniel Brinsmade
   (Stratford)
John Richards (Waterbury)
Samuel Tuthill [New York]
John Cleaveland
   (Canterbury)
Nathaniel Draper [Mass.]
Thaddeus Betts (Norwalk)
Joseph Clarke (Middletown)
Jeremiah Leaming (Durham)
Nathaniel Taylor (Danbury)
Moses Tuttle (New Haven)
John Searle [Mass.]

Class of 1746
Lewis Morris [New York]
Thomas Fitch (Norwalk)
Ezra Stiles (New Haven)
John McKinstry [Mass.]
Enos Alling (New Haven)
John Morin Scott [New York]
Thomas Fosdick (New London)
Ephraim Judson (Stratford)
Ebenezer Bassett (New Haven)
Peletiah Webster (Lebanon)
John Brainerd (Haddam)
Elihu Spencer (Millington)

Class of 1747
Oliver Wolcott (Windsor)
Elisha Whiting (New Haven)
Timothy Pitkin (Hartford)
William Cooke (Fairfield)
Chauncy Graham (Lebanon)
Jedidiah Mills (Stratford)
John Benedict (Ridgefield)
Nathaniel Huntington(Wind-
ham)
Lyman Hall (Wallingford)
John Maltby (New Haven)
Benjamin Tallmadge (New
Haven)
Joshua Chandler (Woodstock)
William Bryant [New York]
Benjamin Fisk (Haddam)
Joseph Clark (Lebanon)
Isaac Lyman [Mass.]
Daniel Sheldon (Hartford)
Jonathan Elmer (Norwalk)
Samuel Lan[gy]on (Berlin)
Job Strong [Mass.]
John Hubbard [Mass.]
Daniel Griswold (Norwich)
John Reynolds (Norwich)
Timothy Todd (New Haven)
Matthias Crane [New Jersey]
James Brown [?]
Daniel DeWolf (Lyme)
Aaron Hutchinson (Hebron)

Class of 1748

Richard Morris [New York]
Jonathan Fitch (Norwalk)
William Johnson (Stratford)
Samuel Seabury (Groton)
John Cornelius Cuyler [New
    York]
Jamison Johnston [New Jersey]
Eleazer Porter [Mass.]
Daniel Hubbard (New Haven)
William Smith [?]
Solomon Mead (Greenwich)
James Wadsworth (Durham)
Thomas Williams (Pomfret)
John Ogilvie [Scotland or New
    York]
David Baldwin (Milford)
John Coleman [Mass.]
Reynolf Marvin (Lyme)
Judah Nash [Mass.]
Israhiah Wetmore (Stratford)
Daniel Stocking (Middletown)
Elijah Lyman (Lebanon)
Hobart Mason (Stonington)
Daniel Bennett (Stratford)
Eliphalet Ball (New Haven)
Michael Todd (New Haven)
John Hotchkiss (New Haven)
Ebenezer Bogue (East Haddam)
Elijah Still (Lyme)
John Shepard (Plainfield)
Joshua Elderkin (Norwich)
Ebenezer Cleaveland (Canter-
    bury)
Thomas Paine (Canterbury)
Noadiah Warner [Mass.]
Naphtali Daggett [Mass.]
John Darbe (Canterbury ?)
Nehemiah Greenman (Fairfield
    or Norwalk)
Moses Gunn [Mass.]

Appendix B:
New Light
Ministers in Connecticut

In the summer of 1743, the following parish ministers in Connecticut signed one of two public statements issued in support of the Great Awakening. While these names do not constitute a complete list of Connecticut New Lights, they do provide a convenient source of reference.

Joseph Bellamy (1719–1789)	Woodbury 3rd	Litchfield
Benajah Case (?–?)	New-Fairfield	Fairfield
Samuel Cook (?–1747)	Stratfield (Bridgeport)	Fairfield
Hezekiah Gould (?–1790)	Stratford 1st	Fairfield
John Graham (1694–1774)	Woodbury 2nd	Litchfield
David Jewett (1714–1783)	New London 2nd	New London
Reuben Judd (?–?)	Woodbury 4th	Litchfield
David Judson (?–1776)	Newtown	?
Elisha Kent (1704–1776)	Newtown	?
Daniel Kirkland (1701–1773)	Norwich 3rd	New London
Benjamin Lord (1693–1784)	Norwich 1st	New London
Hezekiah Lord (1697, 1698–1761)	Preston 2nd	New London
Joseph Meachum (?–1752)	Coventry	Windham
Jedidiah Mills (1697–1776)	Ripton in Stratfield	Fairfield

Samuel Mosely (1708–1791)	Windham 2nd	Windham
John Owen (1699–1753)	Groton 1st	New London
Jonathan Parsons (1705–1776)	Lyme 1st	New London
Benjamin Pomeroy (1704–1784)	Hebron	Hartford
Anthony Stoddard (1678–1760)	Woodbury 1st	Litchfield
Eleazer Wheelock (1711–1779)	Lebanon 2nd	Windham
Ebenezer White (?–1779)	Danbury	Fairfield
Jabez Wight (1701–1782)	Norwich 5th	New London
Solomon Williams (1700–1776)	Lebanon 1st	Windham

For Further Investigation

Paperback collections of source material dealing with the Great Awakening have only recently begun to appear. The most useful of these collections for readers of the present volume is Richard L. Bushman (ed.), *The Great Awakening: Documents on the Revival of Religion, 1740–1745,* (New York, 1970), which is partially focused on events in Connecticut and which contains a variety of correspondence by Eleazar Wheelock and some relevant documents dealing with the separation in Norwich. Another useful (and very large) collection is Allan Heimert and Perry Miller (eds.), *The Great Awakening: Documents Illustrating the Crisis and its Consequences* (Indianapolis, 1967). Two other anthologies are Darrett B. Rutman (ed.), *The Great Awakening: Event and Exegesis* (New York, 1970), and David S. Lovejoy (ed.), *Religious Enthusiasm and the Great Awakening* (Englewood Cliffs, N.J., 1969).

As for nonanthologized primary sources, almost everything published in British America during the Great Awakening is available on *microcard* (a kind of microfilm) under the general title *Early American Imprints.* (This series, which is owned by many larger research libraries, is produced by the American Antiquarian Society in Worcester, Mass., and includes all titles published in colonial and Revolutionary America. A published index to the microcards is also available.)

Of all the individuals to appear in this volume, there is only one whose writings are widely available today: Jonathan Edwards. His works are available in a variety of editions; perhaps the most useful introduction to his intellectual career is Clarence Faust and Thomas Johnson,

Jonathan Edwards: Representative Selections (New York, 1935; paperback edition, 1962).

A number of reference works should prove indispensable for most further investigation. Franklin B. Dexter, *Biographical Sketches of the Graduates of Yale College, with Annals of the College History,* Volume I: 1701–1745, Volume II: 1745–1763 (New York, 1885, 1896) traces the life of every Yale graduate, including many who were already established in their careers by the time of the Awakening (such as Eleazar Wheelock and James Davenport). Many of the same men, and others who did not attend Yale, can very often be traced in William B. Sprague, *Annals of the American Pulpit,* Volume I: Congregationalists Volume III: Presbyterians (New York, 1856), which is limited to men who entered the ministry. Minister or not, if a man received a degree from Harvard College his biography can be found in Clifford K. Shipton, *Sibley's Harvard Graduates,* Volumes IV–XI: Classes of 1690–1745 (Boston, 1933–1960). Most of the men whose names and writings appear in this reader can be found in one of three books: Sprague, Dexter, and *Sibley's.* Finally, a useful compilation of the histories of the individual churches and county associations in Connecticut is to be found in *Contributions to the Ecclesiastical History of Connecticut* (New Haven, 1861).

Accounts of the Great Awakening in New England include Edwin S. Gaustad, *The Great Awakening in New England* (New York, 1957; available in paperback) and C. C. Goen, *Revivalism and Separatism in New England,* 1740–1800 (New Haven, 1962), which concentrates on the separatist tendencies spawned by the revival but which also contains an excellent discussion of the theological issues. Both the Gaustad and Goen volumes append useful and extensive bibliographies. These books do not, however, altogether replace two earlier studies: S. Leroy Blake, *The Separates, or Strict Congregationalists of New England* (Boston, 1902), and—especially—Joseph Tracy, *The Great Awakening: A History of the Revival of Religion in the Time of Edwards and Whitefield* (Boston, 1842). A fascinating but difficult recent volume is Allan Heimert, *Religion and the American Mind from the Great Awakening to the Revolution* (Cambridge, 1966), which makes a connection between the New Light impulse of the Awakening and the democratic impulse of the American Revolution—and a corresponding connection between Old Lights and political conservatives. Perry Miller, *Jonathan Edwards* (New York, 1949) and Ola E. Winslow, *Jonathan Edwards, 1703–1758* (New York, 1940) are both available in paperback. Two general essays by Sidney E. Mead may be useful: "Denominationalism: the Shape of Protestantism in America," *Church History,* XXIII (1954), 291–320; and "The Rise of the Evangelical Conception of the Ministry in America (1607–1850), in H. Richard Niebuhr and Daniel D. Williams (eds.), *The Ministry in Historical Perspective* (New York, 1956).

The most thoughtful analysis of the Great Awakening in Connecticut will be found in Richard L. Bushman, *From Puritan to Yankee* (Cambridge, 1967), which describes the colony's metamorphosis into social and intellectual modernity. Bushman argues that the Awakening was the single most significant event in this metamorphosis. Still very useful after 150 years is Benjamin Trumbull, *A Complete History of Connecticut, Civil and Ecclesiastical,* 2 volumes (New Haven, 1818), especially Chapter VIII of the second volume. (This chapter contains, among other things, an extended account of the New Haven association's struggle against Philemon Robbins, a New Light minister.) One article of interest is Robert Sklar, "The Great Awakening and Colonial Politics: Connecticut's Revolution in the Minds of Men," *Bulletin of the Connecticut Historical Society,* 28 (1963), pp. 81–95. The story of the Great Awakening at Yale College is reported in Louis L. Tucker, *Puritan Protagonist: President Thomas Clap of Yale College* (Chapel Hill, 1962) and, more briefly, in Edmund S. Morgan, *The Gentle Puritan: A Life of Ezra Stiles, 1727–1795* (New Haven, 1962). Tucker's book in particular provides a thorough picture of the context at Yale.

No adequate history of Yale College in the eighteenth century has been written. In addition to the Tucker volume on Thomas Clap, there are a number of essays on the subject in Franklin B. Dexter, *A Selection of the Miscellaneous Historical Papers of Fifty Years* (New Haven, 1918); see also the same author's *Documentary History of Yale University . . . 1701–1745* (New Haven, 1916), and the annals included in his *Biographical Sketches.*

For the separation in the New Haven church, see Leonard Bacon, *Thirteen Historical Discussions on the First Church in New Haven* (New Haven, 1839) and Samuel W. S. Dutton, *The History of the North Church in New Haven* (New Haven, 1842). A thorough and most excellent account of the troubles in Canterbury leading to the expulsion of John and Ebenezer Cleaveland is included in the first volume of Ellen D. Larned, *History of Windham County, Connecticut* (Worcester, 1874). For a less thorough account of the Awakening in the New London area, see Francis M. Caulkins, *History of New London, Connecticut* (New London, 1895).

Finally, Bushman's *From Puritan to Yankee* (described above) contains an excellent bibliography of Connecticut titles from the period of the Great Awakening and earlier, and also an indispensable passage on the location of manuscript collections in that colony.